# Digital and Media Literacy in the Age of the Internet

D0933375

# Digital and Media Literacy in the Age of the Internet

## Practical Classroom Applications

MARY BETH HERTZ

ROWMAN & LITTLEFIELD
*Lanham • Boulder • New York • London*

Published by Rowman & Littlefield
An imprint of The Rowman & Littlefield Publishing Group, Inc.
4501 Forbes Boulevard, Suite 200, Lanham, Maryland 20706
www.rowman.com

6 Tinworth Street, London, SE11 5AL, United Kingdom

British Library Cataloguing in Publication Information Available

Library of Congress Control Number: 2019949772

∞™ The paper used in this publication meets the minimum requirements of American National Standard for Information Sciences—Permanence of Paper for Printed Library Materials, ANSI/NISO Z39.48-1992.

# Contents

# Foreword

Like many of the connections in my personal learning network, my association with Mary Beth began on Twitter back in 2009. As relatively early adopters of the social media platform, we connected there at a time when the idea of Web 2.0 was still shiny and new, and when the online world was fueled by a sense of boundless possibility, where anyone could have a voice and where relationships flourished, independent of time and place.

While the online world has allowed me to remain connected to Mary Beth in the years since our first encounter, I have also witnessed countless shifts in the media landscape in those intervening years. Over time, the utopian vision of the Internet has been tarnished by the erosion of privacy, the increasingly toxic nature of online discourse, and the rise of huge corporations that have privatized and monetized the once "free" web. In 2019, we now find ourselves in a new and complex reality of information proliferation, fake news, and cyberbullying, where every post, comment, and like is etched indelibly into the fabric of history and into our own digital footprints.

It is this new reality that Mary Beth tackles in the pages of this book. Writing from the perspective of both an educator and a parent, she paints a detailed picture of the world in which we live, underscoring in particular the challenges and complications faced by today's young people as they navigate childhood and adolescence. Additionally, the book includes lesson ideas and resources designed to help teachers address the many facets of digital literacy, media literacy, and digital citizenship in K–12 classrooms, developed with the unique attention to detail and critical thinking that Mary Beth brings to the table.

As a professor of educational technology and media, I can confidently say that the book you are about to read addresses the biggest "hot-button" issues facing our society, and our students, today. In fact, when Mary Beth first asked me to consider writing this foreword, I commented that the array of topics included in the text was remarkably similar to the book that I had always wanted to write, only better; reading the final draft has only reinforced that sentiment. And although the digital world we inhabit can be incredibly difficult to navigate, the pages that follow will certainly help to illuminate a path forward for our students and ourselves.

Dr. Alec Couros
professor of education, faculty of education
University of Regina

# Acknowledgments

I would like to thank all of the talented educators who have inspired my teaching over the years. Without the powerful conversations at conferences and the exchanging of ideas and practices through Twitter to push my thinking, this book would not be possible.

I am also grateful to my husband, John, who has endured my years of traveling for conferences and hours spent staring at a computer screen as I pursued exciting learning opportunities, networked with colleagues from across the globe, and feverishly plugged away at this book.

I am thankful for the mentorship and friendship of Marcie Hull and the time that Marcie, Ann Leaness, and Katie Burrows-Stone put into providing feedback on some of the chapters in the book. Writing this book was a huge endeavor and would not have been possible without the knowledge, experience, and tutelage of so many people who cannot all be named here. Pieces of so many friendships, professional relationships, brief conversations, and shared experiences are contained in the pages of this book.

A big thank you goes to my editor, Sarah Jubar, for her patience, and for taking the time to answer my endless questions throughout the process of writing this book, and to Rowman & Littlefield for believing in me and providing me the opportunity to write it.

Finally, thank you to my amazing family, who has always encouraged me to follow my dreams and has never doubted me. I would not be the person I am today without you.

# Introduction

Over the last few decades, educators have had to grapple with a new kind of literacy. Just knowing how to read is no longer enough. Teaching reading must now be paired with teaching how to access, comprehend, and analyze the content students are reading, and content now extends beyond the written word.

The purpose of this book is to provide educators with the necessary background information to teach these new kinds of literacies in their classroom. Each chapter addresses a different topic and contains an overview of general practical applications of the concepts in the chapter for elementary, middle, and high school settings.

By no means does this book cover every possible topic connected to digital and media literacy. Each of these could (and do) have entire books dedicated to them. This book attempts to string these content areas together and provide the groundwork for successful teaching and learning when teaching with and about technology at various grade levels.

## HOW TO READ THIS BOOK

This book can be read from front to back or in pieces depending on the interest of the reader. Toward the end of each chapter, there is a textbox containing lesson ideas tied to the content of the chapter. More detailed, long-form lessons based around these practical applications are located in the Appendix.

These lessons are paired with standards from the International Society for Technology in Education (ISTE), the leading global organization for technology in the classroom. Some chapters also contain case studies of teachers who address the content of the chapter in their practice. Chapters 1 and 9 do not contain sample lessons as they help define digital and media and literacy and are not based around specific content.

## THE ISTE STANDARDS

The ISTE standards for students support technology integration that goes beyond simply knowing how to use technology. The standards provide a framework for students to become responsible and effective creators and consumers of content. A practical guide for integrating the standards can be found on their website (https://www.iste.org/standards/for-students). The standards as a whole can be seen in Table 0.1, and the lessons in the Appendix are paired with some of these standards.

**Table 0.1.  ISTE Standards for Students**

| 1 | Empowered Learner | Students leverage technology to take an active role in choosing, achieving, and demonstrating competency in their learning goals, informed by the learning sciences. | 1a<br>Articulate and set personal learning goals, develop strategies leveraging technology to achieve them and reflect on the learning process itself to improve learning outcomes.<br><br>1b<br>Students build networks and customize their learning environments in ways that support the learning process.<br><br>1c<br>Students use technology to seek feedback that informs and improves their practice and to demonstrate their learning in a variety of ways.<br><br>1d<br>Students understand the fundamental concepts of technology operations, demonstrate the ability to choose, use, and troubleshoot current technologies, and transfer their knowledge to explore emerging technologies. |

2  Digital Citizen  Students recognize the rights, responsibilities, and opportunities of living, learning, and working in an interconnected digital world, and they act and model in ways that are safe, legal, and ethical.

2a
Students cultivate and manage their digital identity and reputation, and are aware of the permanence of their actions in the digital world.

2b
Students engage in positive, safe, legal, and ethical behavior when using technology, including social interactions online or when using networked devices.

2c
Students demonstrate an understanding of and respect for the rights and obligations of using and sharing intellectual property.

2d
Students manage their personal data to maintain digital privacy and security and are aware of data-collection technology used to track their navigation online.

3  Knowledge Constructor  Students critically curate a variety of resources using digital tools to construct knowledge, produce creative artifacts, and make meaningful learning experiences for themselves and others.

3a
Students plan and employ effective research strategies to locate information and other resources for their intellectual or creative pursuits.

3b
Students evaluate the accuracy, perspective, credibility, and relevance of information, media, data, or other resources.

3c
Students curate information from digital resources using a variety of tools and methods to create collections of artifacts that demonstrate meaningful connections or conclusions.

3d
Students build knowledge by actively exploring real-world issues and problems, developing ideas and theories, and pursuing answers and solutions.

| 4 | Innovative Designer | Students use a variety of technologies within a design process to identify and solve problems by creating new, useful, or imaginative solutions. | 4a Students know and use a deliberate design process for generating ideas, testing theories, creating innovative artifacts, or solving authentic problems. |
|---|---|---|---|
| | | | 4b Students select and use digital tools to plan and manage a design process that considers design constraints and calculated risks. |
| | | | 4c Students develop, test, and refine prototypes as part of a cyclical design process. |
| | | | 4d Students exhibit a tolerance for ambiguity, perseverance, and the capacity to work with open-ended problems. |
| 5 | Computational Thinker | Students develop and employ strategies for understanding and solving problems in ways that leverage the power of technological methods to develop and test solutions. | 5a Students formulate problem definitions suited for technology-assisted methods such as data analysis, abstract models, and algorithmic thinking in exploring and finding solutions. |
| | | | 5b Students collect data or identify relevant data sets, use digital tools to analyze them, and represent data in various ways to facilitate problem-solving and decision-making. |
| | | | 5c Students break problems into component parts, extract key information, and develop descriptive models to understand complex systems or facilitate problem-solving. |
| | | | 5d Students understand how automation works and use algorithmic thinking to develop a sequence of steps to create and test automated solutions. |

| 6 | Creative Communicator | Students communicate clearly and express themselves creatively for a variety of purposes using the platforms, tools, styles, formats, and digital media appropriate to their goals. | 6a Students choose the appropriate platforms and tools for meeting the desired objectives of their creation or communication. |
|---|---|---|---|
| | | | 6b Students create original works or responsibly repurpose or remix digital resources into new creations. |
| | | | 6c Students communicate complex ideas clearly and effectively by creating or using a variety of digital objects such as visualizations, models, or simulations. |
| | | | 6d Students publish or present content that customizes the message and medium for their intended audiences. |
| 7 | Global Collaborator | Students use digital tools to broaden their perspectives and enrich their learning by collaborating with others and working effectively in teams locally and globally. | 7a Students use digital tools to connect with learners from a variety of backgrounds and cultures, engaging with them in ways that broaden mutual understanding and learning. |
| | | | 7b Students use collaborative technologies to work with others, including peers, experts, or community members, to examine issues and problems from multiple viewpoints. |
| | | | 7c Students contribute constructively to project teams, assuming various roles and responsibilities to work effectively toward a common goal. |
| | | | 7d Students explore local and global issues and use collaborative technologies to work with others to investigate solutions. |

## SCOPE AND SEQUENCE

Each content area can be taught at nearly every grade level, but it looks different at each grade level. Table 0.2 and Table 0.3 contain sample scope and sequences for both digital and media literacy by grade level. These are cumulative and build on each other, so by high school, students should have mastered all of the concepts that have come before as well as the concepts listed for their grade level.

**Table 0.2. Digital Literacy Scope and Sequence**

| Grade Level | Concepts (cumulative) | Essential Question (cumulative) |
|---|---|---|
| K and 1 | • Understand that the Internet is a way that people can communicate when they are not physically in the same place.<br><br>• Understand that websites are created by people to share information.<br><br>• Know what kinds of information we should not share online.<br><br>• Know how to tell if something is an ad. | What is the Internet?<br><br>Should I be sharing my information online? |
| 2 and 3 | • Understand how people use the Internet to communicate, collaborate, and share ideas.<br><br>• Understand the consequences of giving our information to websites.<br><br>• Know what kinds of information we should and shouldn't be putting online. | How can I learn and lead using the Internet?<br><br>How do my online choices affect me? |
| 4 and 5 | • Understand how to use the Internet to connect with experts and find primary sources.<br><br>• Know that websites and apps track us when we use them.<br><br>• Understand how websites make money from ads.<br><br>• Understand that works created by others are protected by copyright law. | If I am not paying for an app or website, is it truly free?<br><br>Does the Internet have rules? |

| 6–8 | • Understand the purpose behind copyright laws and why they matter. | Why do people use social media? |
|---|---|---|
| | • Know where to find resources that are copyright free. | How do my online choices affect others? |
| | • Understand how websites and apps track us when we use them. | |
| | • Understand what social media is and how it is used. | |
| | • Know how personal information is used for profit. | |
| | • Understand how my online choices affect me. | |
| | • Understand how my online choice affect others. | |
| 9–12 | • Understand the role of IP addresses and how the Internet works. | Who am I and who do I want to be online? |
| | • Be able to explain the pros and cons of social media. | How does social media empower its users? |
| | • Begin to build a deliberate online presence and identity. | How can I protect my privacy online? |
| | • Understand the consequences of plagiarism. | |
| | • Begin to take an active role in protecting individual privacy when using apps and websites. | |

**Table 0.3.   Media Literacy Scope and Sequence**

| Grade Level | Concepts | Essential Questions |
|---|---|---|
| Elementary Grades | • Understand what an advertisement is. | Is this a fact? |
| | • Understand what a fact is. | Is this an ad? |
| | • Understand what an expert is and how to find the author of articles we read online. | What makes someone an expert? |
| Middle Grades | • Understand how the author's purpose affects the reporting of the news. | Why did the author write this? |
| | • Understand and conduct basic CRAP detection. | How do I know that I can trust what I see? |
| | • Understand how images and videos can be manipulated or taken out of context to change their original purpose. | |
| High School | • Understand the difference between false information and manipulated information. | Can news be fake? |
| | • Understand the influence of individuals' biases and beliefs on their interpretation of information. | How do my own biases or the biases of others affect how I interpret what I see? |

*CRAP*, Currency, reliability, authority, purpose.

# I

# DIGITAL LITERACY

# Defining Digital Literacy

In exploring digital literacy, this book attempts to address the big picture and the underlying ways that some technologies work so that educators can be more informed in their practice. The chapters in Part 1 largely focus on privacy concerns in the classroom, something that has become an increasingly important topic as more and more student data is brought online. Understanding these concerns requires a basic knowledge of how the technologies behind the Internet, online ads, and search engines work, especially because many, if not most, of these technologies have a direct effect on students' lives.

## WHAT IS DIGITAL LITERACY?

The American Library Association's (ALA) 2013 Digital Literacy Task Force defined *digital literacy* as "the ability to use information and communication technologies to find, evaluate, create, and communicate information, requiring both cognitive and technical skills."[1] This task force also recommended that libraries form partnerships around digital literacy and bring programs into their spaces to promote digital literacy skills in the communities they serve.[2]

The ALA also runs the website http://digitallearn.org, which is dedicated to providing resources for learning skills such as navigating email, navigating a website, using the Windows operating system, understanding Internet privacy, creating safe passwords, and identifying online scams. These are the kinds of skills that digitalliteracy.gov, a website created by the Obama administration, also focuses on. Like the ALA initiative, http://digitalliteracy .gov provides information on workforce development in communities where a lack of digital literacy skills limits job opportunities.[3]

These interpretations of the ALA definition of digital literacy focus on specific technological skills considered necessary for employment and success in the current workforce. However, these definitions are limited and do not consider the skills necessary for success and employment in the world that young people today will inhabit as adults. This is not to say that these are not vital skills, but they are the bare minimum.

The International Society for Technology in Education (ISTE) describes the evolution of their standards for students over time on their website. In 1998, the organization defined the standards as "Learning how to use technology." Today, it states that the standards focus on "Transformative learning with technology." In the classroom, the expectation is that teaching and learning with technology goes beyond what ALA provides. It is less about how to use technology in general and more about what you can do with technology.[4] So, although knowing how to check your email is an important skill, it is just a jumping off point. More important is knowing how to use email to communicate around projects or with teachers about class concerns or questions.

## DIGITAL LITERACY IN THE CLASSROOM

In the classroom, educators have the unique and complex task of teaching digital literacy through content. Just knowing the skills themselves is the first step, but more importantly, students need to understand how to navigate and apply these skills when completing complex tasks like researching or collaborating with peers. In many schools, libraries have become digital literacy hubs where students learn these skills and have access to technology, similar to the work of public libraries.

However, schools may also invest in computer labs for technology education and dedicate time each week for a technology class. Other schools invest in mobile carts or 1:1 laptop programs where every student can have access to a laptop in the classroom for their work. Often, the setup depends on the school budget and resources, including human resources.

In 2016, the US Department of Education released its policy brief, *Advancing Educational Technology in Teacher Preparation*. It was a call to action for schools of education to build opportunities for preservice teachers to explore and learn about emerging technologies and best practices for using them in the classroom.[5] The brief lists a few examples of schools who currently provide these supports for their future educators.

At the time, Columbia University's Teacher's College, the University of Michigan School of Education, the University of Virginia, and the Dominican University of California School of Education and Counseling Psychology were a few that made the list. The University of Northern Colorado (https:// www.unco.edu/cebs/educational-technology/) and the University of Regina in Saskatchewan, Canada (https://www.uregina.ca/education/programs/ masters-certificates.html) also offer a master's certificate in educational technology and media that focuses on media literacy, digital citizenship, and social media, which is rare for schools of education. It's not clear what the landscape looks like three years after the policy brief was released, but it is clear that there is guidance and model programs out there for others to learn from.

Educators are expected to integrate technology tools into their classrooms, but that can look different depending on the teacher's level of comfort as well as the available resources, the school's collective knowledge of best practices, and the supports provided for teachers as they try new things with their students. If the expectation is that students will "use a variety of technologies within a design process to identify and solve problems by creating new, useful or imaginative solutions," as stated in the ISTE Standards for Students, a number of elements must be in place before a teacher can get to that place. ISTE calls these *essential conditions*. These can be found at https://www .iste.org/standards/essential-conditions. The conditions include things like adequate funding and student-centered teaching, as well as skilled personnel.

Along with the ISTE Standards for Students outlined in the Introduction and included in the lessons in the Appendix of this book, ISTE also has specific standards for educators. The ISTE Standards for Educators, which are aligned with digital literacy skills, state, "Educators inspire students to positively contribute to and responsibly participate in the digital world."[6] To achieve this goal, educators must have a clear and deep understanding of the digital world that they and their students inhabit.

As more and more technology enters the classroom, and teachers are expected to support students through using technology for learning, educators must have an understanding of how the Internet works and how search engines function, as well as the legal and moral responsibilities that they have to maintain student data and privacy. Even more, educators cannot guide students through complex applications of digital skills without understanding students' own experiences with technology and how their use of technology in school and in their personal lives overlap and how they don't. Digital literacy should also extend to social media tools, especially as more and more schools run social media accounts and teachers use social media to connect with students' families. Understanding how young people use these tools is the key to understanding how young people in today's classrooms communicate and connect with each other.

Although skills like sending emails, navigating an operating system, and browsing the Internet are vital for success in today's world, students and teachers must meet the complex demands of today's literacies that go beyond simple reading and writing. It is also more and more important that students and teachers have a deeper understanding of how these technologies work as they evolve. Educators are often provided teaching guides for their disciplines so that they can teach the content better. We do not, however, provide a teaching guide for digital literacy for educators so that they can effectively manage and navigate using digital tools in the classroom and understand the responsibilities connected to using these tools in their practice. Hopefully, this book can fill in some of those gaps.

# 2

# Living in the Digital Age

Most students in today's classrooms have had a much different experience growing up than the adults teaching them. Even high school students born in the early 2000s have never known a world without the Internet, and in some cases, cell phones. Younger students have only ever known the world of ubiquitous smartphones, tablets, and laptops and constant connectivity. Along with this hardware come video and TV streaming services like You-Tube, Netflix, and Hulu, as well as music streaming services like Pandora and Spotify. Facebook and Instagram are household names and many parents use these services alongside their children.

This all means that these young people are exposed to more media on a more diverse set of platforms than any other generation. They have the added challenge of learning how to navigate childhood and adolescence not only alongside these media, but with it as an integral part of their existence. These young people live in two worlds—one physical and one digital. Sometimes these worlds overlap and sometimes they don't. This chapter explores how young people today engage with screens based on a number of research studies as well as important things to consider when living in the digital world, and it peeks into what kids are doing online from their own perspective.

## THE INFLUENCE OF ACCESS

According to an Influence Central study conducted in 2016, parents are providing their children with smartphones at 10.3 years of age and 50 percent of young people have a social media account by the time they are twelve.[1] This means that a large number of young people have access to their peers and the larger Internet community before they even hit their teenage years online. As for Internet access, according to the same study, 42 percent of young people had access to the Internet on their own laptop or tablet in 2012, whereas in 2016, 64 percent of young people have that access. This increase shows that more and more students are connected to the Internet through an individual, personal device rather than a shared family computer, making their connection to the Internet an increasingly personalized and private experience.

A 2017 Common Sense Media (CSM) study reported that the use of mobile devices by kids eight years old and younger has increased by 31 percent since 2011, mostly because of the decline of DVDs and the increased use of online streaming services.[2] This means that younger kids are using mobile devices (although this includes apps that aren't necessarily connected to the Internet) and that they have more autonomy over how and when they access online media.

Although the "digital divide" between families that have Internet access and families that don't has shrunk over the last decade, with 74 percent of low-income families with children ages birth through eight years old having access compared with 96 percent of higher-income families, there are still concerns over this divide. The proliferation of Internet-based homework has left low-income students at a continued disadvantage compared with their peers from high-income families. Furthermore, according to the same 2017 CSM study, lower-income children spend more time in front of screens than their more affluent peers[3]; children from low-income families may be subject to unknown long-term health effects of extended time in front of screens and thus are at higher risk for physical, mental, and emotional issues related to technology use.

One of those health issues is the prevalence of technology-related multitasking among young people with direct access to smartphones, tablets, and computers. A 2015 CSM study reported that nearly two-thirds of teens who multitasked said it had no effect on the quality of their work.[4] However, in a 2018 study also by CSM, 57 percent of teens admitted that social media often distracts them from their homework. In the 2018 study, 54 percent of teens also reported that they admit that their phone often distracts them when they should be paying attention to someone right in front of them. This is up from 44 percent in a similar study conducted in 2012.[5] Research shows that multitasking can have a significant effect on the way the brain processes information and its ability to focus.[6] As later chapters explore, the devices in kids' hands are designed to garner their attention because most social media companies earn money based on ad views.

Despite all this time online, the 2015 CSM study discovered that only 3 percent of teens' digital media time is spent *creating* content. For this reason, the tendency for adults to make assumptions about young people's aptitude around digital technologies and the popular moniker "digital native" is worrisome. Students may be adept at *consuming* media, but they are not always active participants in creating the content that they consume. They also are not inherently aware of the effect that the media they consume has on them. As researcher danah boyd warns in her 2015 book, *It's Complicated: The Social Lives of Networked Teens*, "Teens may make their own media or share content online, but this does not mean that they inherently have the knowledge or perspective to critically examine what they consume." There is still an important role for adults in guiding students through the digital landscapes they inhabit.[7]

## GROWING UP ONLINE

danah boyd, one of the most prominent researchers of teen media use, has talked with teens all over the country about their experiences. She has a powerful explanation for the world that young people live in, which she calls *networked publics*: "Networked publics are publics that are structured by networked technologies. As such, they are simultaneously (1) the space constructed through networked technologies and (2) the imagined community that emerges as a result of the intersection of people, technology, and practice."[8] Young people inhabit these spaces the same way they inhabit physical spaces, and these spaces are very real, just like the physical spaces they inhabit. When adults complain that teens are addicted to social media, boyd explains, "Most teens aren't addicted to social media[;] if anything, they are addicted to each other."

Young people are very intentional about their identities in these spaces in the same ways that teens have been expressing themselves across schools and communities since before the Internet and social media. Their identity may be expressed in their choice of avatar (the image attached to the accounts they curate), as well as their curation habits. Teen social media accounts are not as spontaneous as adults would believe. They often change avatars and usernames to express their current mood or state of mind, and they will remove posts that do not garner enough praise or "likes" from their peers. One teen explained to a group of teachers at the 2016 Educon conference in Philadelphia that she would even empty her entire timeline and start fresh from time to time.

Young people often express themselves differently across different platforms, too. This, however, is not always a case of multiple identities, says boyd. Instead, young people must conform to a particular site's "norms," so their identities seem to vary depending on where the account is held. For example, if they are using Snapchat and they know that their posts won't last very long, their posts may be different than their carefully curated Instagram posts. One explanation that boyd offers for teens' attraction to these spaces is the increase in "helicopter parenting." Teens, she explains, have less and less unmonitored time together. These online spaces provide a private, unmonitored space for teens to interact, especially because it has become harder for them to "hang out" face to face as their parents often did at their age.

Adults have their own "networked publics" as well. Many educators use Twitter to share ideas through hashtags and real-time chats. These educators also join Facebook groups and participate in Edcamps, unconferences that often blend online and face-to-face interactions. A quick perusal of the #edcamp hashtag on multiple social media platforms shows how teachers are leveraging social media to learn together. Content-area teachers also connect through services like Twitter and Facebook to share classroom practices, and the positive effects have been explored by education researchers.[9]

These educators, who are steeped in social media themselves, should have a clearer understanding of the way that teens and young people use and inhabit these spaces. Despite the impression that teens only use these sites socially, they discuss issues and current events through social media, as do adults. For instance, teens have created their own spaces on Instagram called "flop accounts" to discuss and debate issues.[10] A quick perusal of these online spaces can instill both hope and fear for the next generation. Many of the discussions are thoughtful and civil and others can be wildly misinformed or misguided.

This, again, shows the need that young people have for adult guidance in these spaces. They are seeking connections and social experiences but don't necessarily have the skill set to discern between good and bad information or even between genuine accounts and fake ones. They also may fall into social pressures they see online, such as sharing their password with friends. According to a 2015 Pew study, sharing passwords is a sign of trust. As a high school girl in the study explains, "I know they have this game on Instagram where you'd be like, 'Do you trust me? Give me your password and I'll post a picture and then log back off.'"[11] This kind of behavior can obviously lead to huge security issues, but teens don't often think beyond the social pressures they feel and there are rarely adults in their lives helping them navigate these kinds of pressures.

Despite this lack of guidance, and the many stories that we hear about teens (and adults) making poor choices online, these social platforms are, for many young people, a lifeline. For example, high-risk kids like LGBT youth who may be afraid of coming out in their community can connect with others who can support them. Kids who may feel they don't fit in at school can find a community of kids who enjoy the same movies or books or games online. There is also the experience of connecting with someone who is from a place outside of your hometown and learning that geography doesn't have to dictate who you are friends with.

Kids today are also often more aware of what is going on in the world since it is right in front of them (although what they are learning about world events may be very skewed, depending on where they are getting their information—more on that in Chapter 12). It is important as adults that we don't downplay or forget about the positive aspects of online connections while also guiding young people through the pitfalls.

## THE IMPACT OF ONLINE CHOICES

In his 2011 book, *lol . . . OMG! What Every Student Needs to Know about Online Reputation Management, Digital Citizenship and Cyberbullying*, author and tech entrepreneur Matthew Ivester lays out three important concepts for young people to consider when they are navigating and participating in these networked publics. He focuses on *immediacy*, *permanence*, and *lack of control*.[12] These three concepts capture the essence of sharing online and can be easily understood by students across many grade levels.

## SHARING IS EASY . . . TOO EASY

Students aren't often aware of how the ease of sharing increases the odds that they will share something that they regret or that they have not completely thought through. This ease is no accident. Apps are designed to make sharing easy. Most, if not all, of the social media apps that young people use are free. (See Textbox 2.1 for more about social media apps.) As discussed in Chapter 6, "free" just means that the user is the product being sold. By making it easy to share content from an app, a company hopes to garner more users, or in other words, more ad revenue.

There is no incentive for companies to help young people be more thoughtful about what and when they post. In addition to the ease of posting, what people post goes live immediately, and social media allows for the lightning-fast sharing of content with a larger and larger audience. A post that was shared with a small following of thirty friends can easily spread outside of that circle through the simple act of sharing. If one friend shares the post

TEXTBOX 2.1. CASE STUDY

For a lot of my lessons I use the Common Sense Media Curriculum. I implemented the curriculum about five years ago through my elementary to high school classes. We have noticed a significant drop in having to deal with issues regarding students not being responsible digital citizens. Parents were so impressed with the implementation that one parent who works for our local government in ICT had her staff become certified trainers as they reach out to the public schools. I have always been a believer that everyone has a choice to make, with good or bad consequences. If the students are informed of issues, and we talk about it, they will think before acting and posting. Technology is here to stay, and our students need to be able to handle the situations that they potentially face. If they are kept in the dark or we don't discuss them they won't know how to react.

—Lisa Stevens, Mount St. Agnes Academy, Bermuda

and someone else shares it, and so on, then it is exposed to a larger and larger network of people.

## SMALL MISTAKES, BIG CONSEQUENCES

A prime example of the power of immediacy is the story of Justine Sacco, a thirty-year-old public relations executive who was fired from her job over a tweet in 2013. Justine was on a flight to South Africa to visit family and tweeted, "Going to Africa. Hope I don't get AIDS. Just kidding. I'm white!" Justine at the time only had 170 Twitter followers and didn't think much of the joke. In her mind, the joke was a statement on the fact that white people "live in a bubble," and she states that she was playing off of stereotypes that white people might have of South Africans.[13]

Unfortunately for Sacco, by the time she landed in South Africa after her eleven-hour flight, and turned on her phone again, she discovered that her tweet had exploded across Twitter, even spawning a hashtag, #HasJustine LandedYet. People were threatening her safety, demanding that she be fired, and one Twitter user even went to the airport in Johannesburg to catch Justine as she entered the airport after her flight. Eventually, Justine was fired over the incident.

Justine didn't think about how her Tweet might read to those who didn't know her, and Twitter makes it so easy to share our thoughts as they come to us without any delay. This ease of online sharing combined with the ease with which users can share content can easily backfire; taking a moment to think about how what you are posting will sound to people who may not know you is an important step. In an ideal world, tech companies would build this into their platforms, offering a reminder to users—especially if their account is set to post publicly—but it's doubtful that we will ever see such a feature.

Another aspect of Justine's story that is a common thread across many social media gaffes like hers is the extreme to which complete strangers wanted to make an example of her. This ease of sharing widens the audience of what we post. Text without context is often misconstrued, even among friends. When posts are shared widely outside of a friend group and out of context, it opens us up to misinterpretation from people who have never met us. It also opens the flood gates for judgments that are sometimes harsh and unwarranted.

This form of public shaming has become widespread and can be seen as a form of cyberbullying. Some compare it to giving someone a digital Scarlett

Letter or even putting them in metaphorical stocks and pillory, allowing complete strangers to throw insults and hurtful (and sometimes threatening) language at them as passersby would throw mud and rotting vegetables. Often, this punishment is seen as more severe than the "crime" itself. So, although the words we post online matter, sometimes they come back to bite us more than may be warranted.

## WHAT GOES ON THE INTERNET STAYS ON THE INTERNET

More than five years later, a quick online search of Justine Sacco's name still results in articles about her tweet, and that tweet itself is still available online in a myriad of articles and screenshots. This is, as Ivester explains, the aspect of permanence that comes with everything we post online.

Ivester uses the example of Alexandra Wallace, a former University of California–Los Angeles student who posted a video rant on YouTube called "Asians in the Library." The rant contains a number of insensitive comments, was met with death threats and doxxing (posting of her address and other private information online), and led to her withdrawing from the university.[14] It was posted in 2011 and removed soon after it was recorded, can still be found online today because other YouTube users have re-uploaded the video. So even though the original poster removed the video, it is still available. This is also how tweets, Instagram posts, and other social media posts can live beyond their time through screenshots and reposting.

## WHOSE IS IT, ANYWAY?

Once Alexandra and Justine posted to their social media accounts, they discovered that the content that they had chosen to share with what they thought was a small group of their friends was shared publicly across the Internet and soon was out of their control. Even after Alexandra removed the video from YouTube, it was still up on other accounts.

Sometimes, too, we lose control over things that are posted about us or photos of us that we did not take or post. This happened to Lindsey Stone, a caretaker with the organization Living Independently for Elders, who was visiting Arlington National Ceremony in Washington, DC. During the visit, a co-worker snapped a photo of Stone making an obscene gesture in front of a sign that read "Silence and Respect." Unfortunately, her co-worker posted

FIGURE 2.1
Screenshot from https://www.change.org/p/life-living-independently-forever-fire-lind sey-stone-and-jamie-schuh. Accessed February 26, 2019.

the picture to her Facebook account, which, unbeknownst to Lindsey, was set to public. The photo was quickly shared across the Internet and Lindsey soon began to receive threats and calls for her to be fired. There were even two Change.org petitions set up (Figure 2.1) to get her and her co-worker fired, which eventually did happen.[15]

A tragic example of lack of control is the story of Tyler Clementi, a freshman at Rutgers University in New Jersey. One night in 2010, Tyler asked his roommate for some privacy. His roommate went down the hall to a friend's room and connected to his laptop, which was in the room with Tyler, through Skype so that both students could see what was happening in the room. They witnessed a sexual encounter between Tyler and another man and described what they witnessed on Twitter. The roommate encouraged his Twitter followers to tune in by connecting with him on iChat, Apple's instant messaging service. "Anyone with iChat, I dare you to video chat me between the hours of 9:30 and 12. Yes it's happening again," he tweeted.

The next day, Tyler posted "Jumping off the gw bridge sorry" to Facebook and about ten minutes later, he jumped off the George Washington Bridge to his death.[16] Tyler had complained to a resident assistant and was aware of the broadcast, and had requested a change of room, according to his own Internet postings and the testimony of the resident assistant.[17]

Tyler had not posted about the encounter directly himself, but he had no control over the fact that his personal and private life was being broadcast online for the public to see. Tyler had also been outed as gay without his consent. Not only do we lose control of the content we post as soon as we click "post" or "send," but there are times where, in the cases of Lindsey Stone and Tyler Clementi, the posts that others make of us go out of our control and can have a huge effect on our lives.

There is a powerful example here of a large number of people watching these events unfold and saying nothing, or worse joining in on the public shaming or the "fun" at someone else's expense. At what point does the shaming that happens to people online outweigh the mistake that they made? How we react to others' slip-ups or the mistreatment of others is just as important as our own actions. Not reacting or failing to stand up for others is also, in itself, a choice. For this reason, it is vital that we teach young people not just about how their online choices affect them, but also how their online choices affect others.

## LOOKING AHEAD

As the "father of the Internet," Vint Cerf once said, "The Internet is a reflection of our society and that mirror is going to be reflecting what we see. If we do not like what we see in that mirror the problem is not to fix the mirror, we have to fix society. It is much harder to examine broad systemic changes with a critical lens and to place them in historical context than to focus on what is new and disruptive."[18] Young people's lives are intertwined with technology. They live in two worlds that often overlap. Their use of online tools to communicate is often sophisticated and even young people who have limited access still have more access than kids their age had even just a few years ago.

And yet there are few supports in place to help kids navigate this world, and there are important things to consider when communicating online versus face to face. Just as parents help their kids navigate the playground bully or ask them how about their day at school, it is equally important that we pay attention to what our kids are doing online. If we treat social media and online spaces as equal to the face-to-face spaces that our kids inhabit (as they inherently treat them), then they are more likely to ask for help or guidance, or to share when they are being bullied or feeling like they have lost control of something they have posted.

Although many parents want to monitor their child's social media use and will often follow their child on social media to keep tabs on what they are posting, this alone is only so effective. Engaging students in their own spaces can be helpful for understanding their experiences and for helping kids think about what they are posting. This enables parents to have conversations about questionable content.

However, kids often have multiple accounts and maintain an outward facing account for their parents while maintaining private accounts as well. Conversations about what kids are posting are also only helpful when they are two-way and involve both deep listening and parental guidance. Most of the people reading this book can remember having some kind of privacy from their parents in their interactions with their peers, so although this is new territory and digital footprints can follow kids for their entire lives, it is also important to remember that we learned how to navigate social situations with some autonomy and we also had our own private lives that our parents were not involved in that played a big part in our development as young adults.

Helping kids understand the implications of what they do online can help them think through the choices that they and their peers make. This hybrid world is the world that our young people will inhabit and, although it's easy to blame the technology for the kinds of negativity that we see online, we need to look at ourselves first as users of this technology. It is equally important for us as adults to model respectful and responsible technology use and to see the positive aspects of living a digital life. We should listen to our kids and validate the value that they get out of their online life while helping them navigate the gray areas that, in all honesty, are not that different from the gray areas in our analog lives, only magnified and intensified by the technologies they use.

## LIVING IN THE DIGITAL CLASSROOM

With more and more classrooms going online, students are spending even more time using technology to communicate, collaborate, and create. This means that not only are they spending time online with their peers, they are also being required to be online for their classwork.

As educators and adults, we often chide our young people on the time they "waste" online, but we must remember that by assigning them work online, we are opening the door to distraction by putting them directly in the middle of their social lives as well. If you have ever sat down to lesson plan or pay some bills and discovered that, forty minutes later, you are still scrolling through Facebook, imagine what it is like for your students.

This is not to say that we should not be assigning online work or that we should take our classes offline. This just means that we need to be mindful about how we support students through navigating their limited attention and using it effectively. Many teachers use social media tools to communicate with their students, creating a Facebook page for their class or using a hashtag or Twitter account to provide updates. Although many schools and districts prohibit this because of concerns about what may be posted and how teachers may be connecting with students outside of class, many teachers claim that it helps them meet students "where they are."

However, the attention economy is real, and most, if not all, of the digital tools and technologies that students use are carefully engineered to hold their attention.[19] Young, teenage brains are already impulsive and prone to risky behaviors and poor decision making.[20] This makes them more likely to struggle with regulating their use of technology and more prone to fall victim to the techniques that tech companies use to catch and keep their attention.

Renowned author and professor Howard Rheingold, whose specialty is digital technologies, recounted in his 2014 book *NetSmart* how he began to notice more and more laptops showing up in his classes. One day, he decided to record his classroom and then showed this recording to his students so they could see what they looked like during class. It was apparent that there were varied levels of attention during class and the students saw it. He created a "five laptops at a time" rule, which forced his students to be more aware of their own laptop use and attention.

Although this, of course, is in a lecture-based setting, there are times in *all* classrooms where screens are not necessary for learning. There has also been research showing that notetakers who took notes by hand instead of by typing retained more than those who used a laptop to take notes. This is tied to the fact that writing handwritten notes takes longer and requires more information processing to efficiently record it.[21]

There are times when students *need* to use a computer because of learning accommodations needed for success in the classroom, but it appears that, for most students, it may be beneficial to step away from a screen from time to time. This is why, as the *New York Times* reported, parents in Silicon Valley, the home base of some of the world's largest tech companies, are intentionally limiting screen time for their children, including sending them to expensive private schools that focus on face-to-face interactions and outdoor exploration, while screen time in most US schools is rising.[22]

There is no denying that young people today live a dual life and have grown up managing both an online and offline persona. These personae and their online friends and communities are very real and important to them and have undeniable value. Still, there has not been widespread, intentional guidance provided to young people for how to responsibly live in that online world, and the choices that they make there can have serious consequences. Although it is easy to peg the responsibility on young people themselves as the users of these technologies, there is also an irrefutable responsibility on the part of parents, teachers, and tech companies to help children manage their screen time, the interactions that they have online, and their own self-awareness about their online presence.

This book attempts to go beyond the typical conversations around cyberbullying and digital citizenship and explores topics and issues that affect young people and educators when using technology that are often hidden or misunderstood and are rarely explicitly taught in the classroom. Today's students live in a media-saturated world and they live a large portion of their lives online. As more teachers try to meet students where they are to make content more accessible, they must also understand the risks and underlying costs and benefits of the technology they are using in the classroom while also educating their students on these same costs and benefits. The rest of this book attempts to explain how students' online activities are tracked and used for profit, as well as the laws and responsibilities of educators who implement online technologies in the classroom.

We must meet kids "where they are" and engage them using technologies with which they are familiar, but we must also do this with care, understanding what is actually going on when we and our students are using the Internet.

We must also help them navigate the firehose of information and the barrage of media they are exposed to every day. This is on top of the guidance we can provide for navigating their digital lives safely and responsibly and the validation we can offer for the lives they live online.

Textbox 2.2 provides specific ideas for how to guide students at each grade level through these issues and concepts. Although these are not sample lessons, they are practical ways that educators can both consider the digital world in which their students live and also provide supports for students in those spaces.

TEXTBOX 2.2.

### Elementary Grades

Students in the elementary grades often have varied access to technology and personal devices. Some students have access to a tablet at a young age and some even have a smartphone by the time they are in fourth or fifth grade. At this age, simple conversations around how they use these devices and what their purpose is can help guide students toward thinking responsibly about how they use the device. Younger students can discuss how technology can be used to find answers, learn new things, or for entertainment.

Elementary students can also discuss how they feel when using technology, especially more personal devices like tablets or smartphones (many of them may use their parent's phone, even if they don't have their own). They can also discuss how it feels when they have to put the device away or use it before going to bed. Is it hard to do? Does it make it hard to fall asleep? Why do they think that is? Share with them the importance of limiting screen time right before bed.

For older elementary students who may have started connecting with others on social media, or have started exploring social media sites, conversations around the different platforms, how they are used and what they see there can prove a great jumping-off point. Even activities and discussion around how people build their profiles and what kinds of information should and shouldn't go there can be important. Students should also understand that they are legally not supposed to have a social media account without parental permission until they turn thirteen, although most kids just lie about their age when they set up their account. Talk about the implications of this. If they are lying about their age, who else out there is also lying? How do they know who they are talking to online?

It's not necessary to frighten students away from using social media, because it can also be used to connect with experts; find real-time information; connect with others who share their interests; and share their own pursuits, experiences, and accomplishments. Still, a healthy amount of skepticism is important.

## Middle Grades

Once students hit middle school, many of them will have a social media account, many will have smartphones, and they will have begun to build digital "habits." Like any habit, these can be good or bad.

- Are they staying up late scrolling through Instagram or watching videos on YouTube?
- Do they check their phone as soon as they wake up?
- How do they decide who to follow and how do they decide which friend requests to accept? Is their account public or private?
- Do they watch videos or play games while doing their homework?
- Is their homework digital? If yes, how do they stay focused when they are on the computer?

A great question to ask is, "Why do you use social media?" (You may need to help define *social media* with them first.) Many times, kids use social media because they want to see what everyone else is up to, or because a friend told them to. Some of them follow celebrities or use it to connect with others who share their interests. These are all great conversations to have with kids and will definitely offer some eye-opening insight into their digital lives while also providing a pathway for guidance in building good digital habits.

## High School

By high school, young people's digital habits are much more ingrained. However, many of the same questions can be discussed with high school students. In high school, conversations around time management and technology and the research around multitasking and divided attention are important.

If students have iPhones running iOS 12 or later, they can access a feature called "Screen Time." This tool breaks down the amount of time they spend on their phone, how many times they unlock their phone, and which apps they use the most. Android users have a few options for this kind of tool, too, in the Google Play store, or if they are running Android Pie (version 9.0) they can access *Digital Wellbeing*, which is built into the operating system. Teaching students how to analyze their own screen time, set goals, and monitor their own use can help them build better habits.

In high school, students also need to begin to be more deliberate about their online presence as it relates to college and career success. Share stories like Justine Sacco or Alexandra Wallace, described in this chapter. Share the stories of Tyler Clementi or Megan Meier, two young people who took their lives after being victims of online harassment. What if people watching the harassment unfold had said or done something to stop it? Discuss what it means for their posts to be permanent.

Share with them the story of Harvard rescinding admission for ten students who were found to have participated in an inappropriate Facebook group. Have them do an Internet search for their name, or their name and where they live, or their name and their school's name, and discuss what they find (or don't find). These young people are steps away from adulthood and from being treated as an adult. Unfortunately, their online persona and actions can be harshly judged, and their actions can also have a powerful effect on others.

# 3

# How Does the Internet Work?

The purpose of this chapter is to familiarize the reader with the history of how the Internet came to be, as well as some of the basic vocabulary related to the Internet. Many of the discussions that exist elsewhere in the book will be better understood with a "crash course" in the who, what, when, where, and how of the Internet. The first part of the chapter reads like a history book; understanding this history will help readers understand commercialization, net neutrality, ownership of the Internet, cybersecurity, online privacy, access, and even just a simple understanding of what's happening every time a user goes online. (Hint: it's not magic!) The second part explores what happens when the Internet doesn't work, along with troubleshooting tips. The third part explores implications for the classroom, along with some sample lessons. The last part provides a cheat sheet of terms and acronyms for easy reference either while reading the book or for personal use.

So, although this chapter is heavy on technical terms and historical facts and dates and is a longer read than many of the other chapters, it is a precursor to and lays the groundwork for many of the discussions in subsequent chapters. (See Table 3.1 at the end of this chapter for a glossary of technical terms.) Although there is more to "digital literacy" than the Internet, most of the digital activities and work that both teachers and students do is online or using an Internet-enabled device. As more and more mobile devices such as tablets and cloud-based computers such as Chromebooks enter classrooms, understanding the Internet has become parallel to understanding the work-ings of these devices.

## A BRIEF HISTORY OF THE INTERNET

For young people who have grown up with the Internet, it may be hard to imagine that this powerful, global network is only about as old as their grand-parents and may not have been accessible to their parents growing up. In real-ity, the Internet, which was pulled together through a collaboration between universities and the federal government, is, at the time of this book's publica-tion, only about fifty years old. The Internet as we know it is even younger, and the term *Internet* wasn't even officially used until the Federal Networking Council coined the term in a resolution it passed on October 24, 1995.[1]

The history of the Internet and how it came to be is an important story as the world moves into more and more uncharted territory and as new uses for this powerful network are explored and implemented. Many of the key players in its development are still alive and are still involved in discussions and policy around the Internet, which is also a testament to its youth as a technology. As with any young, fledgling twenty-something, the Internet has experienced growing pains and setbacks, and is still in the process of figuring out what it wants to be. Taking a step back can help put the Internet as we know it today into perspective.

In 1958, in response to the Soviet Union's launch of the Sputnik satel-lite, the Eisenhower administration created the Advanced Research Projects Agency (ARPA) to work on developing new technologies for the military.[2] A few years later, mathematician Leonard Kleinrock at the Massachusetts Insti-tute of Technology (MIT) was exploring the idea of using "packets" instead of circuits to share information. He shared this theory with Lawrence Roberts, who was also at MIT at the time.

When Roberts became head of ARPA in 1967,[3] he used Kleinrock's theory to design and direct the development of ARPANET, the first network that connected computers that were geographically separate.[4] The hope was that using this "packet" technology to communicate would allow the government to communicate even if the Soviets took out the telephone lines because communication would be distributed.[5] This meant that, unlike a phone line, which, when cut, loses connection, packets could take multiple routes to their destinations, maintaining connection even if a wire is cut. Communication was already possible through machines in the same building connected to the same computer through a local area network (LAN), but there was no way for these machines to communicate with computers outside of this hyperlocal network, or machines that were not connected to the same main computer.

This new way of communicating required an interface message processor (IMP), or the very first Internet router. This machine would help direct "traffic" between computers. Each location connected to ARPANET needed its own IMP (Figure 3.1) to connect its computers to the network. The IMPs were connected to existing phone lines.[6] Data was transferred through these IMPs in "packets" rather than through circuits, as in our phone lines, where a direct connection is made between two points.

Messages were divided into separate packets that contained the address of the intended receiver (computer). These packets could be delivered over a variety of lines because the intended destination was part of the packet, which made them more efficient than a circuit connection because smaller amounts of data were being transferred at one time, and because there was more than one path for the data to take. These packets were then reassembled once they reached their destination.[7] On October 29, 1969, Kleinrock and one of his students, Charley Kline, sent the first message using this packet switching technology over ARPANET from an IMP at the University of California, Los Angeles, to an IMP at Stanford Research Institute in Menlo Park, California, and thus the Internet was born.[8]

Three more computers joined the ARPANET network by the end of 1969. As more computers joined the network, it became necessary to create rules, or protocols to make communication effective and efficient between more and more machines. One of the most powerful and important aspects of the work being done was that it was publicly documented and archived as "requests for comments" (RFC) at the same time as this new network was being built. The original documentation still exists, alongside current documentation and Internet standards at http://www.faqs.org/rfcs. There, anyone can view the original release date and author as well as the experimentation and inner workings of some of the technologies that we take for granted today.

One of those technologies is the transmission control protocol/Internet protocol (TCP/IP). It was designed and built by Robert Kahn and Vinton Cerf in the 1970s, and was released as an RFC in 1981.[9] The TCP created rules for how data is transmitted and allows computers to connect to each other, and the IP created rules for how packets are handled, making sure that they are sent and reassembled in the correct order and sent to the correct destina-tion.[10] This protocol was widely adopted by ARPANET in 1980, and is still the backbone of the Internet today.[11]

In addition to needing a protocol for sending packets, a protocol was needed so that packets knew where to go. The original system could not handle ARPANET's rapid growth, and a better system for assigning computer addresses and names was needed. In 1983, Paul Mockapetris created the domain name system (DNS) to handle the translation of computer Internet addresses, which were strings of numbers, to more easily remembered names. This automated system replaced a system that required a centralized text file to be updated by one centralized person. In 1986, DNS became the primary way to manage host names on the Internet and it still remains so today.[12]

Another mainstay of the Internet as we know it today is email. Ray Tom-linson, an electrical engineer at the research and development company Bolt Beranek and Newman, is widely credited with creating the first protocols that allowed users to send messages to each other over ARPANET in 1971. He is also credited with using the "@" symbol in the message address.[13] However, V. A. Shiva Ayyadurai, a future MIT engineer, created a program that he called "EMAIL" in 1978 as a fourteen-year-old high school student. He copyrighted the program and the name "email" in 1982. As a result of this copyright filing, Ayyadurai claims to be the actual inventor of email as we know it.[14] However, his invention is seen more as a new user interface, not a new way to send mes-sages, and because Tomlinson's RFC documentation of new electronic mail standards was released in 1973, he is still credited with creating electronic messaging over ARPANET.[15] In any case, both men played an integral role in what is often considered an irreplaceable aspect of modern life.

In 1985, the National Science Foundation (NSF) got involved in build-ing more connections across research institutions to support the work of scientists and researchers across the country. This fundamentally changed the existing network as more and more computers came online. This new network, which came online in 1986, was called NSFNET. The NSF provided it free of charge to universities, researchers, and other institutions. By 1993, the number of networked computers grew from two thousand to more than two million.[16] Still, these connected machines were limited to educational, sci-entific, and governmental organizations, and few people outside of academia or the government knew about ARPANET or had ever seen it.

In 1989, this would change dramatically. British scientist Tim Berners-Lee conceived of the idea of the World Wide Web as a way for scientists to share information while working at the CERN physics lab in Switzerland. In 1990, he built the framework of the World Wide Web, or the Internet as we know it, including hypertext markup language (HTML), which is used to format webpages across the Internet, the uniform resource identifier (URI) now called uniform resource locator (URL), and hypertext transfer protocol (HTTP), which can be found at the beginning of web addresses, and allows for information retrieval across the Internet.

As of this writing, the very first website he set up in 1991 can still be viewed at http://info.cern.ch/hypertext/WWW/TheProject.html. A strong believer in the importance of an open and free Internet, Berners-Lee announced in April 1993 that CERN, the lab where he worked building this new system, would open up the technology to anyone free of charge. In 1994, he moved to MIT where he started the World Wide Web Consortium (W3C) to continue supporting a free and open web.[17] The NSF ended its work with NSFNET and the Internet in 1998, at the same time that the Internet moved over to private, commercial operations. However, the job of assigning domain names, which was originally done by the NSF, was handed over to a nonprofit called Internet Corporation for Assigned Numbers and Names (ICANN), which still runs domain registration today.[18]

Over the next few decades, as the technology improved and became more reliable, standardized, and commercialized, the Internet grew into a global phenomenon, connecting people across continents and opening up conversations about privacy, access, and freedom of speech, and putting pressure on Tim Berners-Lee's vision of a free and open Internet. In 1995, when a small Internet startup in Silicon Valley called Netscape made its public offering, the Internet was changed forever. This was the first time that the world realized that the Internet could make money.[19]

Since 1995, more and more of the Internet has been transferred to the private sector, which is what has sparked the global debate over "net neutrality," or the idea that Internet service providers (ISPs) like Verizon and Comcast should not be able to prioritize content that goes through their servers. Because ISPs are responsible for the building and upkeep of the Internet's basic infrastructure, they argue that companies whose services use up a lot of network bandwidth because they require huge amounts of data to be sent over the network (think YouTube, Netflix) should be helping pay to maintain the infrastructure they depend on and that the ISP has the right to limit this traffic. Proponents of net neutrality argue that, for instance, if Comcast is able to give priority to certain traffic, it will give priority to traffic from websites and services it owns, while making others pay extra to have their data transmitted at that same, faster speed.

In 2015, the Federal Communications Commission (FCC) voted to change the classification of the Internet to a public utility through the Open Internet order, which treats ISPs similar to phone companies. Although this did not change much on customers' bills, or affect how ISPs currently work, it does prevent ISPs from blocking legal content or "throttling" (slowing down) specific services that it thinks require too much network bandwidth. The biggest arguments for and against these new regulations are based on the growth or stifling of innovation. Opponents of net neutrality say that if ISPs cannot control the data flowing through their networks and can't charge more for companies that usurp it, then they will not have the money to invest in new infrastructure or new Internet technologies. Proponents say that if ISPs can throttle certain companies and put their own interests in the fast lane, that it will kill new Internet

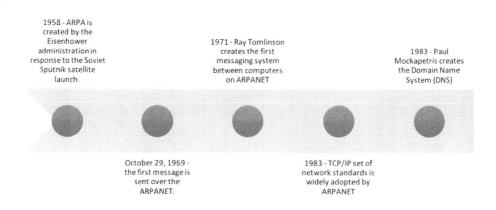

FIGURE 3.1
Internet Timeline

startups because these fledgling companies would not have the resources to enter the "fast lane."[20]

Ajit Pai, the new FCC chairman for the Trump administration, spearheaded new regulatory changes that essentially have done away with net neutrality. The "Restoring Internet Freedom" order took effect on June 11, 2018, and states, "The order replaces unnecessary, heavy-handed regulations dating back to 1934 with strong consumer protections, increased transparency, and common-sense regulations that will promote investment and broadband deployment.[21]

Many of the Internet's original architects believe that maintaining a free and open Internet is vital to its survival. As Berners-Lee stated, "It was simply that had the technology been proprietary, and in my total control, it would probably not have taken off. The decision to make the Web an open system was necessary for it to be universal. You can't propose that something be a universal space and at the same time keep control of it."[22] The concept of who "owns" the Internet and discussions around the openness of the web is a prominent part of the future of the Internet as we know it today, and will most likely continue to be hotly debated as long as the Internet as we know it exists.

1991 - Tim Berners-Lee builds the framework for the World Wide Web (WWW), the precursor to modern Internet.

August 9, 1995 - The tech startup Netscape goes public, and the commercialization and privatization of the web begins.

1985 - The National Science Foundation supports the expansion of connected computers through its NSFNET system, growing the network by thousands of connected computers.

1993 - The CERN lab where Berners-Lee works releases the WWW technology to the world for free.

## HOW THE INTERNET WORKS TODAY

Essentially, the Internet was a grand experiment conceptualized and realized by a small group of people who shared their work widely, which allowed it to grow organically and collaboratively into the network we use today. As the Internet became more widely adopted by those outside of the academic and government spheres, companies like America Online began to offer connection to the Internet for a fee. These ISPs charge a fee to connect customers to the World Wide Web. This is done through cable lines, phone lines, fiber optic lines, or, in more rural areas, a satellite connection.

Phone companies also provide Internet connection to Internet-enabled smartphones through their cellular towers, which translate cellular signals into digital signals and vice versa. Connection to the Internet that is not through a smartphone requires a modem, a technology similar to the IMPs of ARPANET. A modem is a box that converts a digital signal from a computer to an analog signal that can be transferred over a phone or cable line. Many companies rent these to customers for a monthly fee, but a modem can be purchased at an electronics store for use in the home or office. This modem can be connected directly to a desktop computer, gaming system, or wireless router through an Ethernet cable (often called a *Cat-5* or *Cat-6* cable), which transmits the digital signal from the modem to the connected machine. Ethernet is the main way that businesses and schools connect their computers together and to the Internet because it is more reliable than a wireless connection.[23]

Every time a customer accesses a web page, he or she is actually connecting to files hosted on another computer. Clicking on a link sends packets of data (remember the packets from the original ARPANET) to the computer where the website data is stored. These packets know where to go because of the TCP/IP protocols that route the packets to the correct machine. These packets contain not only the IP address (a set of numbers unique to each Internet-connected device) of the intended recipient, but also the IP address of the sender so that, once the packet is received, data can be transferred back to the original sender.

Luckily, because of the DNS system built in the 1980s, users do not have to remember or even know the unique IP addresses of the websites they are trying to access. Instead, because no one is ever going to remember ten numbers and dots in a particular order, these unique identifiers are translated into domain names. For instance, typing 172.217.5.228 into a browser will yield the same result as typing www.google.com.

The IP addresses along with any public information about who owns every website on the Internet can be easily retrieved at the site http://who .is. A quick visit there will also reveal the IP address of your own computer or device at the top of the screen. When a user accesses Google.com, a name server does the work of translating the text into the actual web address (IP address) of the site. These name servers have one of the most important jobs on the Internet, because without them, our data requests would never make it to their intended destination.

Another vital piece of the Internet's main infrastructure is the router. Routers act as Internet hubs, directing traffic across the many different networks that make up the Internet. When packets arrive at a router, it reads the information attached to the packet, specifically the web address that the packet is looking for, and finds the most efficient route to get the packet to its destination. This is how the Internet distributes data across multiple routes so it moves faster through the system. If one pathway is congested, the router sends the packet by another route to its destination.[24]

Packets that are all headed in the same direction don't necessarily take the same route, but when they arrive at their destination, the TCP makes sure that the packets have all arrived and are delivered in the correct order. This is how data that originates in Houston, Texas, for instance, can be delivered to a computer in Memphis, Tennessee in its entirety. Routers make the connections and direct traffic between various networks. We use routers in our own homes to direct traffic, though these are usually wireless routers that manage how our wireless devices connect and send and receive data on our home network.

So how is it that a user in India can access a website hosted in the United States? In an amazing feat of human ingenuity, cables that run across both the Atlantic and Pacific Oceans connect the continents; they are mostly maintained by private companies like Google and Microsoft. These cables, however, are not the first of their kind.

The first successful cable across the Atlantic was completed in 1866 to provide a globally connected telegraph system.[25] Today's cables are made of high-grade fiber optic materials and are laid by an undersea robot that digs a trench while a ship above uncoils the line. The lines must be replaced every few decades for upgrades and because of wear and tear.[26] Communication through these undersea cables works the same as it does aboveground, allowing users on one continent to send packets of data to computers on another continent seamlessly. Because data that moves over fiber optic cables is transmitted as light, this data moves extremely fast (at the speed of light), so even over these long distances, users do not experience a delay.

Anyone who uses a wireless router in the home adds one more layer to the data transfer process. Whereas routers exist within the infrastructure of the Internet, directing traffic and making sure that data packets go where they are supposed to, a *wireless router* is connected directly to the modem and broadcasts its own radio signal to the immediate area. Any device with a wireless card can pick up that signal and connect to it. The broadcast range for a home wireless router is fairly small, so neighbors two blocks away can't "see" or connect to the router.[27] Still, it is best to secure the router's signal with a strong password to keep unwanted guests off of the network.

Connecting to a wireless router does not necessarily mean that a device will connect to the Internet. Many devices in the home use the router to "talk" without using it to access the Internet. For instance, a wireless printer has an IP address and a wireless card and can connect to a computer or other device that is also connected to the router or to the same network that the router is connected to (remember, it is plugged directly into the modem). This printer is not connecting to the Internet, but is connecting directly to another device on the same network, similar to the original LANs of the 1960s. This kind of connection is also called an "intranet" because it is an internal network created between devices that are all connected to the same network.[28]

In contrast, a computer that is connected to a wireless router sends its IP address (assigned by the wireless router) through the router, which then sends the data through the modem to access the Internet using the modem's assigned IP address. IP addresses of machines connected to a wireless router in the home are all very similar since this network is intended to be internal, not external.[29] Similarly, devices like home security systems and even lights in the home can be connected to the Internet through a wireless connection. These devices can be accessed from anywhere because they are connected to the wireless router, which then sends communication back and forth through the modem out onto the Internet.

This new phenomenon is called the "Internet of Things" (IoT), and, although convenient, it also has its security drawbacks. Although it is great to know that you can watch your house from a beach chair at the Jersey Shore, once something is connected to the Internet, the likelihood of someone *else* watching your house increases if they are able to get onto your wireless router or your network.[30] Many of the devices used in the massive attack discussed later in this chapter weren't computers at all, but IoT devices connected to the Internet.

In a nutshell, the Internet is series of connections between computers and other devices across the globe, with each machine connected to the Internet having its own unique IP address (like a home address) and a set of universal protocols (rules) that direct packets of data between these devices. Users pay a company called an ISP (think Comcast, Verizon, AT&T, or Time Warner) to connect them to this network, which requires a box called a modem to translate digital signals into analog signals that can be transferred across phone and cable lines and to satellites.

Users can access the Internet directly through the modem by connecting a computer through Ethernet, or they can use a wireless router that broadcasts a signal to any device within range to allow it to pass data through the modem. Some items in the home use the wireless router to connect to each other rather than connect outside the home to the Internet. All of these processes happen within seconds and are based on the foundations laid out decades ago by innovative pioneers who took an idea, collaborated, shared their discoveries with each other, and built on the work of others to create a tool that connects continents.

### WHAT HAPPENS WHEN THE INTERNET DOESN'T WORK?

Anyone who has ever used the Internet knows that it doesn't always work 100 percent of the time. There are a number ways that the Internet might not "work." A website may not load properly, a computer may have difficulty connecting, the signal coming into a user's home may stop working, a wireless router may go down or go bad. Or there may be more nefarious things going on. Identity theft, hacked email and social media accounts, and even silent, hard to recognize takeovers of devices are all too common in the age of the Internet.

#### Common, Harmless Internet Disruptions

As explained previously, the Internet relies on phone lines, fiber optic lines, cable lines, and satellites. Should anything happen to any of these lines, a user may experience an outage. A construction crew may hit a fiber optic line, or a power surge may cause a router to go down. Even an issue with the line coming directly into the house may cause an outage. These kinds of outages are usually hyperlocal, only affecting those geographically near, and they are usually quickly repaired. Calling the ISP directly usually provides an answer as to whether an outage is related to a line disruption. Another way to know if the issue is related to the ISP is to look at the modem in the home. If it is not showing a connection, there may be an issue.

If it appears that the ISP service is not the issue, there may be an issue with the modem or, if applicable, the wireless router. Like any piece of electronics, modems can go bad and eventually must be replaced. If the user is renting the modem from his or her ISP, calling the ISP for troubleshooting is the best way to find out and get a replacement quickly. If the user owns the modem, calling the manufacturer may be the best way to go. Sometimes, all a modem needs (like any electronic equipment) is a reset. This can be done using the reset button, the on/off switch, or by unplugging and replugging in the device.

If the modem is not showing any sign of loss of connection, the next thing to check is the wireless router. This router, as explained previously, connects directly to the modem and broadcasts a wireless signal that computers and other devices in the house connect to. If the router is not showing a connection, a simple reset like one for the modem may fix the problem. If the router is rented through an ISP, calling the ISP for troubleshooting is the next step; if the router is owned, the customer should call the manufacturer. Wireless routers also go bad and sometimes must be replaced as well. Another trick to try is simply toggling the wireless off on whatever device the user is trying to connect. Turning it off and on again can often restore the connection.

Some common, harmless disruptions are not caused by physical disruptions, but rather data congestion. As explained previously, websites, email, and other online services are run off of servers, which are machines that run the Internet. If a server goes down or is overloaded with traffic, it may cause a website or web tool to stop working properly. Most large companies have multiple servers spread out geographically, so that if one goes down, it doesn't disrupt the whole system, but only a small subset of users. These kinds of outages are often fixed quickly by the company affected and many times the company indicates the outage to its customers. Sites like http://www.isitdownrightnow.com/ show the current status of major websites and allow users to search for specific sites.

**Harmful Disruptions of Service**

Although most disruptions are harmless to the user, some are more nefarious, such as a denial of service (DoS) or distributed denial of service (DDoS) attacks. These are caused when an attacker attempts to overload a server by sending a barrage of requests to the server (requests are attempts to access the site), causing it to crash or preventing it from being able to handle any more requests. This prevents anyone else from accessing the site. This can also be done to individuals' email accounts. An attacker can send a barrage of large files to an email address, making the email inaccessible. When the attack is *distributed*, it means that the attacker has taken control of other computers, forcing them to send messages to the intended target.[31]

The largest DDoS attack in history occurred on October 21, 2016. The attack targeted the servers that control most of the Internet's DNS services. It is estimated that this attack leveraged around one hundred thousand devices around the world, many of them Internet-connected devices such as digital cameras, not just computers. Because DNS services are vital to Internet traffic, this attack caused major websites to go down, mostly across the United States, including sites like Twitter and Netflix.[32]

Preventing your machine from becoming part of a DDoS attack is difficult to prevent without installing antivirus software and setting up a firewall (software that monitors incoming web traffic to a computer and searches for potentially harmful content), but being a victim of ransomware is a bit easier to prevent. When a computer becomes a victim of ransomware, the user can no longer use the machine until a ransom is paid. This usually happens when a user clicks on a link in an email or opens an attachment that contains malicious code. This code then takes over the machine, locking the user out. In general, users should avoid clicking links directly in emails, even if it comes from someone familiar. Often, these emails are sent through compromised email accounts. If you receive an email from an unknown sender that contains a link, try to access the homepage of the site listed or do a quick web search to see if it's legitimate before clicking. In addition, do not open attachments from strangers or that look "fishy" in any way.[33]

Following these tips can also prevent "phishing scams." These are also attempts to either gain access to a user's computer or to a user's account. Usually, the user clicks on a link that connects to a legitimate-looking site and asks the user to log in. The premise of the fraudulent email is often that the user needs to log into his or her bank's website to update information, or that there is an opportunity available by clicking on the link.[34] One recent phishing scam was so sneaky that it emulated the document sharing email sent by Google Docs claiming that someone had shared a file with the user. Users who clicked the link in the email were sent to a login screen that looked like Google to enter their login credentials. This gave the creators of the scam both the victim's email address and password for their Google account.[35]

One of the easiest ways to avoid having personal information compromised online involves everyone's favorite thing: free Wi-Fi. Coffee shops, many cities, public libraries, and even McDonald's offer it. However, there are some dangers to connecting to these networks. The first danger is knowing whether the network being connected to is actually the one provided by the business or location. Sometimes, a nefarious hacker (not all hackers are nefarious, but these definitely are) create an open wireless network of his or her own with a name like "Free Wi-Fi" or "Coffee Shop Wi-Fi." When a user connects, he or she is actually connecting to the hacker's network, giving the hacker access to all of the user's personal information. Make sure to find out what the *exact* name of the location's wireless is.

A dependable coffee shop network will also have some kind of password. However, even connecting to the legitimate network can still be unsafe. If the hacker is also connected to the same wireless router, he or she can use special software to monitor traffic through that router. Using a virtual private network (VPN) to route your Internet traffic through a different, protected server will make the hacker unable to access the data going in and out of your computer. Also, making sure to use sites with addresses that start with *https*, not just *http*, indicates that these sites are secure and will encrypt data going between your machine and the website.[36]

The Internet makes modern life more efficient in many ways, except, of course, when it doesn't do what it's supposed to do or when it is used against the very people using it. Basic protections can help, such as installing antivirus software, setting up firewalls, being careful with links and attachments in emails, and even something as simple as making sure that the wireless router in the home is password protected (and not with 12345 as the password). Unfortunately, there are no real protections against acts of nature, but these interruptions are usually temporary and harmless.

## THE INTERNET IN THE CLASSROOM

Computers were brought into the classroom as early as the 1980s, but it wasn't until the 1990s that classroom computers came online. Part of the early adoption of computers in the classroom can be attributed to Seymour Papert, the innovative and renowned educator, mathematician, and creator of the first programming language for children, Logo. Papert, along with his colleagues, created Logo in 1968, not long before the first transmission over ARPANET.

Papert believed that children could and should program computers, rather than merely using programs on the computer.[37] However, most classrooms lucky enough to have a computer at the time mostly used them for word processing or educational games based on floppy disks or CD-ROMs.

According to a 2006 study by the National Center for Education Statistics, only 3 percent of public school classrooms had Internet connection in 1994. Five years later, in 1999, that number grew to 77 percent.[38] This increased access changed the way that students conducted research and accessed information, and caused a dramatic shift in how information was delivered, consumed, and created in the classroom. Although discussions of technology integration in the classroom and best practices for teaching and learning with technology are beyond the scope of this book, many of the ideas, discussions, and lessons in this book provide a backbone for working with technology and the Internet in the classroom.

## IMPLICATIONS FOR THE CLASSROOM

The who, what, when, where, and why of the history of the Internet has huge implications for how technology and the Internet is used in and out of the classroom. Students should be familiar with and know how to avoid the scams and concerns discussed previously, and having a basic understanding of what is happening when they access a website helps explain the privacy issues involved in using the Internet.

Because a device's IP address is sent with every online request, this becomes a unique identifier for the student as well. This is how YouTube tracks unique views, but it's also how advertisers know who is clicking what and when and where. It is also how "anonymous" users can be traced on the Internet and how law enforcement tracks down cyber criminals. Because many students (and teachers) are online nearly constantly throughout the day, understanding how and when their online activity and presence is tracked and monitored is just as important as knowing how to perform an effective search using a search engine.

Understanding the flat leadership and altruistic intentions of the creators of the Internet and its use as a purely academic and nonprofit tool for more than two decades, should spark conversation around the commercialization of the Internet, government control and regulation of the Internet, and important debates around net neutrality, as well as online censorship and freedom of speech. It is also important to look around the world to see how other countries regulate (or don't regulate) the Internet. Comparing and contrasting the way the United States regulates the Internet with how the Chinese or North Korean governments do is an eye-opening conversation. There is even a section of the new European Union General Data Protection privacy law that gives all EU citizens the "right to be forgotten" by requiring search engines to remove incorrect information about a person from search results.[39]

For lessons at various grade levels centered on this chapter's content, see Textbox 3.1. A sample lesson is provided in Textbox 3.2.

TEXTBOX 3.1.

**Elementary Grades**

In the younger grades, the Internet may be a place where students go to play games or watch videos. They may not be aware of the larger picture of what the Internet actually is. As a class, brainstorm some things that students use the Internet for. What is something they learned while using the Internet? What is something exciting that they found on the Internet? Discuss how the Internet allows people to share ideas, pictures, videos, and music across long distances. Students may also not be aware that some of their favorite services, such as Netflix or Hulu, are Internet based, even if they watch it on their TV.

Ask students where they think the information they find on the Internet comes from. Discuss how content on the Internet is put up by people, that everything they see and hear and read on the Internet was put there by someone. The Internet allows them to access things created by people all over the world. Have them create their own visual depiction of the Internet.

## Middle Grades

Give students a blank piece of paper. Have them, individually or in small groups, draw their understanding of how the Internet works. This can include words, symbols, pictures, and so on. Have a few groups or individuals read out their replies. Show students the Code.org video "What is the Internet?" (https://www.youtube.com/watch?v=Dxcc6ycZ73M) followed by the video "Packets, Routing and Reliability" (https://www.youtube.com/watch?v=AYdF7b3nMto). Then have students flip over the paper and draw how the Internet works. Have them compare their two responses. Pair the activity with an exit ticket asking students to explain in their own words how the Internet works. This whole series by Code.org is excellent if there is time to watch them all.

## High School Grades

Pair this activity with conversations around IP addresses or even a research unit when exploring the sources that students are using. This can be done as a whole class or by individual students. Go to http://who.is and look up your school's website. Discuss the information that students find (or don't find) there. Why might information be missing?

Look up a famous or favorite website. What did you or didn't you find? Did anything surprise you? What domains are for sale? Why do you think that someone would buy a domain that closely resembles a popular domain?

Students can also see what is known about their own IP address by going to: http://infosniper.net. They can discuss the implications of this as a class. What did they learn about IP addresses?

## TEXTBOX 3.2. CASE STUDY

To help her high school students understand how the Internet works, Philadelphia educator Marcie Hull had them use paper cutouts and signs that have the different parts of a network written on them. Students then arranged classmates holding the paper cutouts and signs in order of what is connected to their home modem or router. As a follow up, students then used LucidChart software to create a diagram of their home network, properly labeling every connection, including what kind of wire it uses or if it's wireless. An example can be seen in Figure 3.2 and can be found at https://scienceleadership.org/blog/my_home_internet.

### My Home Internet

Posted by Siawale Vesslee in Technology- Freshmen - Hull - b2 on Friday, November 22, 2013 at 7:06 am

In this quarter, we learned about where our internet comes from in our homes. Because of this, we also had to learn about the different Acceptable Use Policies (AUP) that we, as SLA students, are held under. We learned about the School District of Philadelphia AUP and SLA's AUP. After learning about the AUPs, we discussed about how to make smart decisions when using the internet. To me, this was very insightful because I never knew that my activities on the internet were being monitored. This was a reality check and it kept me informed.

FIGURE 3.2
Screenshot from https://scienceleadership.org/blog/my_home_internet. Accessed March 1, 2019.

**Table 3.1. Glossary of Technical Terms**

| Term | Definition |
| --- | --- |
| bandwidth | Bandwidth is the rate of data transfer across a path. Often in reference to the bitrate or speed that information travels across the Internet. |
| bluetooth | Bluetooth is a radio signal used to connect devices over a short distance. |
| browser | A browser is a program used to display Internet webpages. |
| denial-of-service (DoS) attack | A DoS is any type of attack in which the attackers (hackers) attempt to prevent legitimate users from accessing the service. This is usually done by sending repeated requests to a server, preventing legitimate users from connecting to it. |
| distributed denial-of-service (DDoS) attack | A DDoS attack uses a number of hosts to overwhelm a server, causing a website to experience a complete system crash. This is different from a DoS attack because it leverages multiple hosts (senders). |
| domain | In a simple network domain, many computers or workgroups are directly connected. This includes users, workstations, printers, and other connected devices. For example, www.apple.com is a domain. |
| domain name server (DNS) | The basic function of a DNS is to translate a domain name like www.apple.com into its respective IP address. |
| download | To download a file is to retrieve it from a website so that it is placed directly onto an individual's computer. |
| encryption | Encryption is a way to prevent access to messages sent between users by encoding the original message so that it requires a key to be decoded. |
| Ethernet cable | An Ethernet cable is composed of twisted copper strands used to connect computers in an LAN. |
| fiberoptic cable | A fiberoptic cable is made up of many thin optical fiber strands made of plastic or glass that transmit pulses of light at very high speeds. |
| firewall | A firewall is security technology that blocks access to and from potentially unsafe sources on a network. |
| hypertext | A word, phrase, or chunk of text that can be linked to another document or text. |
| hypertext markup language (HTML) | HTML is the major markup language used to display web pages on the Internet. In other words, web pages are composed of HTML code, which is used to display text, images, or other resources through a web browser. |

| | |
|---|---|
| hypertext transfer protocol (HTTP) and hypertext transfer protocol secure (HTTPS) | HTTP is the protocol that web browsers use to gather web content for users. The browser uses HTTP to communicate to the server and retrieve web content for the user. If there is a letter s after http, then the site is considered "secure." This is often seen with banking websites and other portals that contain private or personal information. |
| Internet protocol (IP) address | An IP address is a logical numeric address that is assigned to every single computer, printer, switch, router, or any other device that is part of a TCP/IP-based network. |
| Internet service provider (ISP) | An ISP is a company that provides customers with Internet access. These are companies like Comcast, Verizon, and AT&T. |
| interface message processor (IMP) | The IMP was the first packet-router. It was part of the ARPANET, the precursor to today's Internet. |
| Internet of things (IoT) | The IoT is a computing concept that describes the idea of everyday physical objects being connected to the Internet and being able to identify themselves to other devices. |
| local area network (LAN) | An LAN is a computer network within a small geographical area such as a home, school, computer laboratory, office building, or group of buildings. |
| malware | Malware is software that intentionally disables or damages a computer. This is often installed accidently through the clicking of links in emails and on suspicious websites. |
| modem | A modem allows computers to connect to the Internet by converting analog signals from phone lines to digital signals that computers understand. These are an integral part of how we connect to the Internet in our homes. |
| network (net) neutrality | Net neutrality is a principle that asserts that governments and Internet service providers should not place restrictions on consumers' access to networks participating in the Internet. In general, net neutrality prevents restrictions on content, platforms, sites and equipment, and modes of communication. |
| packets | A packet normally represents the smallest amount of data that can traverse over a network at a single time. A TCP/IP network packet contains several pieces of information, including the data it is carrying, source destination IP addresses, and other constraints required for quality of service and packet handling. |
| phishing | Phishing is an attempt by a malicious user to gain access to another user's account or personal information (e.g., credit card account information) through deceptive emails that look like they come from a legitimate source. |

| | |
|---|---|
| ransomware | Ransomware is a piece of software that locks a user out of his or her computer and files until a ransom is paid. |
| router | A router is an Internet device that manages how packets of data move around a network. |
| spyware | Spyware is software that hides on a computer and monitors all the activity on the computer, stealing information like credit card numbers and passwords and sending them back to the originator of the software. |
| transmission control protocol (TCP)/ internet protocol (IP) or TCP/IP | TCP works in conjunction with IP to ensure that data is properly delivered on the Internet. IP creates a universal standard for how data is transmitted and TCP ensures end-to-end delivery. Most people refer to this as TCP/IP because they work together. |
| upload | To send a file from your computer to a website. |
| uniform resource locator (URL) | A URL is the address of a resource on the Internet. These are commonly referred to as web addresses and contain the name of the server where the resource is located as well as, if necessary, the specific resource being accessed. For example, www.apple.com/support is a URL. |
| virtual private network (VPN) | A VPN is a private network that is built over a public infrastructure. Security mechanisms, such as encryption, allow VPN users to securely access a network from different locations via a public telecommunications network, most frequently the Internet. This allows users to securely access private networks from any location. |
| virus | A virus is a piece of computer code or a program that can copy itself and spread from computer to computer with the intent of damaging or disabling computer systems. |
| Wi-Fi | Wi-Fi is a technology by which devices connect over a short range through radio waves sent through a wireless access point. This allows devices to connect to each other and to connect to the Internet without needing a direct cable connection. |
| World Wide Web (WWW) | The WWW is a network of online content that is formatted in HTML and accessed via HTTP. The term refers to all the interlinked HTML pages that can be accessed over the Internet. The WWW was originally designed in 1991 by Tim Berners-Lee while he was a contractor at CERN. It is the aspect of the Internet that most people interact with. |

All definitions directly from or adapted from Techopedia (http://www.techopedia.com) and Wikipedia (http://www.wikipedia.com) on October 26, 2018.
"Bandwidth (computing)," Wikipedia, December 6, 2018, accessed December 10, 2018, https://en.wikipedia.org/wiki/Bandwidth_(computing).

# 4

# Search Engines

As explained in Chapter 1, the Internet was originally composed of a small, insular group of scientists and researchers communicating and sharing information. The addresses of the machines they used were listed in a directory and accessed directly. Web pages didn't exist yet and there was no need for search engines because so few people were using the network. Instead, users employed file transfer protocol, a technology that still exists and is in use today to share files, and they accessed digital libraries through a direct connection, or used a tool like "Archie" that indexed files by collating a text-based list of publicly available files on the network.[1]

Archie is widely considered the first search engine, although it lacked the complexity of even the earliest search engines that were born after the advent of the World Wide Web. As of this writing, a copy of it can still be accessed at the University of Warsaw's site (http://archie.icm.edu.pl/archie_eng.html; Figure 4.1), although it hasn't been updated since 1999. A search for "cats" produces a list of files as seen in Figure 4.2. These files date back to 2001, so most likely this version of Archie has not indexed any files since then.

After 1989, when the Internet opened up to a larger audience and web pages became more and more common through the World Wide Web, trying to locate information became more and more difficult and there was no easy way to search all of the new websites coming online. This is where search engines as we know them came in. Many Internet historians point to Excite,

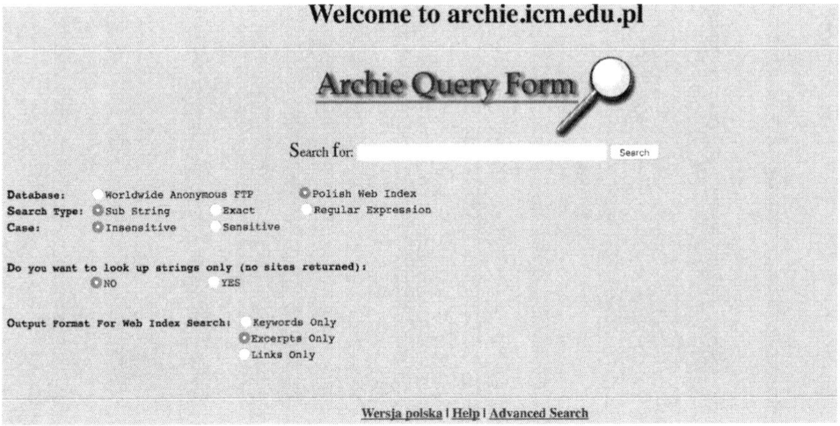

# Welcome to archie.icm.edu.pl

## Archie Query Form

Search for: [_____] Search

| | |
|---|---|
| **Database:** | ○ Worldwide Anonymous FTP    ● Polish Web Index |
| **Search Type:** | ○ Sub String    ○ Exact    ○ Regular Expression |
| **Case:** | ○ Insensitive    ○ Sensitive |

Do you want to look up strings only (no sites returned):
○ NO          ○ YES

Output Format For Web Index Search:  ○ Keywords Only
                                     ● Excerpts Only
                                     ○ Links Only

Wersja polska I Help I Advanced Search

FIGURE 4.1

Screenshot from http://archie.icm.edu.pl/archie_eng.html. Accessed September 4, 2018.

## Archie Query Results

New Advanced Query I New Simple Query

Modify Search : cat

### Found 100 Hit(s)

More Results

*(1)* ftp.task.gda.pl

     *1* /vol/d31/ftp.debian.org/pub/debian/pool/main/s/safecat
     -rw-rw-r--   19906     21:00:00 22 Jun 2001 GMT    safecat_1.8-1_mipsel.deb

*(2)* ftp.man.szczecin.pl

     *2* /disks/disk0/debian/pool/main/s/safecat
     -r--r--r--   19906     21:00:00 22 Jun 2001 GMT    safecat_1.8-1_mipsel.deb

*(3)* ftp.lubman.pl

     *3* /vol/2/linux-debian/pool/main/s/safecat
     -r--r--r--   19906     21:00:00 22 Jun 2001 GMT    safecat_1.8-1_mipsel.deb

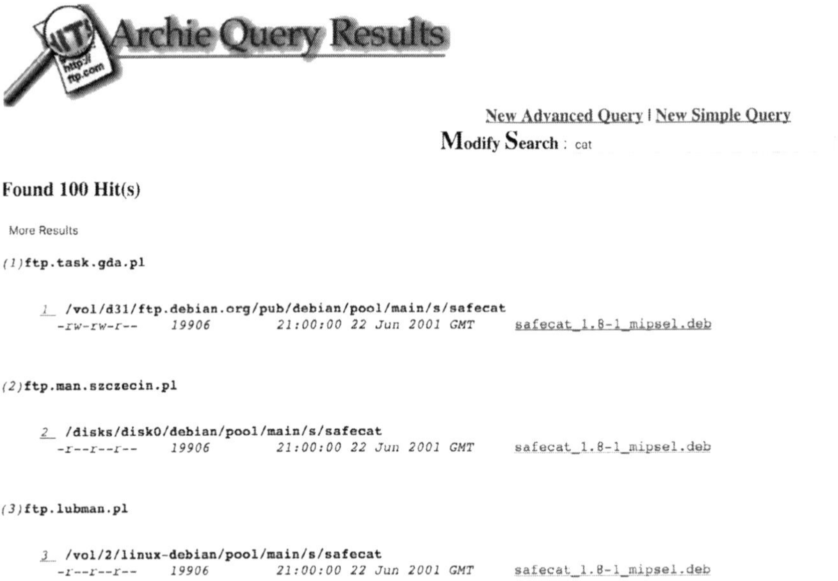

FIGURE 4.2

Screenshot from http://archie.icm.edu.pl/archie_eng.html. Accessed September 4, 2018.

released in 1993, as the first search engine that analyzed the content of a web-page. A year later, WebCrawler came on the scene with the ability to search and index the title, header, and content of web pages all over the Internet. Following WebCrawler was Lycos, which allowed users to change their search results settings to better fit their interests. In two years, Lycos had indexed and archived sixty million websites.[2]

## SPIDERS, WEB CRAWLERS, AND BOTS

The most important technological advances of these search engines were based on how they competed to improve how they discovered and archived content across a rapidly growing Internet. Search engines use software called web crawlers, also known as "spiders" or "bots," to scan the Internet. These spiders follow the links the same way that a regular Internet user would, except they collect all kinds of data from websites they visit, including the URL, the title, content, links on the page, and any other information that the creator of the spider wishes. They then index the sites by creating an individual record for each site, and they archive this information into a large database. This way, each time a spider visits a site, it merely updates the existing information in the database with any new information it finds.

Essentially, any Internet search is actually accessing this database and not the actual website itself. The results that a user sees are based on the data last pulled from a site by the spider or bot and can be customized by the creator of the search engine; in the case of Google (and no doubt others), the user's search history can influence search results as well.

## SEARCH ALGORITHMS

Search engines often rely on proprietary algorithms, or sets of rules, to decide what to show users and in what order. Because search results tend to be shown in list format, they try to show the most relevant and reliable information at the top of the list. The algorithms often depend on the popularity of the site, how many other sites link to the site, and more recently, even if the site is easily viewed on multiple kinds of devices.

In Google's own words, its "algorithms rely on more than 200 unique signals or 'clues' that make it possible to guess what you might really be looking for."[3] All search engines, not just Google, use algorithms. However, each company's algorithm is different. What is often similar across many search engines is the appearance of ads at the top of the search results. Although search engines are a vital and necessary part of the Internet, they are not free to run. This is why, despite the ranking system used by search engines, there will very often be "sponsored results" above the search results. It is important to note the difference between an ad placed at the top of a search results page and the site that the search engine thinks is most relevant to a search.

Google, although the most well known, is not the only search engine out there. The second most used search engine is Microsoft's Bing search engine, released in 2009.[4] A number of search engines are not based in the United States. For instance, according to its Wikipedia page, China's Baidu search engine is ranked as one of the most popular search engines in the world.[5] Another search engine that has grown in popularity in recent years is Duck Duck Go (http://duckduckgo.com), a search engine that markets itself as the search engine that doesn't track you and what you do online.

This kind of tracking is discussed in more detail in other chapters; for now, it's important to understand that tracking is partially related to the customized search results described previously as well as to the advertising users see in these results. Duck Duck Go is not as robust as Google, but many people feel safer using it knowing that their searches are not being tracked. Duck Duck Go's algorithm shows different results than Google for the same search term for this reason.

## BROWSERS VERSUS SEARCH ENGINES

Along with understanding how search engines work and how to best leverage them, it is important to understand the difference between a browser and a search engine. In today's web environment, search engines are so integrated into browsers that sometimes they seem as if they are part of the browser. However, while these tools work in tandem, they serve very different purposes.

Web browsers are the applications that allow users to view web pages on the Internet. They access sites for us and turn lines and lines of code into visual displays of information. Anyone hoping to do a quick Google or Bing search could easily go to Google.com or Bing.com to access the search engine. However, fewer and fewer browsers require users to directly access search engines. Rather, users can choose their default search engine and then use the URL address bar as a search box. This is true whether using a desktop, tablet, or a smartphone.

## DATABASES VERSUS SEARCH ENGINES

Search engines are not the only place to find information online. Scholarly databases like Education Resources Information Center (ERIC) or JSTOR are used by higher education communities and professional communities looking for high-quality, peer-reviewed sources. ERIC is run by the Institute of Education Sciences of the United States Department of Education and has a number of built-in tools to help locate and identify sources. Users can often click on external links that take them directly to the source. Although some of these sources do show up in a general internet search done through a traditional search engine, a direct search of ERIC's database returns only scholarly results. College students and other professionals can usually access these sources for free through an institutional login. ERIC can be accessed through http://eric.ed.gov.

JSTOR is a nonprofit organization that works similarly to ERIC but is not run by the federal government and is specifically geared toward libraries. The organization started in 1995 as a solution for libraries to make room by digitizing their collections.[6] Although public domain searches are unlimited and free, access to JSTOR databases with a free account are limited; the site requires a membership fee for unlimited access to its full database. It does offer different pricing structures for schools, libraries, and individuals. JSTOR can be accessed at http://www.jstor.org.

Google's search engine sometimes lists sources under "scholarly articles." This is because Google has a project called *Google Scholar* (http://scholar .google.com) that allows users to search Google's database of scholarly papers. Some of these can be accessed for free, but many direct the user to the specific journal article where they can read an abstract and request a license to view the entire piece. These articles can often be found by directly searching ERIC or JSTOR.

## KEYWORDS AND SEARCH TERMS

Every Internet search is made up of words. These words are called *keywords*. As the name suggests, not all words play a role in finding information. Keywords are the words in a search that play the most important role in the query. For instance, a search for the world's largest land mammal would have to include the words *largest*, *land*, and *mammal* to produce an accurate result. Similarly, searching for the results of an election or hotels in a specific locale would have to include location information along with the word *election* or *hotel*.

When keywords are strung together to form a search, they become a *search term* or *query*. These queries are what we type into a search engine to find the answer we are looking for. However, knowing what keywords best fit your topic will lead to better search queries and better results.

## INTERNET SEARCH TIPS

So how can someone looking for information find the most relevant information? The first step to a good Internet search is to use the best keywords possible. Keywords are the words that a user types into a search engine to find the information they seek. Often, a user will simply type his or her search term, or string of keywords, as an entire question verbatim into the search engine. However, although Google's algorithm has become so sophisticated that it can analyze a question and display what it believes is the best answer, a quick comparison of the results of *how to peel an onion* and simply *peel an onion* shows that they have almost identical search results. Once the search results appear, users can also see the bolded words that the algorithm focused on for the search. These words are the same whether the search includes the word *how* or not. That's because Google's search algorithm is not focused on every word, but rather searches its database for just the words it thinks matter. This is a faster, more efficient way for the most relevant information to be delivered back to the user.

Keywords are also an important part of narrowing down searches. For instance, a search for *peel an onion* will not necessarily help with preparing that great stew that contains tiny pearl onions. By simply adding the word *pearl*, the search results narrow down the search. Similarly, a search for *South Korea president* will show many resources about the current president of South Korea, Moon Jae-in. However, add the word "corruption" to the end of the search, and the results are completely different. A simple search that included just *president* would have completely omitted much of the news articles related to the recent impeachment scandal involving South Korea's (now former) president.

Search engines, however, have begun to include more layers to their search results. For instance, a search for *South Korea president* on the default search results page may not include a lot of information about the scandal, but by clicking on the *News* option that many if not most search engines have now at the top of the results page, a user can find current events related to his or her search. In addition, most search engines include options for video or image results, and even results that the algorithm believes are related to the original search, helping anyone seeking information to see a variety of results related to their original search term.

Another way to get the most relevant information to an Internet search is by using search commands. For instance, a Google search for *president South Korea* that is then narrowed down by clicking the *News* option on the search results page. However, as shown in Figure 4.3, that results page also contains articles related to North Korea.

This is because of the shared word, *Korea*, is in the search results. A close look will show that the website snapshot gathered by the web crawler has the word *Korea* bolded all by itself without the word *South*. Simply putting the words "South Korea" or "president South Korea" in quotation marks can eliminate these kinds of overlapping yet often unrelated results. Quotation marks tell the Google search engine to only return results that include the words between the quotation marks in that exact order. In this case, the results show all three words in a bolded string, as shown in Figure 4.4.

 Cyr: **South Korea President** Moon Jae-in is key leader in regional ...
Chicago Tribune - 11 hours ago
History encourages persistence, and the **Korean** Peninsula is an especially important example of that principle. The meeting last summer ...

**South Korea** wants to brainwash students to whitewash North Korea's ...
Washington Examiner - 8 hours ago

**South Korea** Plans to Inspect Site of Inter-Korean Road Connection ...
Sputnik International - 8 hours ago

Building Confidence in Denuclearization: A Roadmap for the **Korean** ...
The Diplomat - 9 hours ago

N. **Korea** still mum on S. **Korean** foreign minister's offer to meet
Local Source - Yonhap News - 5 hours ago

Something extraordinary is happening in North **Korea**, and it has ...
In-Depth - The Times - 9 hours ago

Washington E...  Sputnik Intern...  Yonhap News  The Diplomat  The Times  The Asian Age

**View all**

FIGURE 4.3
Screenshot from Google search results. Accessed October 8, 2018.

It is helpful to know search commands to improve search results. These can range from simple quotation marks, as explained previously, to symbols and indicators used to tweak the algorithm itself. To create a more complex search command, include *filetype:* in a search. If a user is looking for a PDF file, a simple addition of *filetype: pdf* along with the keyword or search term will only return results that are in PDF format. Each search engine uses its own commands, and, although some are universal, others are specific to a

**Supporters of ousted South Korea leader outraged over jail for ...**
Reuters - 16 hours ago
SEOUL (Reuters) - Hundreds of diehard supporters of ousted **South Korean President** Park Geun-hye reacted with outrage on Friday after ...

**Will Samsung Case Mark A Turning Point For South Korean ...**
NPR - 10 hours ago
Samsung's chief was just sent to prison by a **South Korean** court ...
Vox - 8 hours ago

**South Korea** court says Samsung leader Lee gave bribe to win ...
Channel NewsAsia - 19 hours ago

Samsung Heir Gets five years for scandal that toppled **South Korean** ...
In-Depth - Financial Post - 12 hours ago

Samsung Verdict Sends a Tough New Message to **South Korea** Inc.
In-Depth - New York Times - 5 hours ago

Financial Post   New York Tim...      NPR            Vox         Channel News...   The Guardian

**View all**

**The sprawling corruption scandal that rocked South Korea**
CNN - 17 hours ago
On it they found evidence that Choi, a close friend and unofficial adviser of then-**South Korean President** Park Geun-hye, had been receiving ...

**North Korea launch of three missiles fails, US says**
CBS News - 18 minutes ago
The JCS says the **South Korea** and U.S. militaries were analyzing the launch. **South Korea's presidential** office has convened a National ...

North **Korea** launches three missiles into sea, heightening tensions
Washington Post - 1 hour ago

North **Korea** Fires Short-Range Missiles in Apparent Failed Test
Bloomberg - 2 hours ago

Living on the edge of oblivion: life along the North **Korean** border
In-Depth - The Guardian - 17 hours ago

FIGURE 4.4
Screenshot from Google search results. Accessed October 8, 2018.

**Table 4.1.**

| Search Command | Example |
|---|---|
| Site: | Site:time.com _____ <br> *Searches the content of the site.* |
| " __ " | "ice skating" <br> *Searches the exact combination of words between quotation marks* |
| Define: | *Finds the definition of the term* |
| Safesearch: | *Shows only content that is considered safe for children* |
| Filetype: | Filetype:pdf <br> *Searches for results that are a certain file type.* |
| Intext: | Intext: kitten <br> *Searches for mentions of a word or phrase in text* |
| Weather: | Weather:19132 <br> *Provides the weather report in a specific zip code* |

search engine's unique algorithm. A simple search for the name of the search engine and the keywords *search commands* will return enough resources to get started with more advanced searching. See Table 4.1 for more search tips.

Search engines have influenced web pages and web content in a huge way. Online marketing experts teach entrepreneurs how to incorporate keywords into the titles of their articles and web content to increase traffic. Websites even hold title information scraped by search engine robots within the code of the website to make sure that the site information is properly displayed in search results, preferably closer to the top of the list. This has also increased the phenomenon of "click bait," in which clicking on what seems to be a relevant article by title alone leads to a fluff article surrounded by advertising. Being found on the Internet is now a complicated and nuanced game played by web publishers, who are constantly updating their sites and services with each change in search engine algorithms.

Search engines are always getting "smarter," and as the Internet expands and millions more sites come online, knowing how to sift through this endless trove of information is becoming a necessary skill and a part of being digitally literate. For lessons related to search engines in the classroom, see Textbox 4.1.

TEXTBOX 4.1.

## Elementary Grades

In the younger grades, research can seem like a daunting task. The most important skills at this age center around understanding how keywords work and being able to decode search results. Some search engines are friendlier for younger students and display search results in a much clearer view than traditional Google or Bing results. Some examples are Sweet Search (http:// sweetsearch.com), a custom Google search that whitelists sites that are credible, kid-friendly, and relevant. Kidtopia (http://www .kidtopia.info) is a similar site that has a more graphic interface. This site is a mixture of a search engine and an online library collection of sites organized by content. Google also has its own kid-friendly search engine, Kiddle (https://www.kiddle.co) that shows the most kid-friendly, easy-to-read search results at the top of the page. Each result is paired with an image.

Students can be given a scavenger hunt, or they can develop their own questions about a topic. Scaffolding is key. Start by doing a few searches with the whole class and analyzing the results. One of the first tests should be whether students can read enough of the sites they find independently. If they can't, then the site may not be a good match for them. They can also practice making sure that the results they are seeing actually match the information that they are trying to find. Although this may seem simple, it is very common for younger learners to take notes on or use information they find online that is not connected to what they are trying to find.

At the elementary level, it is important to start simple and break things down into parts before attempting a research project or larger research assignment. It may also be beneficial to pair students up when doing research at this age.

## Middle Grades

Even in the middle grades, students need reinforcement on using keywords and taking the time to analyze their results. Older students should begin transitioning to a more traditional search engine, which means beginning the gargantuan task of sorting through a myriad of search results, some of which are completely useless. Start with making sure that students know the difference between "sponsored results" and ads and actual content. This can be done as a whole group, so you can model for students how to discern relevant content from advertising.

In the older grades, students also begin experimenting with more complete search terms and keywords. It is helpful to have students write their keywords and search terms down on paper before starting their research. Students often want to type their questions directly into the search engine, but search engines do not process full questions, but rather combinations of keywords that make up search terms. Have students experiment with putting in just their keywords by themselves and analyzing the results. Have them pair keywords together to see how different combinations affect their results. Just as with the younger grades, have students analyze the relevance of their results for what they are trying to find so they can discover the ideal combination of keywords needed to locate the information they are seeking. And, just like with the younger grades, chunk this process so students get to practice on a smaller scale before attempting a larger research project.

## High School Grades

High school students will benefit from many of the same activities and skills practiced in the middle grades. However, at this age students should begin to familiarize themselves with specific searches. For example, if a teacher is asking for a PDF of a primary source, then a student can add "*filetype:pdf*" to the search query. High School students should also be able to spot the difference between an advertisement and opinion pieces like articles or blogs. They should be familiar with generally reliable sources of information and should know how to search for scholarly works such as those found through Google Scholar (http://scholar.google.com) or JSTOR (http://www.jstor.org).

# 5

# Social Media

Many teachers in today's classrooms feel like they are fighting a war for their students' attention. They lament over the way that young people are entrenched in their phones or distracted on their computers. Still, as argued in the Digital Youth Project, which interviewed more than eight hundred young people and spent more than five thousand hours observing youth online behaviors, "to stay relevant in the 21st Century, education institutions need to keep pace with the rapid changes introduced by digital media."[1] So although we are competing for students' attention in a way never seen before, the reality is that these technologies are not going away, and if we are going to compete, we need to bring these technologies into our teaching, even in small ways.

The first step to bringing these technologies into the classroom is to learn more about the technologies young people use. Table 5.1 provides a list of some of the most prevalent digital places where young people are spending their time.

These virtual spaces, defined by researcher danah boyd as "networked publics" (see Chapter 2 for more on these digital spaces that kids inhabit), are fairly new and fall under the umbrella term "social media." These platforms allow for the sharing of text, video, images, and sound between users, which are all traditional forms of media. The difference is the social aspect.

**Table 5.1.   Top Social Media Sites Used by Young People**

| | | |
|---|---|---|
| Facebook | http://www.facebook<br>.com | This social platform allows users to create a detailed profile and then connect with others on the site by sending a "friend request." Users then see all of the posts from the people on their friends list. Users can also create events, fundraise, and create pages for specific interests or organizations. As of the third quarter of 2018, Facebook had more than one billion active daily users. |
| Instagram | http://www.instagram<br>.com | This photo- and video-sharing app, owned by Facebook, allows users to upload photos and videos and create "stories" to share with their followers. Users can apply a variety of filters and other edits to their images before posting them. Users build a photo stream by following other users. They can "like," comment on, save, and share other people's content. Ads are also mixed into this stream, which allows the platform and app to be free to use. Facebook acquired Instagram in 2012. |
| Pinterest | http://www.pinterest<br>.com | This platform is both web-based and has an app. Users create "boards" composed of "pins," which are linked to sites they visit. Boards are like collections and are organized visually in a grid-like format with thumbnail photos that link back to the source. Users can "pin" images and videos to specific boards to organize resources, and they can keep these boards private or make them public. Other users can "repin" things that they see on someone else's board to organize it into one of their own boards. This site turned the practice of social bookmarking into a visual experience. |
| Snapchat | http://www.snapchat<br>.com | This was one of the most popular social media sites for tweens and teens in 2018. Snapchat allows users to post videos and photos that disappear seconds later. Users can also create "stories," or ongoing public posts over the course of a day that can be viewed for twenty-four hours. "Snaps," as the posts are called, can be set to stay longer than a few seconds, and they can be altered using filters and additions like bunny ears and hearts. Users can send each other snaps directly, maintaining "snap streaks" between them. Snapchat also introduced the ability for users to pay each other through the platform. |

| | | |
|---|---|---|
| Tumblr | http://www.tumblr.com | Users of this site can create their own online space in the form of a blog. It is often used to share artwork or other creative pursuits. Content can be explored on the site by scrolling through "tiles" of featured posts, similar to Pinterest. This is a popular place for young people to connect around shared interests. |
| Twitter | http://www.twitter.com | This social platform allows users to post words and links up to 280 characters. Users can also attach files to their posts. Users "follow" each other, and they view all of the "tweets" of the people they follow in one stream. Twitter allows for searching of tweets that all contain specific words and hashtags (phrases that start with #), so users also use hashtags to create conversations around specific topics. Users can save (favorite) and "retweet" tweets sent by others. They can also send direct messages, or private messages, to other users. |
| WhatsApp | http://www.whatsapp.com | This app is a free messaging service, owned by Facebook, that allows encrypted messages to be sent between individuals and in group "chats." Users can share video, images, text, and even voice recordings. |
| YouTube | http://www.youtube.com | This video sharing site, acquired by Google in 2006, allows users to upload videos, watch videos, create curated playlists, and comment on videos hosted on the site. YouTube also has a built-in video editor for simple editing needs. Users can also follow other users and "like" or "dislike" videos. Many TV shows have their own YouTube channels and a number of famous "YouTubers" make a living off of the advertising that runs on their highly popular channels. |

"Facebook Q3 2018 Earnings," Facebook Investor Relations, October 30, 2018, accessed November 9, 2018, https://investor.fb.com/investor-events/event-details/2018/Facebook-Q3-2018-Earnings/default.aspx.

"Facebook to Acquire Instagram," Facebook Newsroom, April 9, 2012, accessed November 9, 2018, https://newsroom.fb.com/news/2012/04/facebook-to-acquire-instagram/.

Elise Moreau, "Hottest Social App Trends for Teens," Lifewire, October 25, 2018, accessed November 09, 2018, https://www.lifewire.com/hottest-social-app-trends-for-teens-3485940.

For most of the Internet's short life, it was considered "read-only." Users could look for information and read it or view it, but they could not *interact* with it. In the late 1990s, sites started to experiment with letting users create profiles and connect with each other. One of those sites, LiveJournal, which started in 1999, still exists today.[2] In 2002, the social networking site Friendster came on the scene, which allowed people to create a profile, connect with others, and share posts similar to the way Facebook works today. Friendster grew so quickly that it eventually couldn't handle all of the traffic through the site and began to make changes that users did not like. In 2003, MySpace launched and began to attract former Friendster users. Facebook, which launched to the public in 2005, drew users away from MySpace and grew exponentially, although both sites still exist today.[3] These sites are different from their predecessors because their sole purpose is to connect people and allow users to find other users. Many of the earlier social media sites were based around blogging (online writings that vary from informational posts to posts similar to personal journal entries) or sharing of ideas and discussion between members.

Social media has now become the primary way that young people connect with each other and, as the Digital Youth Project discovered, "The digital world is creating new opportunities for youth to grapple with social norms, explore interests, develop technical skills, and experiment with new forms of self-expression."[4] The *Merriam-Webster's Dictionary* definition of social media includes the term "online communities," which is what these spaces have evolved into over time.[5] Both young people and adults use these spaces as virtual communities that are very real and often play a large role in their lives. These communities even have their own language and slang, the most easily recognizable term being "lol" for "laughing out loud." For more of these abbreviations, see Textbox 5.1.

How people "live" in these online communities is, however, varied. Each space has its own norms and parameters, sometimes based on the way the platform itself is designed. Often, however, it is defined by the users themselves. For instance, Instagram lends itself to more curated content that is carefully modified using the tool's built-in filters. Content on the platform tends to be highly stylized and staged, whereas a platform like Twitter, which

## TEXTBOX 5.1. TEXT MESSAGE AND SOCIAL MEDIA ABBREVIATIONS

| | |
|---|---|
| 4EVA | Forever |
| <3 | Love/a heart |
| A/S/L or ASL | Age/Sex/Location |
| AF | As f*** |
| ATM | At the moment |
| B4N | Bye for now |
| BF or BFF | Best friend or Best Friend Forever |
| BRB | Be right back |
| CMB | Call me back |
| CTN | Can't talk now |
| CU | See you |
| DKDC | Don't know, don't care |
| FB | Facebook |
| FFS | For f***'s sake |
| FML | F*** my life |
| FTW | For the win |
| FWIW | For what it's worth |
| GTFO | Get the f*** out |
| GTG | Got to go |
| HBD | Happy Birthday |
| ICYMI | In case you missed it |
| IDK | I don't know |
| IG | Instagram |
| IKR | I know, right |

| | |
|---|---|
| ILY | I love you |
| IMHO | In my honest opinion |
| IOW | In other words |
| IRL | In real life |
| JK | Just kidding |
| K | OK |
| LH6 | Let's have sex |
| LMFAO | Laughing my f***ing a** off |
| LMK | Let me know |
| LOL | Laughing out loud |
| LULZ | indicates a joke |
| MBS | Mom behind shoulder |
| MEH | Just OK or "so so" |
| NOYB | None of your business |
| NSFW | Not safe for work |
| NVM | Never mind |
| OFC | Of course |
| OH | overheard |
| OMG | Oh my God |
| PAW | Parents are watching |
| POS | Parent over shoulder |
| PPL | People |
| ROFL | Rolling on floor laughing |
| SMH | Shaking my head |
| SOWM | Someone with me |

| | |
|---|---|
| STFU | Shut the f*** up |
| SU | Shut up |
| TBH | To be honest |
| THX | Thanks |
| TMYL | Tell me your location |
| TTYL | Talk to you later |
| UHGTBSM | You have got to be s***ing me |
| VN | Very nice |
| WAM | Wait a minute |
| WC | Who cares |
| WRU | Where are you |
| WTF | What the f*** |
| WYCM | Will you call me? |
| YOLO | You only live once |

Some definitions adapted from Carly Stec, "Social Media Definitions: The Ultimate Glossary of Terms You Should Know," *HubSpot*, accessed October 3, 2018, https://blog.hubspot.com/marketing/social-media-terms.

allows users to post quickly composed short messages in seconds, leads to more spontaneous, less thought-out posts.

Still, according to a 2015 Pew Research Study, 40 percent of teens reported that they felt pressured to only post things that would make them look good to others viewing their posts. The same study reported that 39 percent of teens say they feel pressure to post things that will receive lots of comments or likes.[6] So, no matter the platform's design, the norms and pressures of online communities can have a powerful influence on young people. For a glossary of some social media terms that can be found in these spaces, see Textbox 5.2.

TEXTBOX 5.2.   SOCIAL MEDIA TERMS

**AMA**: An acronym for "ask me anything." Users on various social media platforms use the term to prompt questions from other users.

**Block**: A user on a social media platform prevents another user from viewing, posting to, or interacting with the first user's profile or account.

**DM/PM**: Direct message or private message sent through a social media platform.

**Emoji**: Small images used in text-based messages to indicate emotion or represent ideas.

**Favorite**: A way to indicate on a social media post that a person likes or enjoys a post. Also can be a way for a user to save a post to view for later.

**Follow**: The act of adding a user to one's social media feed to see the posts made by the user.

**Followers**: People who add a user to their social media feed to see what they post.

**Friends**: On Facebook, users who mutually follow each other's posts.

**Graphics Interchange Format (GIF)**: A moving image, often a movie or TV clip, that can easily be shared on social media. There is debate over the pronunciation of the word; some say "jif" and some saying it "gif" with a hard *g*. Both are considered correct.

**Handle**: On Twitter, this is the username that users tweet from.

**Hashtag**: A word or phrase preceded by a hash mark (#), used within a message to identify a keyword or topic of interest and facilitate a search for it.

**Like:** A way to indicate approval, enjoyment, or other emotion related to a post. This can be in the form of a heart or thumbs up or other emoji, depending on the platform.

**Meme:** A cultural idea or behavior that is shared and spreads from person to person. On social media, this often comes in the form of images paired with words in humorous ways.

**Mention:** On Twitter and other social media platforms, a post that includes another user to garner their attention to content or indicate that the user is with the person. On many platforms, these put an @ in front of a username.

**Post:** As a noun, an online message shared to an online platform. As a verb, the act of sharing a message to an online platform

**Private:** An account setting that only allows a user's followers to see posts. The user must approve all followers.

**Reply:** A user responds directly to another user publicly.

**Repost:** A user shares content from another user to his or her own social media feed.

**Retweet:** To share or forward someone else's message on Twitter.

**Selfie:** An image taken by a user of himself or herself.

**Shaming:** The act of responding to an online or offline gaffe by posting negative comments or personal or private information to a person's social media account or in connection to a person's account. Often the shaming is more extreme than the gaffe itself.

**Story:** A way for users to create a collection of images and videos that often only last twenty-four hours. These stories exist in addition to the user's traditional social media posts.

**Tag:** A way to indicate that someone is in a post, image, or video by labeling the content with the person's username.

**Troll:** As a noun, an Internet user who intentionally posts attacks, insults, or other content with the intent of inciting anger and retaliation from the victim or other users. As a verb, the act of posting negative comments or content with the sole purpose of inciting anger or retaliation from the victim or other users.

**Viral:** Content that spreads widely and quickly across social media.

## SOCIAL MEDIA AND MENTAL HEALTH

A 2017 Royal Society of Public Health (RSPH) study of 1,500 young people in the United Kingdom ages fourteen to twenty-four years old found that Instagram had the most negative effects on young people's mental health.[7] Because of the highly stylized and edited content, teens reported that it had a negative effect on body image. The ability to follow others' experiences in real time also led to high levels of "fear of missing out" (FOMO), as young people worried that if they didn't keep scrolling, they would miss something important. This, obviously, also had a negative effect on sleep (which was common across all platforms).

The 2018 movie *Eighth Grade* is a great look at how teens use social media to escape their insecurities, the pressure that they feel when using these platforms, and the power these platforms give them to create and re-create their own identities. In the movie, a young girl, Kayla, who is an introvert and quiet at school, has a YouTube channel where she is bubbly and talkative and gives advice. Her character struggles with who she is and who she wants to be and how her offline and online personalities reflect different parts of her identity.[8]

These online communities created through social media are no different than peer groups older people engaged in before social media and the Internet. We can remember a time when we found out that we had missed a party or a get together because we hadn't been invited and how that felt. Now imagine that you could watch that party or get together unfolding in real time and even see who is there.

Feelings of anxiety and depression aren't just linked to specific apps. Another 2017 study found that "48 percent of teens who spend five hours per day on an electronic device have at least one suicide risk factor, compared to 33 percent of teens who spend two hours a day on an electronic device."[9] It's not clear if those with mental health issues tend to spend more time on their devices or if more time on devices triggers more mental health issues, but it is clear that there is a link between screen time and mental health.

Young people are highly social. They crave peer interactions and approval. Online communities like SnapChat, Instagram, YouTube, and Facebook are where they connect with each other. If that is where their friends are, it is no wonder that they want to spend time there. However, there seems to be a happy medium (no pun intended) between screen-based and non–screen-based interactions, and the more time they spend looking at a screen, the higher the levels of anxiety and depression the teens in the study reported.

Another important aspect of the conversation around kids' use of social media are the platforms and companies themselves. These apps are designed to be addicting. They are designed to keep users on them. Former Google engineer Tristan Harris explains that these apps are designed like slot machines, sending endorphins to our brains with each refresh of the app as we wonder, "What will I get?"[10]

Many social media apps are designed to encourage the user to scroll mindlessly through content. Others, like SnapChat, use this psychology to keep people "hooked." SnapChat users can create "streaks" with other users. The app tracks "snaps" sent between the users and puts a little fire symbol up along with a number indicating how many days in a row the two users have sent snaps to each other. This is an obvious way to keep users coming back to the app and using it.

This is also one reason that the RSPH study suggests that apps have built-in alerts when a user has spent a lot of time on the app (a "heavy usage warning").[11] This warning could prove helpful, especially for young brains. As a 2011 report from the American Academy of Pediatrics explains, "[B]ecause of their limited capacity for self-regulation and susceptibility to peer pressure, children and adolescents are at some risk as they navigate and experiment with social media."[12]

No conversation about social media is complete without discussing the risk of cyberbullying that occurs on these platforms. Like the playgrounds of the past, online spaces are prone to typical childhood behaviors like teasing, social ostracizing, and harassment. Sadly, many of these behaviors are conducted by adults, not just young people. The hardest part about these incidents of bullying is that they follow the victim home. Victims carry cruel words, gossip, and hateful posts around in their pocket.

FIGURE 5.1
Artwork by Mary Beth Hertz. Copyright 2019.

It is important to teach young people to use the tools available within platforms to address cyberbullying. Blocking and reporting is an easy first step, although, if the posts are really egregious or threatening or have continued repeatedly for days or weeks, the first step should be to screenshot the messages. See Figure 5.1 for a simple graphic that lays out these tips.

These screenshots are evidence of what was said in case the bully takes down or removes his or her posts. It is important, when using any social media in the classroom, to lay down the expectations around decorum and to have well-thought-out, clear consequences for students who break that decorum. Students should also consider what they are posting and who might see it. For more on this, see Chapter 2.

## THE GOOD SIDE OF SOCIAL MEDIA

Despite all the negative issues that we often hear around social media, it is not all bad. Like anything, including TV or laptops or even sugary drinks and alcohol, if we know that something has the potential to hurt us or damage our health, we must use it in moderation. Before we adults judge young people's use of social media, we should think about the last time Netflix asked us, "Are you still watching?" as we binge-watched our favorite show. Adults are not immune to the addictive qualities of social media, even if our brains are slightly more formed than teens and tweens.

The same RSPH study showed that YouTube actually had a positive effect on community building and awareness. Users felt more connected to others and felt more connected to quality health-related information. Even Instagram showed a positive effect on self-expression, as did nearly all of the social media sites studied.[13]

This positive influence can be seen in the "It Gets Better Project" started by Dan Savage and his partner, Terry Miller. The campaign started with a simple video of the two sharing their experiences as gay men and telling young lesbian, gay, bisexual, and transgender people that "it gets better." As of this writing, more than sixty thousand people have shared their "it gets better" stories. Many of these stories can be viewed on the project's YouTube channel at https://www.youtube.com/user/itgetsbetterproject.

After the 2018 shooting at Marjory Stoneman Douglas High School in Parkland, Florida, some of the Parkland students began to use social media to speak out about the tragedy and policies that they believe made the tragedy possible. These students had used Twitter for sharing personal quips and communicating with friends, but as their accounts gained popularity as a result of their direct challenges on the platform to powerful people like President Trump or Senator Marco Rubio, they had to learn how to leverage their newfound power. As student Delaney Tarr stated in a *New York Times* article after the shooting, "The fact is that I have to represent our movement. It's not just me tweeting whatever I want to tweet about. It has to be drawn back to who I am to the media, to who I am to the country."[14] Social media not only gave these students a voice, but taught them deep lessons about messaging, branding, and self-awareness.

Social media also has the potential to make it easier for introverts, people who may not feel comfortable speaking up in a large group or who refrain from sharing ideas with others, to connect with people in a safe and less intimidating way. It also allows people to find and make connections with those who share their interests when they don't live in an area or town or attend a school with anyone who shares their interests. And, although social media gets a bad reputation in many studies for increasing feelings of loneliness, it also has the potential to alleviate loneliness, especially when those digital connections cross into the "real world." In addition, for people with disabilities, social media can be a great equalizer, allowing them to interact with online communities without stigma.

On a larger scale, social media is also a great place to find breaking news or to follow important events in real time. One of the most famous examples of this was the use of social media to organize and inform participants in the "Arab Spring" uprisings in 2011. Many of the citizens of countries like Tunisia, Iran, or Egypt used social media because it was out of the reach and control of the state-run media. Social media has since proven to be an ideal way for information in traditionally isolated or highly controlled nations to be shared both inside and outside of the country.[15] These platforms also allow family members, dispersed because of civil war, unrest, or economic hardships, to connect across oceans and time zones.

Social media can also be used to "attend" events or even participate in them without being physically present. "Hashtags," or words or phrases that start with a hashmark (#) and identify topics or facilitate searching and grouping posts, allow for in-person attendees to share what they are discussing and seeing and for virtual attendees to participate almost as if they were there. The experience of in-person attendees can be enhanced through "backchannel" discussions that happen on social media simultaneously with the live event.

In some ways, social media has removed the need for a physical space to learn, laugh, debate, discuss, or share, and in other ways it augments in-person experiences by allowing users to pose questions, share insights, and discuss in real time. Some would argue that this takes the focus away from what is going on in the physical room, and they aren't wrong. Backchannels can be distracting, and like anything, should be used in moderation. In the classroom, students could hold backchannel discussions while watching a movie in class to share analyses without disrupting the viewing experience.

## BRANDING VERSUS NETWORKING MINDSET

Social media is also used by companies to get their products in front of young, impressionable minds. These companies are experts at branding and marketing. This branding mindset is often reflected in personal accounts as well. Users feel pressured to maintain a specific online identity, their "brand," or to cultivate a persona to "sell" themselves to others. This can be a highly stressful way to use social media because every single post needs to fit into an expectation that the user has set up for his or her followers, and it can also eat away at the good side of social media—the building of community and relationships.

**Table 5.2.**

| Branding Mindset | Networking Mindset |
|---|---|
| How can I get noticed? | How can I become connected with a community? |
| How can I be visible on every social media platform? | Which social media platforms are used by people in my field? |
| How can I create an impressive "look" and "feel" to increase my followers? | How can I create ongoing relationships through technology? |
| What will people offer me because of my brand? | What can I offer to the community? |

Source: Reprinted with permission from Digital Citizenship in Action, by Kristen Mattson, copyright 2017, ISTE (International Society for Technology in Education), www.iste.org. All rights reserved.

If everyone is marketing something and broadcasting his or her brand, then there is no room for networking, for making connections.

If the purpose of social media is to forge connections and to build online communities that share interests, ideas, and resources, then users must have a "networking mindset" when using these platforms. Otherwise, scrolling through your Facebook feed or your Instagram or Twitter feed will start to just feel like "noise," a bunch of people sharing highly curated versions of themselves to solidify and sell their "brand." These accounts are easy to spot because they often post constantly and rarely interact. It is important for students to understand the difference if they are to truly reap the benefits of social media.

As students get older, sites like LinkedIn and Twitter may be places where students meet a potential employer, or places where they connect with experts for research or other endeavors. Every good business person knows that it's not what you know, it's who you know, and the relationships that you build along the way. Table 5.2 provides an easy way to help students understand the difference between a "branding mindset" and a "networking mindset."

## USING SOCIAL MEDIA AS EDUCATORS

Social media has been described as the modern day "water cooler" where people talk about gossip, news, politics, or life experiences. Twitter itself is often referred to as a "cocktail party," a space with a large gathering of various people having brief discussions in a crowded room. Anyone can jump into a conversation and conversations are easily overheard. The conversations also tend to be animated and lively.

Aside from bringing social media into the classroom as a way to "meet kids where they are," educators are also connecting through social media to share and learn with each other. There are Facebook groups for subject-area teachers or for projects like the Global Read Aloud (https://www.facebook .com/groups/GlobalReadAloud), where teachers from across the globe agree to read the same book to their students and connect their classrooms through technology.

Teachers also use Twitter to share and discuss ideas and to "meet" educators from all over the world. There are real-time and asynchronous chats like #edchat or #digcit (a chat dedicated to topics related to Digital Citizenship). Retired librarian Jerry Blumengarten has a wonderful page that lists all the active education chats on Twitter, which can be found at https://sites.google .com/site/twittereducationchats/education-chat-official-list.

Twitter is a great place to find resources or make direct connections with experts or see how other educators address concepts and issues in their classrooms. Social media tools like Twitter or classroom blogs are also a great place to share what is going on in your classroom. Many parents appreciate being able to see what kids are learning and these stories are also a great window into how different teachers approach the same content. It is vital, however, to protect student privacy by not posting photos of students without permission. See Textbox 5.3 for an example of how elementary educator Linda Yollis uses Twitter with her students.

Social media can be used to connect classrooms in the same school or district or across countries and oceans. In their study, published in 2017, Dr. Renee Hobbs and Dr. Sait Tuzel followed the experiences of two middle school teachers, one in California and one in Turkey, connecting their students through a "Getting to Know You" activity on social media. They discovered that this experience made students more comfortable talking with someone whose first language is not English, and it allowed American students to see the Turkish students as kids like them, not just "foreigners." It also allowed American students to question some of their beliefs about the Middle East. Students were able to connect in real time and to share images, links, and other media with each other.

TEXTBOX 5.3.   CASE STUDY

Educator Linda Yollis in California has her classes use Twitter to connect with other classrooms across the globe. Her students participated in a Twitter project in which they sent class mascots and told about their adventures using the hashtag #globalpal to classes in New Zealand, England, the United States, and Australia. You can see the adventures here: https://twitter.com/hashtag/globalpal?src=hash

Her students also participated in a Twitter project celebrating poetry and color. Each week they tweeted out poems of color. Here is a blog post with samples from the "What is Red?" week: https://yollisclassblog.blogspot.com/2016/04/wrap-up-what-is-red-clrpoem.html.

The students in the United States also discovered that American popular culture is well known by the Turkish students, whereas American students know very little about the Turkish culture; thus the American students were able to understand how little access they have to pop culture from other countries.[16] The two teachers, through this connection, created a unique and powerful experience for their students.

As discussed previously, social media can be used to participate in events in real time even from a distance. This is common at education conferences as well as "unconferences" like Edcamps. Participants tweet out resources, quotes, and questions based on the conversation in the room, and virtual participants, following the hashtag, can access these resources, learn, and even ask their own questions. Given the cost of large, national conferences and district budgets and teacher salaries, social media has proven to be a great solution for educators to engage with conferences and conference goers when they can't afford to attend in person.

In conclusion, social media is where kids live these days. It has huge potential for connecting classrooms and connecting students to primary, real-time

Table 5.3.  Using Social Media Tools in the Classroom

| Social Media Tool | URL | Classroom Uses |
| --- | --- | --- |
| Diigo | http://www.diigo.com | Students can use this social book-marking tool to bookmark and annotate sites with peers. |
| Goodreads | http://www.goodreads.com | Students thirteen years old and older can create an account and build their virtual library of books to read and books they have read. They can leave reviews and see the book lists of classmates for ideas. |
| Hangouts | https://hangouts.google.com | Students can use the video feature to join into conversations virtually. The chat feature can be used for backchannel purposes or for asynchronous resource sharing and discussion. |
| Kidblog | http://www.kidblog.org | Students can write blog posts and leave comments for each other. |
| Pinterest | http://www.pinterest.com | Students can curate their own "board" of resources to share with the class. |
| Twitter | http://www.twitter.com | Students can follow the tweets related to a news event by having them follow a specific hashtag. |
| Youth Voices | https://www.youth-voices.live/ | Students can upload their work and read and comment on the works of others. |

sources. Although there is a dark side to social media, and educators must plan accordingly, using these tools in the classroom can open the door for important conversations around digital citizenship. Like any technology tool in the classroom, how social media is used is just as important as which platforms are used. See Table 5.3 for some ideas on how to incorporate various social media tools in the classroom. Textbox 5.4 provides some guidance on lessons that incorporate social media.

TEXTBOX 5.4.

## Elementary Grades

Younger students who are starting to type their work can begin to use a platform like Kidblog to share their work with their class, their parents, or the world. Blogging is a great way to motivate students to write because there is an immediate potential audience. Eventually, with enough guidance, students can even begin to comment on each other's work, taking a foray into the social aspect of the tool. Some blogging platforms like Blogger and Edublogs allow for family members and others outside the classroom to leave comments and provide teachers with tools to protect the privacy of their students.

## Middle Grades

Blogging is also a great tool for middle school. In addition, middle schoolers can use social media to participate in live events or even invite experts in the classroom through Skype or Hangout. Have one student in charge of posting questions that the class may have to the chat area of the conversation. In middle school, teachers can create curated Pinterest boards with resources related to what students are learning and make them publicly viewable so students can see them without needing to log in. Remember, students must be thirteen or older to sign up for social media accounts without parental permission, and it is good practice to check with parents regarding their child's use of social media even if they are 13 or older.

## High School

Students in high school can engage more in social media in the classroom simply because of their age. Most major social media platforms require students to be thirteen or older. At this point, many students will have social media accounts anyway, and it is now acceptable for a teacher to ask them to use those accounts in the classroom. Students can follow a hashtag on Twitter, or even tweet their own discussions using a hashtag of their own. They can curate their own Pinterest boards or use a social book-marking tool like Diigo to share bookmarks and annotations with classmates. They could even create their own blog where they share ideas or contribute to a site like YouthVoices to share their writing with other teens. They can connect with each other on Goodreads to build book lists and see their friends' book lists. The class or school can use a YouTube channel to share news or highlight projects or special events.

# 6

# Targeted Online Advertising

Anyone who has browsed online recently can empathize with the somewhat creepy feeling that someone is looking over your shoulder based on the ads you are seeing. It's as if someone was tracking everything you type and giving you ads based on your every action. Not to alarm anyone, but they are.

It's no coincidence that a search for a specific shoe online leads to a barrage of ads on every site a user visits for that same shoe. Invisible tools are at work that make that possible, and most of them are so hidden that very few users even know they are in play. This chapter explores how this technology works, its influence on the consumer and on society, and how it benefits both the company and the consumer.

These kinds of specific, tailored ads are called "targeted ads" or "interest-based ads." They allow users to view much of the web's content free of charge. However, these ads may not cost users tangible money, but online, if something is free, the user is the product.

## HOW ONLINE ADVERTISING WORKS

Search engines and websites often earn a specific amount for each click on the ad content they host. This is called *pay per click.*[1] Advertisers buy space on a website similar to the way they purchase space in a newspaper. However, the host of the ad only gets paid when someone clicks on the advertisement.

Advertisers also pay for their ads to appear in search results, using the keywords related to their target audience to place their ads in a way that targets their customers. Google, for example, makes most of its revenue through its Google Ads, which allow advertisers to leverage Google's sophisticated search algorithm.[2]

You don't have to be a huge search engine, however, to leverage Google's technology to earn money from advertisers. Google also works with individuals to place ads on their sites to earn revenue through their Google AdSense program. This allows individuals to earn revenue the same way (through ad clicks). Google works with advertisers to place ads on individual websites and provides code for users to put on their sites so that the ads appear.[3]

Google is not alone. Amazon also offers similar advertising opportunities, as does Facebook. This revenue from advertising allows these companies to offer their services for "free." The users of the site pay for this service, however, in clicks and views. In fact, many times, websites earn money based on "impressions," or how many page views a site receives. For instance, Ad Age's 2018 Media Kit shows that for every million views of an ad on their website, the Cost Per Mille, or cost per one million views, is $49. An ad with one hundred thousand views would earn $4.90.[4] Your eyes are quite lucrative to these companies.

## HOW THESE ADS KNOW YOU

### Web Cookies

So how is it that these companies are able to put that pair of shoes you looked at once on Amazon in front of you on every website you visit and every search you complete? The main way is based around little files called *cookies*, which are placed on your machine when you visit Amazon or any other site that uses cookies.[5] These cookies store information about you and your machine and identify you to the website. This is why you can close a tab with a full cart and return to the site later to find those same items in the cart.

Cookies have been around for decades, and the word comes from the term "magic cookie" that programmers as early as the late 1970s and early 1980s used to describe "token" data packets sent between machines.[6] Their original intent was to improve the user experience by allowing for faster loading times because the site was able to access existing information rather than try to optimize for each device each time. The average user wasn't even aware that cookies existed or were being used, and sites weren't even required to tell users that they were placing the small file on their computer.[7] Browsers allow users to manage and delete cookies, but the average user rarely accesses that area of their browser settings.

When the new privacy regulations stipulated in the European Union General Data Protection Regulations went into effect in May 2018, Internet users across the globe began to see messages on websites they visited alerting them that the site uses cookies and allowing the user to accept or decline that use. Although US users are not protected under the regulations, this increased transparency has played an important role in US citizens' understanding of how often sites use these little files to track them.

### Through an Active Log-In Session

One simple way for advertisers to tailor ads to a user is simply for a user to be logged into, for instance, his or Google or Facebook account. When users are logged in, the advertiser can easily access basic profile information about a person as well as what a user has been posting. Facebook even has a tool called Facebook Pixel that puts a small dot on partner websites that tells Facebook when you visit the site when you are logged into Facebook. This prompts Facebook to show you ads based on the content of the sites you visit.[8] If this sounds frightening, a Chrome Extension made by Facebook called Pixel Helper (https://developers.facebook.com/docs/facebook-pixel/support/pixel-helper) allows you to see which sites have this installed on their site.

### CONCERNS

One of the biggest concerns around targeted advertising and children is that advertising data collection doesn't distinguish between a user who is a child and an adult user. This means that companies are collecting information about young people to target them with ads. Companies are also not usually transparent about whether they sell their users' identifying information.

Another concern is centered around the content of ads. Following the 2016 presidential election, investigators discovered that Facebook had featured several ads planted by Russian groups attempting to influence the election.[9] These advertisers were able to leverage the same targeting tools as any other legitimate advertiser to put their ads in front of their desired audience.

To combat these kinds of deceptive practices, Congress introduced the Honest Ads Act in October 2017, "to enhance transparency and account-ability for online political advertisements by requiring those who purchase and publish such ads to disclose information about the advertisements to the public, and for other purposes."[10] Although there has not yet been a vote on this proposal, many legislators see the proliferation of misleading advertising as a national security issue.

Online advertisements create issues around credibility and trustworthy information simply due to their whole premise. Because a website can get paid based on every ad click or based on how many people visit a page, there is an incentive to entice people to visit the site. This has led to the prolifera-tion of sites that exist solely to garner ad revenue. They host content with sensational headlines or fluff articles that target specific audiences. They may even contain false or misleading information.

This kind of content is often called *click bait* because it exists solely to get site visitors to click on it and earn the website ad revenue. You might recognize these kinds of headlines at the bottom of news stories or articles. They often use the name of the city you are in and may even be related to recent searches you have done. This click bait and the fluff websites that go along with it can be problematic for educators and their students conduct-ing research projects. If students can't differentiate between viable content and fluffy, click bait websites, they may be accessing incorrect or misleading information.

## A BETTER INTERNET?

Proponents of online advertising stress that, although ads can be a nuisance, the Internet as we know it exists because of online advertising. These ads allow us to browse content for "free," and show people what interests them. If websites couldn't make money from advertising, then they would probably introduce a paywall and require membership to view content. Some sites already do this, and some claim that by requiring membership, they are free-ing themselves from the constraints of working with advertisers, as well as potential conflicts of interest and privacy concerns. Sites like Medium have a business model that intentionally does not include advertising revenue. Its "About" page totes its dedication to its readers, not advertisers.[11] It's hard to know if ads make the Internet more accessible to everyone with some privacy and nuisance trade-offs, or if an ad-free Internet would be a better place. For now, ads are here to stay.

## OPTING OUT

As more and more light is shone on the way that online advertisers and large tech companies are collecting and profiting from our data, companies like Google and Facebook have been pressured to offer ways for their users to opt out of targeted ads. Facebook has introduced a setting that allows users to opt out of seeing ads targeted directly to them. As of the writing of this book, the setting is under *Ads*.[12]

The National Advertising Initiative has an online tool that allows you to opt out of third-party advertising across the web. It can be accessed at http://optout.networkadvertising.org. It scans your browser and shows you which advertisers may be showing you "interest-based ads." You can then prevent these advertisers from showing you tailored ads. You will instead have an "opt-out" cookie in your browser. You will still see ads, but they will not be tailored to your web searches, social media posts, or browsing history.

The Digital Advertising Alliance runs a similar tool: http://optout.aboutads.info. It is an eye-opening experience to see how many advertisers are connected to you through the cookies that they place in your browser when you visit a website. Opponents of this kind of intrusion often argue that this kind of advertising should be "opt-in," not "opt-out" to protect users' privacy.

## MANAGING YOUR INFORMATION

The easiest way to manage how advertisers track you through cookies is to manage them yourself directly in your browser. This can be done in the settings of any browser and most allow you to remove all of the cookies saved at once or select specific cookies to remove. For instance, you may find some cookies that save your information across sites helpful while others are merely tracking you and serve no other purpose.

Another way to thwart potential "interest-based" tracking is to clear your browsing history on a regular basis. Because Google and Facebook, for instance, track the sites you visit and profile you based on your search history, deleting it can help minimize how they use that information.

When advertisers put a cookie on your machine, they are usually doing it through another site. This means that when you go to a website that has targeted ads on it, you are not only receiving a cookie from that site, but also from the advertisers on the site. These are called *third-party cookies*. Now that sites are complying with EU regulations, you can easily deny these cookies. In some cases, however, these cookies may improve or even facilitate user experience and interaction on the site, so your experience using the site may be affected.

One way that people often *think* that they are browsing without cookies is through the use of an *incognito* or *private* browser window. Unfortunately, in nearly all cases, private browsing simply means that your search history is not saved on the machine. Sites can still install cookies when you are browsing privately.[13] An exception is Firefox's tracking protection feature and Apple's Safari browser "do not track" feature. These, however, are settings within the browser and are not necessarily connected to private or incognito mode at all.[14]

Ad-blocking tools that prevent ads from showing up on webpages have become prevalent and popular over the last few years. As ads become more intrusive, users turned to these tools to improve their web browsing experience. These tools, however, wreaked havoc on sites that depend on advertising for revenue. This is why some sites use pop-up messages asking visitors to "whitelist" their site by turning off the ad blocker for the site.

Forbes.com has engineered its site to require that ad blockers be turned off to enter the site at all and provides visitors with directions on how to change

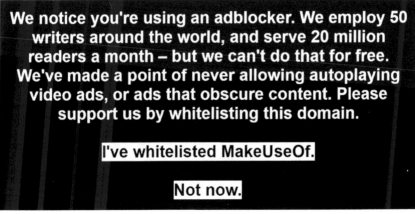

FIGURE 6.1
Screenshot. Make Use Of. Accessed October 6, 2018. http://makeuseof.com.

the settings in their ad blocker.[15] Forbes was included on a list that Google released in June 2017 of sites containing "overwhelming or intrusive" ads.[16]

In 2018, Google included ad blocking in its Chrome browser, claiming that it was improving user experience by eliminating bloated ads that slowed load times on pages and prioritizing sites that load quickly in its search results. Since most of Google's revenue comes from ads, this was a big shift, but it also was part of a larger movement by tech companies to improve user experience overall through the Coalition for Better Ads.[17]

### ONLINE ADS IN THE CLASSROOM

Despite our best efforts, students will be exposed to advertising in our classrooms. This means that educators have a responsibility to guide students through navigation of content they access online. Just as students are provided with scaffolding and strategies for decoding text or reading nonfiction text or magazines, they must be provided similar supports when reading online.

Tools that help eliminate the often distracting presence of advertising are available. Browser extensions like Mercury Reader (https://mercury.postlight .com/reader) load pages as simple text on a white background, eliminating distractions and displaying web-based articles as plain text.

There will also be moments when inappropriate ads surface in the classroom. Students can be given strategies to handle this. They can reload the page or, if there is an option to close the ad (usually a little "x" in the corner of the box), they can remove content that makes them feel uncomfortable. Many schools have filters that block ads or inappropriate content. This is both a blessing and a curse. No ads means less distraction, but no ads also means that students are not given the opportunity to build good habits around managing the distracting content.

Schools that use Google Suite for Education (formerly Google Apps for Education) will find that the default setting for these Google accounts is "Do Not Track." Google is not allowed to employ tracking tools with Google Suite for Education accounts. However, Google has been sued over concerns that it was tracking students' online behavior, and, because its operations are not transparent, there is no way to know what it is tracking.[18]

For instance, Google rolled out its Smart Compose feature to Google Suite for Education users in September 2018.[19] Smart Compose uses the content of your email, including the recipient information, to help you compose an email. It will predict sentences for you so you don't have to type them out yourself. In order for this to work, Smart Compose must read your emails. This raises some privacy issues for students. If Google is reading their emails, what other information is it collecting or accessing?

Finally, ads have influence. How can we support kids in understanding how ads affect their perception of themselves and others? How does ad placement affect how they interpret what they are reading? This is especially true if those ads are tailored directly to them.

Imagine the effect of certain ads only being shown to certain people. This can have a silo effect on large groups of people. It also raises the question of free will. If students only see ads that are similar to ads other kids their age with the same demographic see, there is a serious silo effect beyond anything we've ever seen. Advertisers are curating these young people's self-image like never before. For ideas on how to address and consider targeted ads in the classroom, see Textbox 6.1.

TEXTBOX 6.1.

**Elementary Grades**

Young children are easily fooled by flashy, colorful ads on the websites they visit. In fact, they often don't realize that they are ads at all. For instance, a kindergarten or first grade student may be alarmed when they are suddenly whisked away to another site and can't figure out how to get back to where they were. One way to help them avoid these mishaps is by teaching them how to tell the difference between ads and legitimate content. This can be done as a whole class by projecting a site like coolmath.com on the board and having kids come up to point out the ad.

Remind students that clicking on an ad will take them away from the site they were on, so they want to avoid it. Also come up with a list of traits that ads have (they are usually colorful, in boxes, and have the letters "A" and "D" in them somewhere small). Reinforce these traits and observation skills when students are using a computer individually by pointing to content on their screen and asking them if they think it's an ad or not and by guiding them through the process of analyzing the content of the site they are on.

## Middle Grades

In the middle grades, students can begin to understand why ads are on websites and how students are being tracked online by advertisers. Have a discussion about whether they think the tradeoff of ads and tracking for "free" content is worth it. Students also benefit from analyzing a webpage and identifying "sponsored content" that is baked into the articles they are reading.

This content is often camouflaged as legitimate content, so older students must be guided to look for the signs that what they are reading may be an advertisement. They can look for the words "AD" and "Sponsored," and they can also use their judgment to analyze tone and content. Does it feel like someone is selling them something?

## High School Grades

Once students enter high school, it is still important to reinforce the same lessons from the middle grades while also guiding them through managing cookies, installing ad blockers, and taking preemptive measures to protect themselves from being tracked online. Students should also understand the tradeoffs of sharing their data with sites they visit and why ads seem so tailored to their interests.

# 7

# Privacy in the Digital Age

Using the Internet requires large data transfers. This data includes the user's location (for accurate information on maps or to find the nearest store); the unique, identifying Internet protocol (IP) address of the device; and even information about what the user clicks on and information the user fills out on websites. Over the last decade, both private companies and public institutions have invested in ways to tap into this data and use it, sometimes transparently but often without the user even knowing it's happening. There is so much data that special technologies are employed to make the data useful and to sort through it effectively and efficiently.

These large sets of data are often referred to as "big data," and are defined by *Merriam-Webster* as "an accumulation of data that is too large and complex for processing."[1] In the private sector, companies often track both consumers' online and offline purchases, which are both processed through a digital database. This is how stores market products to consumers based on previous purchases. It's why consumers receive coupons for items similar to those they just purchased. It's why, in 2012, a father discovered that his teenage daughter was pregnant not from the girl herself, but through the mailings being sent home by Target, where the girl shopped.[2]

Target, and most retailers, create identification numbers that are attached to credit cards, addresses, and phone numbers that customers use in the store. This helps them to create a profile for each customer based on where they shop, when they shop, and what they buy. Online, this tracking is directly tied to advertising that users see when they surf the web.

## BIG DATA IN THE PUBLIC SECTOR

In June 2018, the Supreme Court made a landmark decision regarding how specific kinds of data can be used in criminal investigations. The US government obtained the location data from Timothy Carpenter's cell phone in connection with a 2011 criminal investigation. This data was used to convict Carpenter in court. He appealed with the help of the American Civil Liberties Union and as a result, the case escalated to the Supreme Court where it was ultimately decided that the government had broken the Fourth Amendment when it obtained the records without a warrant. This case is one of the first in the deeper discussion around the privacy of information that we share with tech companies to use their services.

In another example, police investigating a 2016 murder case requested access to anything that an Amazon Echo at the scene of the crime may have heard.[3] Amazon pushed back, citing First and Fourth Amendment rights. (To see what an Echo or other Amazon Alexa–enabled device has heard, a user can simply go to the device history in the app.) Cases pop up daily that test the limits of what kind of data the government can ask for from companies that manage the personal and often private information of their customers.

Public institutions inside and outside of law enforcement often incorporate big data into their daily operations. Many police departments collect, review, and analyze crime data to identify "hot spots" or to identify patterns of behavior to help put resources where they are most needed. Public transit agencies track their ridership to plan for expansions, scale backs, or restructuring of bus and train lines. Even the US Census, which is conducted every ten years, is a form of big data collection to help inform public services and direct (or redirect) funding to where it is needed.

## WHAT DOES PRIVACY MEAN?

Privacy-related issues have a long history here in the United States. The parts of the US Constitution that prevent search and seizure and the quartering of soldiers in private homes show that US citizens have always valued their privacy. In the digital age, more and more private information is shared both with and without users' consent. With the advent of social media, the line between what is *personal* information and what is *private* information is also being redrawn. People share the personal details of their daily lives freely through their social media accounts through tweets about everything from their daily commute to Instagram photos of what they had for lunch (often including a location tag of where they ate this lunch). These kinds of experiences, which used to be limited to face-to-face interactions, are now shared with millions of strangers.

So what is private in this age of sharing? More and more, "private" information refers more to things like your social security number, home address, health information, and financial information. This private information is often referred to as "personal identifiable information" (PII). The US Department of Labor defines PII as "[a]ny representation of information that permits the identity of an individual to whom the information applies to be reasonably inferred by either direct or indirect means."[4] Most technology companies define PII similarly. They maintain that the data they are collecting cannot be traced back to an individual. Still, we often share information across technology platforms that can easily be traced back to us due to our online profiles, location data or other identifying factors. This can make it difficult to decide what is private, and it also creates a gray area around the role of tech companies and the role of users in protecting private information.

## THE INTERNET OF THINGS

One of the more recent technological developments that has become widespread in the last five to ten years is the Internet of Things (IoT). This refers to noncomputing devices that are connected to the Internet to enhance their performance. Some examples are home security systems, lights, voice-activated assistants (e.g., Amazon Echo, Google Home) and even baby monitors. These devices allow us to remotely access important aspects of our daily lives and make daily tasks easier. However, anything that connects to the Internet could easily be accessed by a third party because the device is connected to the Internet and is constantly sending information through servers connected online.

These devices have been hacked, sometimes for nefarious reasons and sometimes by "white hat" hackers who help organizations find holes in their security. Most often, this happens when users do not change the default password that the device is shipped with (often just *admin* and *password*). This also happens when device manufacturers do not take precautions to properly secure their devices.

In June 2018, a mother claimed that her baby monitor had been hacked and that someone had been potentially watching and listening to her family. The site SEC Consult was able to explore how this may have happened and discovered that the manufacturer was sloppy with their security set up.[5] In 2016, a "white hat" hacker named Thomas Brewster gained entry to the entire security system of a nonprofit center because they had never changed the password.[6] He was able to access the security alarms and even the closed-circuit TV cameras. He alerted the center and they fixed the security issue, but many victims aren't so lucky.

In 2016, a widespread distributed denial-of-service attack called *Dyn* leveraged potentially one hundred thousand devices, many of which were IoT devices, caused a huge Internet outage. These kinds of attacks overwhelm web servers, taking them offline. This attack was unique in that it took control of IoT devices, allowing the attack to be much more powerful. This, too, was due to the fact that many users had not changed the default password on their IoT devices. This raises the question of whether the technology or the user is to blame; in many cases, these devices are not built securely to protect them from being infiltrated.

Although consumers definitely need to do more to take the proper precautions to secure their devices (and potentially their own homes), there is also the added security issue that these devices are connected to third-party servers that could potentially sit on the open Internet completely unsecured or poorly secured. That is the responsibility of the companies that run them.

In the end, the IoT is here to stay. In many cases, it makes our daily lives easier by allowing us, for instance, to let in the housekeeper or a relative when we aren't home, or allowing us to turn off the lights if we forget to when we go on vacation or a business trip. Amazon is already working on a way for Amazon delivery workers to be able to use a code to unlock your door to put packages inside your house, and it already sells technology that allows you to see who has entered and exited your house from anywhere.[7]

It is now up to us, the consumers and the companies, whom we trust enough to put these devices in the most private of all places—our homes—to continue the hard work of securing these devices. Nothing that is connected to the Internet is ever 100 percent secure, but the current state of security must get better.

## ARTIFICIAL INTELLIGENCE

Many IoT devices use a form of artificial intelligence (AI) to function. AI is, essentially, the process of teaching machines how to learn and function similar to human beings. Although AI has been a favorite subject for science fiction writers for decades, the technological capabilities of AI have ballooned in recent years.

The most prevalent use of AI is in the digital assistants that so many people depend on, including Apple's Siri and Amazon's Alexa. However, Google just wowed audiences at a recent conference when it demonstrated the capabilities of its AI tool, Google Duplex, to not only place phone calls, but to navigate making a hair appointment or a restaurant reservation.[8] The amazing, human-like interactions the digital assistant created while making the phone calls, including "umms" and "hmms," were possible because programmers fed it thousands of recorded conversations from customer service calls (remember that recorded message that tells you that the "call may be recorded for quality assurance purposes?")

This is a privacy red flag. AI needs data and examples to learn from. Where will this data come from? In the example of Google Duplex, what if the person on the other end doesn't know that he or she is talking to a bot? What are the privacy concerns and implications? Privacy concerns are especially relevant if any transcript or recording is kept of the conversation.

AI is now creeping into classrooms. Microsoft offers a number of helpful classroom tools that aid students with translating in real time so they can understand what is going on if they are not fluent in the language,[9] or even if they are deaf or hard of hearing. Microsoft also has an app that describes the world to visually impaired students through photos the students take.

These are powerful tools that allow students to access the classroom in ways they never could before. Still, these tools use Microsoft's Azure service (their cloud-based storage system) to run. This means that everything students are hearing and seeing is being sent to Microsoft's servers for processing, which, as explained in the discussion around the IoT security, means that Microsoft now has a whole bunch of data on its servers. If a student is listening in a classroom and doesn't tell anyone that he or she is using the app, what are the implications for the student's peers and the teacher whose words are being sent to a Microsoft server without their knowledge?

Bill Gates has had his eye on applying AI to learning for a while. In a 2016 interview with *The Verge*, he described a form of "personalized learning" in which an "AI tutor" could give students feedback on their writing or help students work through difficult content, which Gates described as allowing students to move at their own pace through content.[10] In order to get "smarter," AI needs data. Lots and lots of data. In a school setting, this data often comes from students. In the case of the AI tutor, it must collect data from students on their progress to be able to provide support. Again, this raises the significant question of where this data is stored and whether there is transparency about its collection.

Although not an example of AI at work, Tacoma Public School District in Washington State is hosting large amounts of student data in Microsoft's Azure storage to allow it to analyze, predict, and make changes based on the data in the same way that a large corporation would. This allowed the school district to boost its graduation rate by identifying students who were at risk of not graduating.[11] This is proof that mass uploading of student data is already happening.

As more AI is incorporated into schools, it is important that corporations be transparent about what data is being fed to these AI systems and what happens to that data. It's not clear how Tacoma Public Schools communicated this process to families. One of the most infamous examples of a similar attempt to centralize student data is the InBloom venture in 2013 and 2014. InBloom, an education technology (EdTech) startup company funded by the Gates Foundation, had the ambition to streamline how schools and districts operate across the country. InBloom recruited nine states to participate in the project. These states agreed to upload student information to the database, but none of the districts communicated the process well with families and communities and, as in the case of New York State, some did not plan on getting parental consent at all.

This project also coincided with many high-profile data breaches, which sounded the alarm for many parents. In fact, the pushback against InBloom spawned the Parent Coalition for Student Privacy (https://www.studentprivacymatters.org), a national organization dedicated to student privacy, and opened up the conversation around the Federal Educational Rights and Privacy Act (FERPA) and how student information is shared with EdTech companies.

## ADVERTISING AND THIRD-PARTY APPS

As discussed in Chapter 6, "Targeted Online Advertising," ads are another place where privacy can be compromised. During the 2016 US presidential election, a company connected with the Trump campaign collected personal information about millions of Facebook users without their permission through an online Facebook personality test. The test was created by a Cambridge professor, Dr. Aleksandr Kogan, who created an app that allowed users to log in with Facebook to take the personality test. The test was taken by 270,000 users and Kogan eventually shared this data with the company Cambridge Analytica to use in their efforts to help get Donald Trump elected.[12]

Because users logged into the app using their Facebook credentials, they granted the app access to things like their location, likes, photos, interests, and possibly more. This is how the "log in with Facebook" feature works on all sites, although the amount of data that each app or site asks for varies. It is, Facebook contended, the responsibility of the user to approve that access, so Facebook was not responsible for the data being misused.

Since then, Facebook has changed how third parties can access user data, and it has allowed users to download all of the data that Facebook has gathered about them. Some users were shocked when they discovered that once they synced their contacts with the Facebook app, every single contact in their address book, even those without Facebook accounts, were uploaded to their profile. Many articles appeared with accounts of people's experiences opening the downloaded file, and one even described it as a "digital folder of my humiliating past."[13]

Google also allows users to download all of the data that is connected to their profile (https://takeout.google.com/settings/takeout?pli=1). If a user's location is turned on, he or she can scroll through every single place the user has ever taken his or her phone, which can be somewhat terrifying to think about. The data that can be downloaded from Google and Facebook is, essentially, what you look like to an advertiser. Facebook has even created a tool to allow users to adjust their own ad settings. Users can go to https://www.facebook.com/your_information/ to see all of the information he or she has on Facebook and download it. There is also a tab under "My Information" that allows users to see how they are categorized to advertisers based on what they post, click on, and share both on and off Facebook.

All this information that users provide to these services is valuable data. Often, data is thought of as numbers, as something quantifiable. However, data is becoming more and more qualitative as it is used to tailor ads to specific users. This data, and essentially our privacy, are the currency we are paying to access the many "free" sites and services that we depend on. This is why it is important that users read a site or service's privacy policy before signing up and why it matters that companies make their privacy policies more accessible and easier to read by the average user.

Privacy policies are required by law in the United States, although there is no one law that governs their existence. Instead, privacy policies address a number of laws aimed at protecting children and consumers, which are enforced by the Federal Trade Commission (FTC).[14] Many privacy policies are written in "legalese" and can be hard to understand. However, to see an example of a clearly written policy, look no further than the FTC itself, which has created a model for other sites, apps, and services to follow (Figure 7.1).

A good privacy policy tells the user when and how a site or service is collecting information as well as what kind of information is being collected and if or how it is shared. If that information is unclear when reading a privacy policy, it may be worth it to think twice about using a service.

## HOW WE ARE TRACKED

It has become increasingly obvious that companies, law enforcement, and even complete strangers are capable of tracking people online, but it is not always as clear how that tracking happens. Every device that connects to the Internet has a unique identifier, an IP address, that is sent out every time the device accesses a site or logs into an app. (See Chapter 3, "How Does the Internet Work, Anyway?") This IP address usually has a location attached to it, and, of course, the Internet service provider (ISP; e.g., Comcast, Verizon) knows exactly who is attached to which IP address and where that user lives (physical address). However, people are also tracked in other ways.

### Global Positioning System

The easiest way to track someone is through the global positioning system (GPS) on the user's phone. GPS uses satellites to pinpoint the position of objects on Earth. Most users keep their GPS turned on nearly all the time because it's what allows them to use apps that require GPS to

# Privacy Policy

## WHAT DOES THE FTC DO WITH YOUR PERSONAL INFORMATION?

### Our Privacy Policy

Federal law requires us to tell you how we collect, use, share, and protect your personal information. Federal law also limits how we can use your personal information. Protecting the privacy and security of consumers' personal information is very important to us. Please read this notice carefully to understand what we do with the personal information we collect both online and offline.

When you contact us to help you with a problem, we may collect personal information about you. We collect and use only the information necessary to respond to your concerns and conduct investigations. In most instances, we collect minimal personal information, such as name, address, telephone number, or email address. In limited cases, depending on the nature of your request or of our law enforcement investigations, we also may collect other personal information such as Social Security numbers, account numbers, or mortgage or health information. We also may collect information about your visit to our websites for security and internal operations purposes.

## WHEN DO WE COLLECT PERSONAL INFORMATION?

### When you contact us...

- to order publications, obtain redress, or register for the National Do Not Call Registry.
- to file a complaint or seek help for possible consumer fraud or identity theft.
- to file a public comment or participate in a rulemaking, workshop, or community engagement project.

### When we contact you...

- to ask if you will participate in a consumer survey.
- to provide information in response to a subpoena or other legal process.

### When we contact others...

- to collect information about potential victims when we investigate possible law violations.

## WHERE DOES YOUR INFORMATION GO?

### Within the FTC...

- we use consumer information to further our law enforcement investigations.
- our contractors use your information when they perform certain services, such as operating the National Do Not Call Registry or our Consumer Response Center, processing redress claims, or fulfilling your order for publications.

### To other government agencies (federal, state, local, international)...

- we work with our partners to investigate complaints, coordinate law enforcement investigations, cooperate with oversight investigations, or follow up on ID theft reports.

### To others outside government...

- we post public comments and transcripts, including names, state of residence, and other non-confidential information, on the FTC website in a rulemaking, workshop, blog, or other public FTC proceeding.
- we provide information to credit bureaus for complaints about consumer fraud, ID theft, or credit reports.
- we provide only your phone number to telemarketers to enforce the National Do Not Call Registry.
- we provide information to businesses or individuals in response to court orders, subpoenas, discovery requests, or Freedom of Information Act requests, or to resolve complaints.
- we use third-party services on our websites to assist in communicating or interacting with the public.

FIGURE 7.1

Screenshot. Federal Trade Commission. Accessed November 3, 2018. https://www.ftc.gov/site-information/privacy-policy

function—usually a map or driving app that is giving them directions. However, when this is turned on, it also means that your location may be attached to images you take and to social media posts you make, and your location is often sent to websites so they can show you ads based on your location.

### Cell Phone Towers

However, your GPS does not need to be turned on for someone to track your movements. The smartphones that so many people depend on every day are constantly connecting to a cell tower. As a user moves around a city or the country, his or her phone "pings" cell towers nearby to maintain service. This means that the operator of the cell phone tower has a record of which devices connected to the tower and when. Cell phones connect to towers using regular radio waves, which are then converted to digital signals and transported along fiber optic and eventually underground landlines. To properly connect calls, the towers must know which devices are connected to which towers. (This is how Timothy Carpenter, mentioned at the start of this chapter. had his every move was tracked by law enforcement.)

### IP Addresses

When someone accesses the Internet, whether by cell phone, desktop PC, tablet, or laptop, the user is not only transmitting an IP address and letting the site know where the user is, but he or she may also be transmitting information about the device being used. This is called the "user agent," and it is how browsers and sites know how to optimize, or provide the ideal user experience, for a particular kind of device.

In July 2017, the Trump administration requested the records of every single person (1.3 million) who accessed the website http://disruptj-20. org, a site calling for protests at President Trump's inauguration, a few of which were violent. The Justice Department was granted a warrant for the request, but the site's host, Dreamhost, refused to release the records, which added up to millions of people. In Dreamhost's view, this was overreach because it would ensnare people who casually visited the site along with those who may have accessed it in connection with any crimes committed at the protest. These records would have released the IP address (essentially the location), and the kind of device being used by anyone who accessed the site.

In August 2017, a federal judge agreed and, although he did require Dream-host to turn over information regarding who had accessed the site, he limited the release to specific dates and without most IP addresses, and focused mostly on emails and messages sent through the site's domain.[15] This is just one example of how simply visiting a site leaves a trace of the visitor behind.

### Cookies

Users are also tracked online through small files called "cookies" that websites install on a user's computer to help pages load more quickly and to remember information across pages and sites. These cookies are the reason why a user may visit a shopping site, place items in the virtual cart, and find that twenty-four hours later those same items are still in his or her cart. It's also how advertisers can track browsing activity across the Internet and show ads that are specific to users' interests. An explanation for how cookies work can be found in Chapter 6.

### Search Engines

When someone does a basic Internet search using Google, Bing, Yahoo, or other large search engines, the search engine sends the search terms, the words the user typed in to conduct the search, to the website being accessed as part of the transaction. This information may also be sent to any third-party advertisers on the site (advertisers who pay to have their content displayed on the site), who can then show ads related to the search terms. This search history can travel with a user across multiple sites, influencing the kinds of ads they see. Advertisers call this "search retargeting."[16]

### Internet Service Providers

Most people don't think about their ISP as a privacy concern, and for the most part, ISPs, like Comcast and Verizon that provide Internet service, aren't generally sharing the private information of customers with advertisers. However, ISPs do send anonymized data collected from their clients to advertisers. This means that ISPs take information such as location, IP address, IP addresses accessed (websites), age, and any other information provided by the customer without tying this information to customers by name. Advertisers may, however, want to know how many men ages twenty-five through thirty-five have accessed a particular website or kind of website in a particular part of the country in the last thirty days. ISPs can provide that data for a cost.

In April 2017, Congress rolled back rules protecting the privacy of broadband customers, essentially opening the door for ISPs to share their customers' personal information without the customers' permission.[17] The argument was that this put ISPs on a level playing field with companies like Google and Facebook who regularly make a profit off of their users' personal information.[18] It's not clear what customer data ISPs are sharing or how they are sharing it, but the reality is that it is happening.

## IMPLICATIONS IN THE CLASSROOM

In the classroom, individual educators can't do much about how companies and ISPs track their students because browsing the Internet often requires users to give up some of their privacy. Schools do not use virtual private networks (VPNs) to mask IP addresses (more on that later) and in the age of Google Suite for Education (GSFE), Chromebooks, and a number of educational software and cloud-based tools, student information is part of that playing field.

In 2014, Google was sued for scanning the emails of students using its education service.[19] Google claimed that the scanning helped with virus protection and spell check. However, this scanning occurred without notifying the users and, although GSFE is ad-free and Google claimed that none of the scanning was related to targeted advertising, the plaintiffs in the case were not convinced. After the lawsuit concluded, a group of educational technology companies banded together to create the Student Privacy Pledge, a public pledge to maintain the privacy of K–12 students who use their services.[20] As of the writing of this book, over 340 companies have signed the pledge, which holds companies legally responsible for protecting the privacy of the students they serve. Google's current policy states that they do not scan student emails for advertising purposes.[21]

The year 2014 was important for student privacy. It was also the year that Class Dojo, an online classroom management tool that allows teachers to create student profiles to track and manage student behavior, was under fire for how it collected information about student behaviors in class without much transparency about how that information was stored or shared.[22] Class Dojo has since updated its privacy policy and has, it appears, made every effort to jump through every privacy hoop to reach a high standard of transparency and care with how it treats student information.[23] The company has also signed the Student Privacy Pledge.

Privacy concerns in the classroom aren't limited to data scraping from apps and websites, however. In October 2017, the EdTech publication Edsurge reported on a company that built headsets that track students' brain waves and report the activity to a teacher through a dashboard.[24] The idea is that teachers can easily measure engagement by seeing students' brain activity. It also markets the device as a way for students to train their brains to learn better. The company, BrainCo, is also working on building a database of brain waves to increase the potential of the devices they make.

The privacy concerns around the kind of data being collected by the company from users, including those younger than thirteen, has earned the company a lot of negative press. Their privacy policy has a long list of information it collects from users, including things like "dominant hand" and the electroencephalographic (brain wave) raw data.[25] Although the company has a page dedicated to explaining its commitment to user privacy, BrainCo is not a signatory of the Student Privacy Pledge. Most of its pilot programs have occurred in China, where privacy protections are much different than in the United States. Still, as more devices like this are brought into the classroom, it becomes even more important to consider what kind of data are being sent to EdTech companies, especially as that data moves from simple email scanning into the storing of biometric data about children younger than thirteen.

Another consideration is what will happen to that data if a company is sold. Does the company have a clear policy on how student data is handled in the case of a hand-off? If the rules aren't clear, these transactions may make it easy for the acquiring company to turn a profit from the data they have inherited.

Classroom teachers should also consider student privacy when using tools that teachers implement in the classroom. Some tools allow teachers and administrators to view communications between students. Any school that uses GSFE can easily view all of the emails, chat messages, documents, and other information attached to a student account. In addition, some classroom tools such as Schoology (http://www.schoology.com) allows students to message each other. If there are concerns about bullying or inappropriate content, a system administrator can reset a student's password and login to see what messages a student may have sent. School- and district-based acceptable use policies should make this lack of privacy clear and this should be communicated to students before they start using any service that allows administrator access.

## PRIVACY POLICIES

According to *Business Dictionary*, a privacy policy is a "[s]tatement that declares a firm's or website's policy on collecting and releasing information about a visitor. It usually declares what specific information is collected and whether it is kept confidential or shared with or sold to other firms, researchers or sellers."[26] The FTC requires privacy policies for some sites, such as financial institutions, but, at the time of this writing, there are no laws in the United States that require companies to have a privacy policy.[27]

Many companies provide a link to the policy and require users to check a box stating that they have read the policy. Even if a site clearly posts its policy, for instance, in the footer, that policy is usually written by lawyers and is not worded for the average person to understand. These practices make it hard for the average person to manage privacy online and even understand exactly how information is being used.

## PROTECTING OUR PRIVACY

The extent to which Internet users give up their privacy to access the world's largest community and public space can be scary. With more and more transparency around how personal data is collected and used, there are also more and more ways for people to attempt to protect their privacy online. The following are some ways to manage and protect your online privacy.

### Virtual Private Networks

The easiest way to protect one's privacy online is to use a VPN. There are loads of options to choose from, but a simple Google search for "best VPNs of [insert year]" will help narrow down the options.

VPNs protect the data of the user by first encrypting the data (converting data into strings of code) before it leaves the computer. Then the data is sent through a private server before being sent to the website, ISP, or other entity being accessed. These private servers can live all over the world, so when the data is sent, it looks like it is coming from wherever that server lives instead of the actual IP address of the sending device. In many countries whose governments censor the Internet, a VPN allows citizens to access sites that they could not access from an IP address in their own country. This also prevents ISPs from tracking a customer's web traffic because the customer's IP address may be constantly changing or may not be directly linked to their actual location.[28]

### Other Tools to Mitigate Data Tracking

There are also several tools out there that work inside a web browser to block third-party tracking that occurs when you visit a site. One example is Ghostery (http://www.ghostery.com), a browser extension, which runs in the background while a user browses the web. It alerts users to whether they are being tracked and blocks advertisers and sites from tracking you.

Firefox, the free browser run by the Mozilla Foundation, also has a "do not track" setting that can be turned on inside the browser to protect users. However, as Mozilla states, this is a voluntary action and websites do not have to comply with the "do not track" request.[29]

Google's Chrome browser also has this feature, but again, it is up to the individual websites to honor this request. At this time, most don't because there is no fine or official consequence. There is a Firefox add-on called Startpage that provides search results without tracking your searches (https:// addons.mozilla.org/en-US/firefox/addon/startpage-privacy-search-engin/).

The search engine Duck Duck Go (http://www.duckduckgo.com) is built around the model of private web browsing. The company says that it does not send search terms to websites users visit and it does not store search histories as Google, Bing, and other large search engines do. Search results from Duck Duck Go are not as tailored to the user, as would be expected, but users can still see predictive searches shown in a drop-down menu when they use the search engine.

The most private way to browse the Internet by far is through the Tor (an acronym for the onion router) network, often called the *deep* or *dark web*. Tor was originally created through a project of the US Naval Research Laboratory.[30] This network allows for anonymous connections between users. No identifying information is passed when connections are made, so user information is safe. Users can download the browser at https://www.torproject .org. A consortium of libraries called the Library Freedom Project (https:// libraryfreedomproject.org/) is working to bring Tor into their spaces by running "exit servers," computers that serve as the last place that Tor traffic "bounces" off from before it accesses a website. Libraries are unique in that they operate under "safe harbor" statutes and are legally protected in case something illegal comes through their server. This is their way of playing a part in protecting the privacy of citizens.[31]

If someone wants to find out whether their information has been compromised, or wants to know where their information may be stored, tools like deseat.me (https://www.deseat.me) and haveibeenpwned.com (https://haveibeenpwned.com) allow users to search by email address to see how their information may be compromised. At deseat.me, users can see what services are connected to their email address and disconnect them directly from the site. At haveibeenpwned.com, a search of an email address will return any sites where that email has been used that have been part of a data breach. Users then need to navigate to the site to change their password or delete their account.

## ATTITUDES TOWARD PRIVACY

Most adults see how the younger generations handle privacy and says that they are borderline narcissistic and "overshare" their lives. They take selfies, post to Instagram and Snap Chat constantly, and share everything from what they ate for lunch to personal posts about stress and anxiety. Although older generations may believe that young people have no regard for privacy these days, the truth is, kids care a lot about their privacy, but they have a nuanced perspective on what privacy is and means. They also understand the "trade off" when it comes to connecting with their peers and maintaining their privacy.

Despite the stereotypes, according to a 2015 Pew Research Center Study, 88 percent of teens who use social media think that they see people share too much about themselves online.[32] In a 2018 *Education Week* interview, Claire Fontaine, a researcher at Data and Society, described what she learned in her conversations with students. "Across the board, the young people we spoke to were deeply concerned about privacy and had a great appetite for adult guidance." [33]

According to Fontaine, students feel anxiety around their online presence. "A 12-year old," says Fontaine, "shouldn't have to present herself as an employable white-collar worker when she goes on to social media for the first time in middle school. I think that's the project of adulthood, not adolescence. We're seeing the adultification of teenage-hood." Young people don't necessarily understand the larger implications of privacy online when they first start their accounts and they often find it stressful to keep track of what is being shared across the platforms they use.

Many social media platforms, including Facebook until recently, set the default privacy setting to "public." Facebook changed this in 2014 after some pushback from users.[34] Still, recently, Facebook discovered a bug that set millions of users' posts to public without their knowledge.[35] Venmo, an online payment platform run by PayPal that allows people to pay each other through a social media-esque app, was in the spotlight recently because of its policy of marking all payment public by default.

Mozilla Fellow Hang Do Thi Duc decided to track all of these public payments and was able to piece together intimate details of people's marriages as well as payments made to drug dealers. She eventually created the *Public by Default* project in which she profiles the stories of Venmo users based on the data they shared publicly.[36] Social media companies do not prioritize their users' privacy. Young people who are just starting out with these tools may find privacy settings complicated or they may not even know how to access them.

Researcher danah boyd has been studying how young people use technology and the Internet to connect and socialize for many years. In her 2015 book, *It's Complicated: The Social Lives of Networked Teens*, she explains, "There's a big difference between being *in* public and *being* public."[37] For example, imagine that Twitter was a large cocktail party with groups of people milling about and chatting and a few people sitting on the side eavesdropping or people watching. In this case, being at the party is being *in* public. There is no expectation that the conversations being had at the party are for public consumption or sharing. Can they be overheard? Sure. But imagine walking up to an intimate group of friends as a complete stranger and joining their conversation. This is how many young people view and experience online spaces. When talking to a friend on a bus, they expect a certain amount of privacy, even if they are in a public space, and the same is true when they are communicating with their friends in public, online spaces. They are *in public*, not *being public* with their information and conversations.

Young people have a nuanced understanding of privacy and they also understand the "trade off" when it comes to using technology tools to connect with their friends. They have a basic understanding that companies may have access to what they say or post, but they don't necessarily have a clear sense of what that means. Claire Fontaine describes the misplaced responsibility when it comes to tech companies and privacy: "Too often, schools frame online privacy primarily as a matter of personal responsibility, feeding young people's sense that they are responsible for achieving something that Silicon Valley's current business practices and a lax regulatory environment make structurally impossible."[38]

In other words, schools spend a lot of time telling kids how to manage their online personas and teaching them responsibility for what they share online. This puts the onus on students to manage their own privacy online instead of requiring tech companies themselves to take responsibility for protecting their users' privacy. When privacy is not "baked into" the tools that young people use, it is asking a lot for them to understand how to navigate those settings, especially when they are different across multiple platforms.

## EUROPEAN PRIVACY REGULATIONS

In April 2016, the European Union Parliament passed the European Union General Data Protection Regulation (GDPR). This law, which went into effect on May 25, 2018, "applies to all companies processing and holding the personal data of data subjects residing in the European Union, regardless of the company's location."[39] Once the regulation went into effect, websites and online services that catered to or were used by EU citizens had a responsibility to maintain transparency about tracking and other privacy-related practices. For this reason, visitors to these sites are bombarded with messages about cookies used on the site and suggestions to visit the companies' privacy policies. For users in the United States, this has become an important reminder of how our information is used by companies, even if they aren't protected under the EU regulations. Time will tell whether the United States will follow suit or introduce its own regulations around its citizens' privacy, although US companies that do business with EU customers are already directly affected by the new regulations.

## PRIVACY IN THE CLASSROOM

It is the responsibility of educators to consider their students' privacy when introducing new tools into the classroom. However, all responsibility should not fall solely on educators. Districts and schools should have their own privacy policies and plans for how to handle and protect student privacy when using digital tools. Schools are already used to the rules around protecting student data, so considering technology tools should not require much more work. At the bare minimum, schools should be able to provide an approved list of digital tools for teachers to use *as well as* a way for teachers to suggest and propose tools they find that they want to use, and a smooth and timely process for approving these requests.

Schools and districts also have the responsibility to alert families of data breaches involving student information; families should also be alerted to how their child's information is being used in digital or online situations. For more on how to incorporate and address privacy issues and concerns in the classroom, see Textbox 7.1.

TEXTBOX 7.1.

**Elementary Grades**

In the younger grades, students may not yet understand what "private" actually means when it comes to sharing information about themselves. Have students make a T-Chart listing things about themselves that they would tell a stranger on the left and things that they would not tell a stranger on the right. You may need to give them an example to help them get started. For instance, "my favorite color" might go on the left and "my home address" might go on the right. Have them list at least three on each side. Then have them compare lists with a partner.

Ask students to share examples of what they wouldn't share with a stranger and what they would share. Ask them if there were any examples of something they wouldn't tell a stranger that their partner would be willing to share. Explain that things that they would not share with a stranger are considered "private information," and often include your full name, your address, your phone number, your birthday, your age, and the names of your parents and siblings.

The items on the left that they would share with a stranger are called "personal information," and while they are unique to each student, they would not put the student or his or her family in danger of any kind. These items might include a favorite color, a favorite food, the last movie the student saw, or the last book he or she read. Students can then be guided to make connections between the information they give websites when they sign up for their services and their private and personal information lists.

### Middle Grades

As students enter middle school, they may already have a social media account, or they may be aware of social media tools and see posts even without an account. Whereas elementary students are still learning the difference between private and personal information, tweens are grappling with what to share and what not to share, and often base their choices on their peers' choices or the things that they see others post online.

This is a good time to talk with students about "oversharing," or how the private information they are sharing, including their location, could be used against them. They also should consider the privacy settings on their account and they should be familiar with privacy polices. They should also think about the kinds of things that they say online. Have them make a T-Chart comparing things they would talk about on a bus or in a coffee shop versus things they would talk about in their bedroom with a close friend. Sometimes, tweens (and teens and adults) forget who may be "listening" when they are posting to social media.

### High School

By the time students reach high school, they may have been using social media for several years. Now is the time to reflect on how they've been using it and consider how what they are posting could affect them as they enter adulthood. They should be well versed in privacy settings and be clear about what kind of information is private and what is more geared toward a public audience. They should assume that nothing they post on any electronic device, including a computer or phone, is ever private.

In high school, students should also be aware of how they are being tracked through GPS on their phone and through the sites that they visit, and they should be familiar with privacy policies on sites that they visit. They can download their data from Facebook or Google to see what those companies have been collecting about them over the years, and they can turn off location services for sites and apps that they use regularly. They can also use a search engine like Duck Duck Go or a browser like Firefox that has strong policies around protecting user data.

# Laws in the Digital Classroom

As more and more technology enters the classroom, and as more and more of that technology is online and tied to online services and accounts, it is vital that educators understand the responsibilities that come with using these digital tools. Protecting students' information and protecting students themselves from inappropriate content is not only the responsible thing to do, it is also the law. Educators must also consider the materials that they use in their classrooms and how they are using materials that they did not create. This chapter provides an overview of the three major laws that protect students and a close look at copyright laws and how they relate to the classroom along with resources and best practices for protecting students and modeling professional use of learning materials.

## STUDENT PRIVACY LAWS

### Family Education Rights and Privacy Act

In 1974, President Gerald Ford signed the Family Education Rights and Privacy Act (FERPA) into law. This new law took a huge step toward protecting students' private information and giving families more control over how schools and other institutions used student information.[1] After the advent of the Internet, FERPA is still the primary law that governs how schools and other organizations handle students' private information. It allows for families to access, view, and dispute their child's information, and it requires schools and other entities to get permission to disclose this "directory information." Directory information is a student's "name, address, telephone listing, date and place of birth, major field of study, participation in officially recognized activities and sports, weight and height of members of athletic teams, dates of attendance, degrees and awards received, and the most recent previous educational agency or institution attended by the student."

At the 2018 conference for the International Society for Technology in Education (ISTE), a panel of student privacy experts explained that educational technology (edtech) companies can fall under one of the exceptions in the FERPA law and be considered a "school official." This allows the school or district to release student directory information to these companies without parental consent, provided that it is solely for an educational purpose.[2] This is evident in the rollout of Google Suite for Education services across many districts; parental permission is not required to issue students Google accounts through the service.

Still, these companies must follow each individual state's guidelines for handling student data and the school or district must maintain control of that data. ISTE panel member Michael Hawes, the director of the Student Privacy Policy and Assistance Division at the U.S. Department of Education, stated, "There is no such thing as a FERPA seal of approval" for edtech companies because the regulations differ from state to state.

FERPA protections should be taken seriously in the classroom. Violations of this law are subject to legal action and, when using a new digital tool in the classroom that requires any kind of identifying student information, it is best to check with an administrator first.

### Children's Online Privacy Protection Act

Student privacy online in the United States is protected by the Children's Online Privacy Protection Act (COPPA) of 1998. This law and its accompanying regulation was created to protect the personal information of children younger than thirteen. "Personal information" is defined as:

1. A first and last name;
2. A home or other physical address including street name and name of a city or town;
3. Online contact information as defined in this section;

4. A screen or user name where it functions in the same manner as online contact information, . . .;
5. A telephone number;
6. A Social Security number;
7. A persistent identifier that can be used to recognize a user over time and across different websites or online services. Such persistent identifier[s] [include], but [are] not limited to, a customer number held in a cookie, an Internet Protocol (IP) address, a processor or device serial number, or unique device identifier;
8. A photograph, video, or audio file where such file contains a child's image or voice;
9. Geolocation information sufficient to identify street name and name of a city or town; or
10. Information concerning the child or the parents of that child that the operator collects online from the child and combines with an identifier described in this definition.[3]

The regulation requires parental permission for the use of any personal information collected from a child younger than thirteen. It also requires a certain level of security with this information and requires that information only be held onto for a "reasonable" amount of time and that the data must be securely deleted. These regulations hold true across all websites, even those not marketed to children, who may even inadvertently collect personal information from a child younger than thirteen. The Federal Trade Commission (FTC) enforces COPPA regulations.

Although similar to FERPA, COPPA is limited to the online use of student information and it is more specifically geared toward companies and websites and how they collect and store student information.

### Children's Internet Protection Act

Anyone who has attended or worked in a public school or library has experienced the "blocked page" Internet warning. This is the result of the Children's' Internet Protection Act of 2000 (CIPA). Schools and libraries receive special federal funding for their Internet infrastructure through the Universal Services Fund (USF). This fund was created as part of the Communications Act of 1934, which stated that all US residents should have access to affordable and efficient communication services.[4] It is paid for by consumers on

**Table 8.1.   Protecting Students Online**

| | |
|---|---|
| Children's Online Privacy Protection Act (COPPA) | Requires parental permission for children to use websites and apps that collect information from anyone younger than thirteen. |
| Children's Internet Protection Act (CIPA) | Requires entities like schools and libraries to protect children (minors younger than eighteen) from content that is obscene, child pornography, or harmful to minors. |
| Family Education Rights and Privacy Act (FERPA) | A 1974 law that gives parents the right to access, review, and dispute information held by schools and other educational institutions. It also prevents students' "directory" information from being shared by these institutions without parental consent. |
| E-Rate | A program funded by the Universal Service Fund that helps schools and libraries purchase and maintain telecommunication equipment. This fund is paid for by telecommunication consumers and is included as a small charge on their telephone bill. |

their monthly telephone bill, and is often listed as a separate charge on the bill, although Federal law does not require that telecommunication companies itemize the fee.

In 1996, the act expanded to include support for schools and libraries to build and maintain their telecommunication systems, including broadband Internet. This program is called the "E-Rate" program, and it plays a huge role in how schools connect to the Internet. Under CIPA, all entities that receive E-Rate funding through the USF must have protective measures in place to shield children from content that is obscene, child pornography, or "harmful to minors." Schools have the added responsibility of monitoring the online activity of their students and providing a comprehensive digital citizenship curriculum. These protective measures come in the form of content filters that block inappropriate sites (Table 8.1).

### Privacy and Protection Laws in the Classroom

In April 2018, advocates for student privacy filed a complaint with the FTC regarding YouTube, which is owned by Google, stating that Google is collecting information from children younger than thirteen when they access YouTube.[5] Although YouTube has its own app for kids, many kids, the

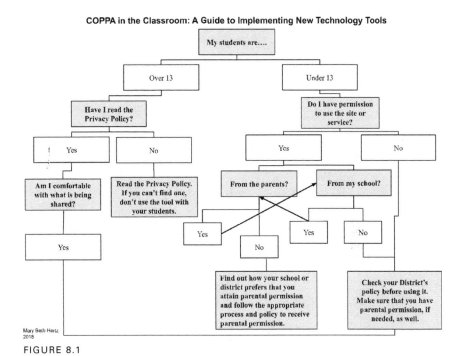

COPPA in the Classroom: A Guide to Implementing New Technology Tools

FIGURE 8.1

complainants argue, access regular YouTube on a daily basis. Some lie about their age when signing up for the service and others are accessing YouTube while not logged in (which does not mean that they are not being tracked). Many of these children access YouTube content at school for assignments, to get on-the-spot tutoring, or even to upload their own content.

Other classroom tools may specifically ask for student names and the name of their school, and still others are used at the district level for online assessment and collect large amounts of information on each student through their district records. In fact, Pearson Education, one of the largest education companies in the world, highlights its use of student data within its products to adapt learning experiences to the individual student.[6] Figure 8.1 provides a simple guide to use when considering implementing a new digital tool in the classroom while also considering student privacy.

**Other Classroom Considerations**

Aside from knowing the laws that protect student information and having a basic understanding of what is being shared, how it is being shared, and with whom, there are a few other things to consider. Teachers often share their classrooms with a wider audience through social media to trade tips and techniques with other educators and to share "good news" with parents and families. However, this kind of sharing must be done with caution. If a teacher shares a photo or video of his or her classroom with a public audience, they must also consider the privacy of the students in the photograph or video. Have the students consented to having their image posted online? Have their parents (especially if their children are younger than thirteen)? Teachers use tools like Skype and Google Hangouts to connect their classroom with experts, authors, and even other classrooms. These are powerful uses of these technologies that make enduring learning experiences. Still, it is important that educators alert their administrator and parents and, if necessary, collect the necessary parental permission.

There are ways to share what is going on in a classroom widely while still protecting the privacy of students. Some educators edit the images to blur out faces or other identifiers (e.g., name tags, room numbers, or other information specific to the classroom or student). Others may use a service like Tadpoles (http://www.tadpoles.com) or Remind (http://www.remind.com) to share information within a closed group. Still, any image or text shared digitally can be easily screenshot or downloaded and reshared or reposted, so no service is truly private.

It is important that educators take responsibility for protecting their students' information, but schools and districts can also easily shoulder some of that responsibility by providing educators with specific guidelines around how student information is shared and even by providing sample apps, websites, and other digital tools that are known to handle student data securely. This takes the guesswork out of the process of implementing new tools in the classroom.

For instance, the Puyallup School District, located outside of Seattle, Washington, requires all "digital vendors" to sign an agreement for how they will handle student data.[7] This is a prudent practice, but does also limit the kinds of technology that teachers can use in the classroom. According to a teacher in the district, this means that schools cannot use tools like Flipgrid run by larger tech companies like Microsoft, who won't sign the agreement.

On the flip side, schools and districts that dictate which apps and websites educators can use with their students may be seen as stifling innovation. More and more edtech companies are reaching out directly to teachers in the classroom to pilot their tools. These pilot programs are important for making tools better and finding new ways to implement technology. However, it is vital that schools and individual educators ask outright how the company handles student data and read the privacy policy carefully.

The company should also require a signed waiver if it is collecting data from students younger than eighteen. Even well-known companies with transparent procedures can fall prey to hacks and data breaches. In 2017, the edtech company Edmodo was hacked and thousands of student accounts, including emails, usernames, and encrypted passwords were put up for sale on the "dark web."[8] As LeeAndra Kahn from Brooks Middle School in Chicago explained in a 2017 *Edsurge* article, teachers are under pressure to make academic progress, and often make impulsive technology purchases hoping that the new technology will boost student scores.[9] Teachers must do their homework, and better yet, partner with their school or district before piloting a brand new technology in their classroom as well as read over the privacy policies of sites and apps they want to use very carefully.

It is important for educators to know their school and district policies around student data before trying out a new tool in the classroom, even if their students are thirteen or older. If, for example, a data breach is due to teacher carelessness, the school could be held liable for the error and, although FERPA does not provide a pathway for parents to take legal action against a school or company (they can only file a complaint), notifying families and following data breach protocols can be costly. It is equally important to know your state's specific laws around student privacy. Many states have passed their own student-privacy laws that provide more local guidance beyond the Federal COPPA law on how student information may be used and must be protected.

Issues around student privacy don't just occur at the classroom level. In August 2015, the Electronic Frontier Foundation, a nonprofit dedicated to "defending civil liberties in the digital world," wrote a letter to the Roseville City School District on behalf of the parent of an incoming fourth grader with concerns about the school forcing his daughter to use a school issued Chromebook and Google account. The district implemented the devices, which require a Google account to log into the machine, without parental consent. The parent was concerned that, although Google Suite for Education (GSFE) states that it does not collect student information or sell it to advertisers, this only applies to the Google apps covered under the GSFE umbrella. Other apps, like YouTube, do not make this promise. In addition, he felt that the district was teaching his daughter complacency about giving her information over to a company like Google with no questions asked.

The parent requested that the district provide his daughter with a different machine and a different, non-Google email account. At first, the district denied his request, but eventually, after several meetings, agreed to the parent's request, although it stated that it would not make such a waiver the following year.[10] Even districts, who are responsible for the data of often thousands of students, may decide that the benefits of technology tools outweigh concerns about student privacy.

The new fad of providing "personalized learning" through software that adapts based on student responses has taken hold in many schools, including those attended by the children of Silicon Valley employees. This adaptive technology is seen as a way to individualize instruction for every student in a class based on the student's understanding of content. However, this software is adaptive because it is collecting massive amounts of data on each individual student to show him or her content on the student's "level." It's not clear that districts are alerting parents to the fact that this data is being collected, and it's not clear that districts are being thoughtful about the security measures that the software companies like Lexia are taking with student data.

A 2017 paper from the National Education Policy Center warns about the "lure" of personalized learning and "lax regulation" that puts children's privacy at risk.[11] The contracts between schools and large tech companies like Microsoft, Google, and Apple, also help these companies ensure that young people continue to use their services into adulthood, providing more advertising revenue for the companies.

### CIPA Compliance in Schools

Schools that receive E-Rate funding, as explained previously, must have a digital citizenship curriculum and must teach students about being safe and responsible in a variety of online settings. This means that schools need to have a schoolwide plan for teaching this curriculum, which can feel like "just one more thing" that teachers have to do in the classroom. Luckily, Common Sense Media has created an easily searchable, comprehensive, grade level–specific curriculum that can be implemented even in schools with limited technology resources. The curriculum can be accessed at https://www.commonsense.org/education/digital-citizenship.

CIPA also requires schools to use protective content filters to qualify for E-Rate funding. These filters are often a source of contention for educators who feel that the "harmful to minors" criteria can lead schools and districts to block sites that, although noneducational, are not necessarily harmful. Many districts blocked YouTube for years before bending to the pressure from educators who found it a vital classroom resource, and most block social media sites like Instagram and Facebook. These filters are actually a piece of software that acts as a shield between the user and the open Internet. They are often preloaded with specific sites and domains and are also programmed to recognize certain keywords and even block sites by category (social media, games). This is why filters often seem to randomly block harmless sites along with the harmful ones.

In many districts, teachers can either bypass the filter with a password or there is a process in place for them to request a site be unblocked for educational reasons. Opponents of filters argue that filters threaten students' and teachers' First Amendment rights because permissible content is decided by the filter manufacturers and not the users themselves.

## COPYRIGHT LAW IN THE CLASSROOM

Although many teachers are provided with textbooks and other materials to use in their classrooms, every teacher, at some point, finds himself or herself reaching outside of these materials to help students access the content. This might come in the form of an article, a video, an image, or text. Some educators mistakenly believe that, if something is for educational purposes, it can be copied and shared in its entirety with students.

Copyright laws also apply to teachers, though there are some small allowances. Teachers can share copyrighted material in small amounts with their students; photocopying an entire book is outside of these allowances. Use of copyrighted material in the classroom generally falls under fair use, a gray area of copyright law. Under fair use, copyrighted materials may be reproduced if the following are considered:

1.  the purpose and character of the use, including whether such use is of a commercial nature or is for nonprofit educational purposes;
2.  the nature of the copyrighted work;
3.  the amount and substantiality of the portion used in relation to the copyrighted work as a whole; and
4.  the effect of the use upon the potential market for or value of the copyrighted work.

The fact that a work is unpublished shall not itself bar a finding of fair use if such finding is made upon consideration of all the above factors.[12]

Essentially, is the work being used for nonprofit or educational purposes? Is it nonfiction or a creative work? How much of the work is being used and will the use of the work negatively influence the value or market for the work? Generally speaking, the use of works that are nonfiction tend to be more easily defended as fair use because the dissemination of facts can be considered a public benefit and because there is less argument for creativity or individuality of the work.

Fair-use guidelines dictate that the less of the work that is used, the more likely fair use can be argued. However, this may not be true if the portion used is, for instance, the hook of a famous song. As for the market value of the work, this is considered in terms of whether the use of the work could cause the copyright holder to lose income from the work. For instance, in 1985 a court ruled that the *Nation*, which published a previously unpublished excerpt from former president Gerald Ford's memoir, could not claim fair use because they published the excerpt weeks before it was scheduled to be published (with Ford's permission) in another magazine. This negatively affected Ford's marketing of the book.[13] In general, unpublished works do not tend to fall under fair use because it is considered the author's right to publish the work for the first time.

Another aspect of fair-use guidelines to consider is the transformative quality of the work. In other words, has the new work changed the purpose or intent of the original work? This is why parody is usually considered fair use. For instance, Paramount Pictures created a promotional poster for its 1994 film, *Naked Gun 33⅓* that parodied a famous 1991 image of a pregnant Demi Moore that was featured on the cover of *Vanity Fair*. The studio recreated the image using a different pregnant model and edited the actor Leslie Nielsen's head onto the woman's body. The original photographer sued for copyright infringement but lost her case because the court decided that the Paramount image was a parody and a transformative work and did not impede on potential earnings from the original work.[14]

Fair use rulings can seem unpredictable and they can sometimes seem to contradict each other. They are decided on a case-by-case basis and often depend on the position of a specific judge. However, certain uses of copyrighted works are definitively not fair use, even though we see them a great deal. For instance, creating your own video and using your favorite (copyrighted) song as the soundtrack is not a transformative use of the song and it has the potential to impede on potential earnings for the original artist.

In 1998, Congress passed the Digital Millennium Copyright Act (DMCA), which provided copyright holders a way to hold Internet companies accountable for taking down content that infringed on their rights to works. This is why YouTube often takes down videos that use copyrighted music or are merely uploads of entire Hollywood movies. It is common to see disclaimers or simple links online when people use work that is not theirs. However, simply stating where a work comes from does not relieve one of the responsibility that comes with using a copyrighted work without permission. Schools can find themselves faced with take-down notices if, for example, a student work contains copyrighted material that does not meet fair-use guidelines.

Publishing a written work in its entirety online without permission from the copyright holder would also not be considered fair use. Although the educational use guidelines state that teachers can reproduce text for student in their class, these reproductions cannot be made to replace the original text. Examples of unacceptable use include photocopying an entire textbook rather than purchasing a textbook for the classroom or photocopying an anthology of poems in place of purchasing the anthology.

There are also limits to the amount of text that can be reproduced and how many times a teacher can reproduce these works. Reproductions of a poem are limited to two hundred and fifty words and/or up to two pages. Articles, stories, and essays are limited to 2,500 words and prose is limited to one thousand words or 10 percent of the work. Only one chart, graph, diagram, drawing, cartoon, or picture book is allowed per book or periodical. Any photocopies should also contain the copyright information of the work.

Teachers are rarely instructed on copyright law before they enter the class-room. Professors at the college level often provide photocopied "coursepacks" to their students, which are usually licensed and require a fee. Students are often unaware of this licensing agreement, and so they may create course-packs for their own classrooms, unaware that they could potentially be break-ing copyright law.

Copyright law and the DMCA walk a fine line. In some ways, these laws help protect the intellectual property of creative people. On the other side, it allows large companies to protect their intellectual property to an extent that sometimes prevents competition or hinders free expression. Because these companies have the money to file lawsuits, individuals may be intimidated and may prevent them from even attempting to build on (transform) exist-ing works in creative ways, thereby creating new works. This is, some would argue, how art is made—building on work that has come before. Still, the DMCA does provide a "safe harbor" for Internet providers so they can't be sued if a user uploads illegal content through their service. This has allowed for more free expression online because the providers are not afraid of law-suits and allow users to take responsibility for what they post.

### Modeling Appropriate Use of Content

In general, educators should be modeling best practices around using copy-righted material in the classroom. Students should be aware of copyright law and fair use and how to properly cite their work. They should understand the ramifications of misuse of copyrighted material and they should also have a basic understanding of why copyright matters.

Students will often argue that because they are students, copyright law does not apply, especially because they are not making money from the copy-righted work. However, educators should discuss the concept of copyright with their students. How would they feel if someone used their work with-out their permission? What if they made money from the work? We teach students about citation but it is important that we pair this with discussions about *why* we cite and why we avoid using materials that we don't have the rights to use.

The case of Shepard Fairey's Obama poster is a great place to start those conversations with kids. Unfortunately, the case was never actually decided along copyright lines, but it is an example that students will recognize. During the 2008 presidential election, renowned street artist Shepard Fairey, whose company, Obey, is popular with young people, created an iconic poster of candidate Barack Obama's face with the words "HOPE" at the bottom. He was summarily sued by the Associated Press because the poster used an AP image of Obama that Fairey had not gotten permission to use.

Because the posters were being sold, it was argued that the poster infringed on the AP's potential income from the photograph and that Fairey was gaining financially from an image he did not have permission to use.[15] Unfortunately, the case was focused around Fairey's attempts to destroy documentation showing that he had used the image without permission rather than copyright law concerns. Ideas for how to guide students through a conversation around copyright and fair use centered on this image and others can be found in Textbox 8.2 at the end of the chapter.

Luckily, students can get videos, music, and photographs that are free to use by anyone from a number of sites. Sites like http://pexels.com and https://commons.wikimedia.org provide a database of free images that can be downloaded directly from the site. Flickr can also be searched for "Creative Commons" images. These are images that the author has designated as free to reuse, and sometime remix or even use commercially, depending on the license. You can learn more about this licensing at http://creativecommons.org.

If your school uses GSFE, the "Insert image" option in Google apps allows students to search the web right inside of their Google Doc or other Google product. This search returns only copyright-free images by default. For a list of websites that offer copyright-free materials, see Textbox 8.1.

### Open Educational Resources and the Lesson Plan Marketplace

In recent years, sites like Teachers Pay Teachers and We Are Teachers have provided a platform for teachers to sell the materials and lesson plans they create for use in their classrooms. On one hand, it is every teacher's right to make money outside of the classroom. On the other, many of these teachers walk a legal fine line. If their materials are based on a book they are reading with their students, they may need the author's permission to sell materials that contain references to the works that might compete with licensed materials in the marketplace.

In addition, the Copyright Act of 1976 considers work that teachers create in their classrooms "works for hire," meaning that they actually don't belong

TEXTBOX 8.1. COPYRIGHT-FREE
RESOURCES FOR THE CLASSROOM

### Open Education Resources

- *New America* database of OER resources: https://www.newamer
  ica.org/in-depth/prek12-oer-in-practice/resources-get-started/
- OER Commons: https://oercommons.org (this organization
  does charge for its professional development services)

### Copyright-Free Images and Video

- Pexels: https://pexels.com
- Pixabay: https://pixabay.com/videos
- Wikimedia Commons: https://commons.wikimedia.org
- Creative Commons Search (students will still need to verify the
  license but it cuts down on the time): https://search.creative
  commons.org
- MorgueFile: https://morguefile.com
- Videvo: https://www.videvo.net

### Copyright-Free Music

- YouTube Audio Library: https://www.youtube.com/audiolibrary/
  music
- Royalty-free music on SoundCloud: https://soundcloud.com/
  royalty-free-audio-loops
- Bensound: https://www.bensound.com/royalty-free-music/2

to the teacher at all, but to the district for whom they teach. Some of the materials are also adaptations of licensed materials from textbooks or other materials purchased by the school. Although copyright is not an issue for everything for sale on sites like these, it is a widespread issue. Another side to this practice is the fact that selling their work in this fashion breaks down the collaborative nature of the field, because teachers can be in direct competition with one another for dollars.[16] One popular solution? Pay teachers more.

Educators can avoid the copyright and fair-use conundrum altogether through the use of open educational resources (OER). These are easily searchable repositories of lesson plans and other materials shared by educators across the country. According to the Hewlet Foundation, which invests in building these databases, "Open Educational Resources are teaching, learning and research materials in any medium—digital or otherwise—that reside in the public domain or have been released under an open license that permits no-cost access, use, adaptation and redistribution by others with no or limited restrictions."[17] This movement began in tandem with the advent of universities like the Massachusetts Institute of Technology, Stanford, and Harvard offering free courses in the form of "MOOCs" (massive open online courses), which allowed anyone to audit a course (take it without receiving college credit) at a prestigious university for free.

In 2015, the Department of Education launched the #GoOpen campaign to raise awareness about the huge availability of free resources through these databases and to bring more districts and classrooms into the sharing community. Through the campaign, 116 districts across the country have agreed to replace one licensed textbook with an OER.[18] Those passionate about this movement argue that OER is a great equalizer for districts who may not have the resources to spend on expensive textbooks and other materials. For more information on OER databases, see Textbox 8.1.

## PLAGIARISM

Guiding students toward legal and responsible use of materials they find online should be paired with guidance on the consequences for misuse and plagiarism. All schools should have a plan for how to instruct students on plagiarism and how to avoid it. Paraphrasing and proper citation should be incorporated into instruction in any classes that require students to conduct research or use materials or ideas that are not their own. Appropriate modeling of these practices and a clear and transparent academic integrity policy should be paired with this instruction.

With the prevalence of digital assignments and online research, students often fall prey to the ease of copying and pasting and, without proper instruction, they may think that just putting quotes around something or just saying where it comes from suffices as proper citation. With colleges using tools like TurnItIn (https://turnitin.com) to scan student papers for plagiarism, it is also easier than ever to catch plagiarism when it happens. Even a savvy teacher can put a phrase from a student paper into a Google search to find out where it may have come from and whether it is the student's own words.

Academic integrity policies lay out students' responsibility to be thoughtful and careful when using information or ideas that they find elsewhere and clearly state what happens when a student fails to meet those expectations. In colleges and in the professional world, plagiarism has serious legal consequences, so building good habits in the beginning is important. If your school does not have one, you can look at academic integrity policies from universities like Harvard (https://college.harvard.edu/academics/academic-integrity) or Rutgers (http://academicintegrity.rutgers.edu/academic-integrity-policy/) for ideas. If schools are not sure how best to teach students citation, Citation Machine (http://citationmachine.net) is a great tool for students to create citations in a number of citation styles.

To drive home the importance of avoiding plagiarism, point students to the story of Monica Crowley, who was selected in 2017 by President-Elect Donald Trump for a National Security Administration position. Investigators discovered that Crowley had plagiarized large portions of her PhD dissertation and she was forced to step away from the position once the plagiarism accusations surfaced. *Politico*'s report on the issue contains a side-by-side comparison of Crowley's work and the work she plagiarized, which is a great tool for showing what plagiarism actually looks like in practice.[19]

Often, students aren't even aware that they are plagiarizing, and being able to show them a concrete example helps them make connections to their own work. This could similarly be done through teacher-created materials. More ideas for addressing plagiarism in the classroom are in Textbox 8.2 at the end of the chapter.

## LEGAL RESPONSIBILITIES IN THE CLASSROOM

Many educators may not be aware of the legal issues that permeate their classroom. However, it is important now, more than any other time in the teaching world, for them to know the laws and to adhere to them, and to help their students understand them as well. The digital world we live in is redefining how personal data is shared, and how copyrighted materials are used and shared (both legally and illegally). We will probably see incremental changes in copyright law as it catches up with new, digital technologies, so this work may never really be done.

TEXTBOX 8.2.

### Elementary Grades

Conversations around intellectual property can start as young as elementary school. Simply discuss ownership around content that students have created in the classroom. Or share examples of images, music, and videos online and discuss the author and the purpose of the work and even the work that went into creating the content paired with a basic explanation of copyright law and how it protects works created by anyone, published or not.

### Middle Grades

By middle school, students should know how to find copyright-free images online and how to incorporate them into their projects and creative works. Have students use sites like Pexels (http://www.pexels.com), Pixabay (http://www.pixabay.com), Wikimedia Commons (http://commons.wikimedia.org), or Creative Commons Search (https://search.creativecommons.org). Make it a requirement for an upcoming project that they use copyright-free images or have them complete a poster, public service announcement, or other visual project using copyright-free images that include citation.

### High School

Students at the high school level should know how to put information they find in their own words, paraphrase sources, use direct quotations, and cite their work. They can incorporate all these skills through the creation of an infographic using the site

Piktochart (http://www.piktochart.com) or Canva (http://www .canva.com). You can assign students a specific topic or allow them to choose their own. Require them to include a small amount of text that should be in their own words based on their research. Have them include a direct quotation from a source and have them include citations of their sources formatted according to Modern Language Association style.

# II

# MEDIA LITERACY

# 9

# Defining Media Literacy

Before delving into specific media literacy topics, it is important to define what is meant by the term. Dictionary.com defines *media* as "the plural of medium. The means of communication, as radio and television, newspapers, magazines, and the Internet, that reach or influence people widely."[1] Media literacy education, like traditional literacy education, involves teaching students how to decode, comprehend, and navigate media in the same way one would provide students with the necessary toolkit that they need to be successful and empowered readers.

In looking at definitions across a number of organizations, a few consistent terms and concepts emerge. Three major organizations that work closely with the topic of media literacy are the Center for Media Literacy, Common Sense Media, and the National Association for Media Literacy Education. All three organizations use the exact same three words in their definitions: *access, analyze*, and *evaluate*.[2] They also reference the diversity of messages and forms of communication (print, video, Internet-based) that students are exposed to. You can read and compare these definitions in Table 9.1.

Other common threads across two of the three definitions is the connection between media literacy and the larger society and the role that media literacy plays in building active and informed citizens. As Elizabeth Thoman and Tessa Jolls from the Center for Media Literacy state in their 2004 article, "The convergence of media and technology in a global culture is changing

**Table 9.1.   Defining Media Literacy**

| | |
|---|---|
| Center for Media Literacy | Media Literacy is a 21st century approach to education. It provides a framework to access, analyze, evaluate, create, and participate with messages in a variety of forms—from print to video to the Internet. Media literacy builds an understanding of the role of media in society as well as essential skills of inquiry and self-expression necessary for citizens of a democracy.[1] |
| Common Sense Education | Media literacy: the ability to access, analyze, evaluate, create, and communicate using information in all forms. Media literacy comprises competency in understanding and using fundamental dimensions of communication, including but not limited to: authorship, message construction, message purpose (both implicit and explicit), audience, aesthetic and technical elements of production, and message effects.[2] |
| National Association for Media Literacy Education | Media literacy is the ability to ACCESS, ANALYZE, EVALUATE, CREATE, and ACT using all forms of communication. |
| | In its simplest terms, media literacy builds upon the foundation of traditional literacy and offers new forms of reading and writing. |
| | Media literacy empowers people to be critical thinkers and makers, effective communicators, and active citizens.[3] |

1. "Media Literacy: A Definition and More," Center for Media Literacy, accessed July 17, 2018, http://www .medialit.org/media-literacy-definition-and-more.
2. "Topic Backgrounder: News and Media Literacy," Common Sense Education, https://d1e2bohyu2u2w9 .cloudfront.net/education/sites/default/files/tlr-asset/topicbackgrounder-newsmedialit_2017_final.pdf.
3. "Media Literacy Defined," National Association for Media Literacy Education, March 10, 2017, accessed July 17, 2018, https://namle.net/publications/media-literacy-definitions/.

the way we learn about the world and challenging the very foundations of education. No longer is it enough to be able to read the printed word; children, youth, and adults, too, need the ability to both critically interpret the powerful images of a multimedia culture and express themselves in multiple media forms."[3]

Young people have more and more access to media and they are accessing it on a more independent level than ever before. Whereas in the past, families watched TV together or shared newspapers and magazines in the house, they are spending more time on their own personal devices and curating their own, individual content, often without even knowing what other family members are reading, watching, or listening to. In addition, the advent of "user-generated content" means that much of the content that we consume has not been filtered through an expert of some kind. This has been both a blessing and a curse, allowing for more voices to be heard that may have been silenced in the past, but also allowing for voices that may have been silenced for good reason to have the world's largest communication platform at their fingertips.

The following chapters explore the misinformation and disinformation that is found online, as well as new technologies that make the job of accurately analyzing media more and more difficult. This new media landscape also requires educators to incorporate media literacy skills and add them to students' toolbox across content areas. For those not sure where to start, the Center for Media Literacy's Construction and Deconstruction Chart provides a great framework. You can see this framework in Tables 9.2 and 9.3.

**Table 9.2.   Questions to Guide Young Children: Deconstruction**

|   | Core Concepts | Key Questions | Questions for Young Children |
|---|---|---|---|
| 1 | All media messages are constructed. | Who created this message? | What is this? How is this put together? |
| 2 | Media messages are constructed using a creative language with its own rules. | What creative techniques are used to attract my attention? | What do I see or hear? Smell? Touch or taste? What do I like or dislike about this? |
| 3 | Different people experience the same media message differently. | How might different people understand this message differently? | What do I think and feel about this? What might other people think and feel about this? |
| 4 | Media have embedded values and points of view. | What values, lifestyles and points of view are represented in, or omitted from, this message? | What does this tell me about how other people live and believe? Is anything or anyone left out? |
| 5 | Most media messages are organized to gain profit and/or power. | Why is this message being sent? | Is this trying to tell me something? Is this trying to sell me something? |

Used with permission, (c) 2018, Center for Media Literacy, www.medialit.org.

**Table 9.3. Questions to Guide Young Children: Construction**

|   | Core Concepts | Key Questions | Questions for Young Children |
|---|---|---|---|
| 1 | All media messages are constructed | Who created this message? | What am I making? How do I put it together? |
| 2 | Media messages are constructed using a creative language with its own rules. | What creative techniques are used to attract my attention? | What does it look, sound, smell feel, taste like? What do I like or dislike about this? |
| 3 | Different people experience the same media message differently. | How might different people understand this message differently? | Who do I want to get this? What might other people think and feel about this? |
| 4 | Media have embedded values and points of view. | What values, lifestyles and points of view are represented in, or omitted from, this message? | What am I sharing about how people live and believe? Have I left anything or anyone out? |
| 5 | Most media messages are organized to gain profit and/or power. | Why is this message being sent? | What am I telling? What am I selling? |

Used with permission, (c) 2018, Center for Media Literacy, www.medialit.org.

Media literacy goes beyond just understanding whether we can trust what we are consuming. It also involves understanding how media is created and how it appeals to our senses and our biases to sell us products and ideas. One of the best ways for students to access this knowledge and understanding is to have them both deconstruct different forms of media and to also construct media to experience the process and thereby better understand how and why media is created and how the purpose and creator of that media plays an influential role in the message that the media is conveying.

The kinds of questions that educators ask and the way that they guide their students through the process of analyzing, deconstructing, and constructing media is important. In their 2008 guide to media literacy education, *Literacy for the 21st Century*, Thoman and Jolls provide a series of guiding questions that they attribute to Dr. Faith Rogow.

Am I trying to tell the students what the message is? Or am I giving students the skills to determine what they think the message(s) might be? Have I let students know that I am open to accepting their interpretation, as long as it is well substantiated, or have I conveyed the message that my interpretation is the only correct view? At the end of the lesson, are students likely to be more analytical? Or more cynical?[4]

The job of educators when teaching media literacy is to teach kids how to think about media, and how to reflect on their own perceptions and the impact that media has on them and on society at large. One of the best ways to get kids to understand these complex concepts is to have them make media themselves. The simple act of creating their own commercial or their own advertisement, having them Photoshop or alter an image in some way to change the message that the image conveys, or even having students use tools like Mozilla's Thimble (https://thimble.mozilla.org) or X-Ray Goggles (https://goggles.mozilla.org) to see how the web is built and how it can be manipulated, can have an effect on their own perception of the barrage of media messages they are subjected to every day.

Media literacy education also plays a role in preparing students with the required skillset to be skilled communicators in a world that communicates in an increasingly visual way. Students who understand the nuances of sound, color, video shot angles, word choice, and the various media-sharing platforms can easily amplify their voice and be heard. This is on top of the career-related communication skills that will no doubt be required when they enter the workforce.

Although charts and guides and frameworks are helpful, this can feel like an overwhelming task for educators on top of the content they are already teaching. Luckily, there are workshops and programs that can support this work. The Media Education Lab at the University of Rhode Island has a digital literacy graduate program specifically geared toward practicing educators (https://mediaeducationlab.com/graduate-certificate-digital-literacy). They also offer webinars and a summer institute centered around digital literacy. These programs encompass both digital and media literacy and are taught by leaders in the field.

This book does not cover every aspect of media literacy or media literacy education. In fact, it barely penetrates the surface. The following chapters are meant to serve as a jumping-off point and focus specifically on skills and concepts directly related to technology and the Internet. For more resources, check the websites of the Center for Media Literacy (http://medialit.org), the National Association for Media Literacy Education (http://namle.net), and Common Sense Education (https://www.commonsense.org/education).

# 10

# Analyzing Information

According to the site Internet Live Stats, there are over 1.9 billion active websites as of January 2019.[1] Search engine results can span dozens to hundreds of pages. We are swimming in information online, and searching for quality information can feel like drinking from a firehose. It is imperative that students of all ages are provided the tools necessary to be critical consumers of content.

## CAN I TRUST WHAT I'M READING?

Online knowledge is nested under the blanket of *information literacy*, a term coined by Paul Zurkowski in 1974 in *The Information Service Environment Relationships and Priorities, Related Paper 5* for the National Commission on Libraries and Information Science.[2] The American Library Association defines "information literacy" as the ability of individuals to "recognize when information is needed and [to] have the ability to locate, evaluate, and use effectively the needed information."[3] In the digital age, so much of the information that we consume is in video, audio, or other visual format that information and media literacy go hand in hand.

Another big change in the digital age is the way that content is published. In the past, media and information we consumed went through a publisher of some kind (a book publisher, newspaper editor, content publisher, scientific peer review) before being widely released to the public. The process in the digital world has nearly flipped, with content often being pushed out and vetted after the fact. Anyone can publish an article containing medical information or direct quotations that are contrived or misleading without any kind of prepublishing vetting process. In a sense, we, the consumers, are the vetting process and the responsibility now lies on media and information consumers themselves to know what is quality and what is junk.

This is especially hard when information is disguised as trustworthy or unbiased. Take, for instance, a site like the National Vaccine Information Center (https://www.nvic.org/), which looks like a legitimate place to get information about vaccines. A deeper look, however, reveals that many of the links are broken and many link back to the same website, and a search for the organization leads to a Wikipedia article about the group that states, "The National Vaccine Information Center is an American 501 anti-vaccine organization which has been widely criticized as a leading source of misinformation and fearmongering about vaccines."[4]

A deeper look at the group behind the site reveals that few of the site's authors have notoriety beyond the group itself and few are practicing medical experts. A search of a few of them show only sites with negative information regarding their stance on vaccines. As Carl Sagan stated in his book, *Science as a Candle in the Dark*, "there are no authorities; at most, there are experts."[5] This is to say that the best we can do is discern whether the person sharing the information has knowledge and expertise related to the topic.

Many reporters, as media literacy expert Howard Rheingold explains in his 2012 book, *NetSmart*, "triangulate" their information. This means that they always confirm information through three different reputable sources before reporting it. This could mean researching an expert in the field and contacting them directly, or going to a known reputable source of information like a scientific journal or even someone who is located in the area affected by the story. By triangulating evidence, reporters do their due diligence before sending information out to the public.

However, we are seeing more and more reporting that takes short cuts as the news cycle becomes more and more relentless. With social media and newsfeed apps creating a 24-hour news cycle, news outlets feel pressured to be the first to break a story, which can cause them to take shortcuts. In 2017, three CNN reporters left the news organization after CNN was forced to retract a story they reported related to connecting Trump administration officials and a Russian investment fund. CNN admitted that "editorial processes were not followed."[6]

## CRAP DETECTION

The author Ernest Hemingway is quoted as saying, "The most essential gift for a good writer is a built-in, shockproof, shit detector."[7] As students move into middle school, they are tasked with more complex research assignments and are expected to synthesize information in more nuanced ways. In addition, they may be reading more on their own about topics that interest them and joining online communities tied to their interests, and are beginning to grow and formulate their own world view.[8] This also requires them to be able to tell whether what they are reading is genuine and accurate or, to put it less politely, crap. Table 10.1 provides students an introduction to "CRAAP detection," a simple way for students to analyze pretty much anything they read or consume in any media. Educators may also find guidance for teaching media literacy skills from authors Jim Wasserman and David Loveland in their book *Middle Schoolers, Meet Media Literacy.*[9]

Developed by Sarah Blakeslee at California State University in Chico, California, the CRAAP Test[10] can be used to help students through the process of analyzing sources. "C" refers to *currency*. How recently was the information published? "R" refers to the *reliability* of the source and the publisher. The first "A" refers to the *author*. Does this person have any experience or professional knowledge of the content? The second "A" refers to *accuracy*. Is the information factual? Are there references for statistics or quotes? The "P" refers to the *purpose*. Why was this written? What is the purpose behind the content? Does it feel like someone is trying to sell you something? Does the language in the source feel neutral or does it feel emotional or opinionated? Students can use these guiding questions as a kind of litmus test for any content that they come across, no matter what format.

Howard Rheingold, who has been on the forefront of media literacy since the 1990s, uses the term "crap detection" as a way to describe the necessary skills needed to consume media of any kind. In 2009, Rheingold said,

> Unless a great many people learn the basics of online crap detection and begin applying their critical faculties en masse and very soon, I fear for the future of

the internet as a useful source of credible news, medical advice, financial information, educational resources, [and] scholarly and scientific research.[11]

Almost a decade later, this fear is getting closer to becoming a reality.

CRAAP detection pulls together all of the major elements of being a savvy
consumer of media as well as all of the preceding essential questions laid out
in this book's Introduction. If students are pushed to fill out the template and
reflect on these four areas whenever they are doing research or even just looking for information, it will become second nature. Even just asking, "Who is
the author and what are their credentials?" or "Where is the evidence that this
is a reliable site?" will reinforce the idea that students can't always trust what
they read and that everything should be read with a critical eye, even if (or
even especially if) students agree with it.

One of the easiest tricks is to find the "About" page for any website. This
is usually a quick way for students to better understand what they are reading. If the About page is missing, that is a red flag for the authenticity of the
information. A quick glance at a URL may include the text "opinion" or
"blog," which is an indication that the content is not a news story. Although

**Table 10.1.   CRAAP Detection**

| | |
|---|---|
| **Currency** | How recent is the information? When was the website last updated? Is the information current enough for your topic? Do the links work or are they outdated and broken? |
| **Relevance** | What kind of information does the resource contain? Is the resource relevant to your topic? Is the resource at an appropriate reading level for your needs? |
| **Authority** | Who is the author and what are the author's credentials? Is the author reputable? Who is the publisher and what interest might the publisher have in the content? |
| **Accuracy** | Does the resource contain sources for data or quotations? Can you find the information anywhere else? Are there spelling and grammar mistakes? Is the resource primarily opinion or is it balanced? Does the URL say .gov, .edu or is it a Weebly or Wordpress site? |
| **Purpose/ Point of View** | Why was the site or resource created? Could it be biased? Is the publisher or author trying to sell you something? Could the author or publisher gain anything from the information? Are there advertisements? |

Sarah Blakeslee, "The CRAAP Test," LOEX Quarterly 31, no. 3, Article 4. Available at https://commons
.emich.edu/loexquarterly/vol31/iss3/4.

the CRAAP Test is great, it is not definitive. Students may find that a site passes some of the tests and fails others. As long as students are aware of the limitations of the information they are looking at, they are able to decide how to use it. Just because something is highly opinionated doesn't mean it can't be used; it just has to be used carefully and intentionally.

## CRAP DETECTION IN THE YOUNGER GRADES

In elementary and even middle school, teachers may find the use of the word "crap" to be too mature. If so, the acronym can be altered to say *PARCA*. Although not as catchy as *CRAAP*, it still allows for an easy way to remember each of the tests when doing research. See Table 10.2 for an example of a *PARCA* table.

## CONCLUSION

The work of crap detection is never done. It is important to model for students how each question can lead to another. Has the student found the author? Who is the author? Where else has he or she written? What kinds of organizations does the author write for? Can you find any social media accounts? What kinds of things does the author post? It is also important

**Table 10.2.  The PARCA Method**

| | |
|---|---|
| **Purpose/ Point of View** | Why was the site or resource created? Could it be biased? Is the publisher or author trying to sell you something? Could the author or publisher gain anything from the information? Are there advertisements? |
| **Accuracy** | Does the resource contain sources for data or quotations? Can you find the information anywhere else? Are there spelling and grammar mistakes? Is the resource primarily opinion or is it balanced? Does the URL say .gov, .edu or is it a Weebly or Wordpress site? |
| **Relevance** | What kind of information does the resource contain? Is the resource relevant to your topic? Is the resource at an appropriate reading level for your needs? |
| **Currency** | How recent is the information? When was the website last updated? Is the information current enough for your topic? Do the links work or are they outdated and broken? |
| **Authority** | Who is the author and what are the author's credentials? Is the author reputable? Who is the publisher and what interest might the publisher have in the content? |

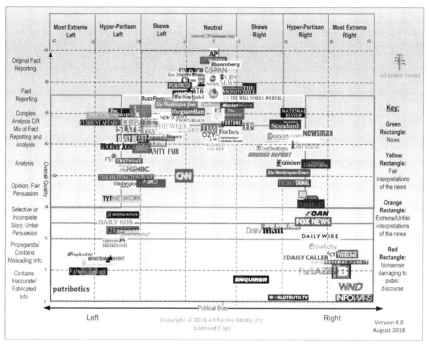

FIGURE 10.1

Media Bias Chart 4.0. Used with permission from Ad Fontes Media.

for students to understand that everything has bias and that bias isn't inherently a bad thing. Knowing what kind of bias something has and how much is important.

Even more important is understanding our own biases, which influence our trust of a source and can cause us to trust things that we shouldn't. For this reason, it is also important to understand vocabulary like "conservative" or "left-wing" or "progressive," and to understand where we fall on the spectrum. By evaluating the kinds of media we enjoy reading, we can start to discover our own bias. See Figure 10.1 for a media bias chart that can help students with this process. This chart, created by Ad Fontes media, uses a methodology based on policy positions and jargon (i.e., "snowflake" or "taxes") to rank sources by their bias and by how factual they are.[12] Although this chart itself has its own bias, it is a good jumping off point.

Analyzing sources is hard work, which is why a ninth grade student in Philadelphia stated, "I wish there was a way to just put in a site and have it automatically tested for CRAAP detection." Perhaps that day will come, but even that will be affected by bias because humans build technology and so all technology has a touch of human influence. We must be able to use our own brains to analyze the media we consume on a daily basis.

In sum, as the American Library Association states, "Ultimately, information-literate people are those who have learned how to learn. They know how to learn because they know how knowledge is organized, how to find information, and how to use information in such a way that others can learn from them. They are people prepared for lifelong learning, because they can always find the information needed for any task or decision at hand."[13] To be *literate* means being able to find relevant, accurate information, using that information in positive ways that have a positive influence on others, and never stopping on that quest to learn new things. This is what we want for all our students. To see sample crap detection lessons for the classroom, see Textbox 10.1.

## TEXTBOX 10.1.

### Elementary Grades

In the elementary grades, students can start the process of learning how to read a webpage to find information. Treat this like a scavenger hunt by giving each student or pair of students a checklist of things to find on a page. For instance, ask students to find the "About" page or find out when the site was last updated. Find an author or a date of publication. Even finding an advertisement can be helpful, especially if it is expertly hidden inside of the regular content.

### Middle Grades

Students in the middle grades should go beyond simply identifying the information to begin analyzing it using the *PARCA* or *CRAAP* detection methods. Try splitting the class into teams and have them dig deeper into the author, the publisher, the references on a site, the links, and so on. Then have each group report back on what they found. They can then decide as a class whether they would use the site or not based on the evidence they find. This can be done with a real site or something like *All About Explorers* (https://www.allaboutexplorers.com/) or *DHMO. org* (http://www.dhmo.org/)

## High School

By high school, students should be able to independently analyze sources using the *CRAAP* detection method. Provide them with a checklist or template to fill out while they are vetting sources for a project or have the class analyze the same few articles together in preparation for a research project. After a few times using the template or checklist, students should become familiar with the process and be able to analyze sources on their own.

# 11

# Deconstructing Images

According to a 2015 study by Common Sense Media, "Tweens (8- to 12-year-olds) use an average of about six hours' (5:55) worth of entertainment media daily."[1] That's about as much media every day as an average night's sleep. It is no wonder that this new generation of young people is considered one of the most visual generations ever, and that they consume more types of media than previous generations. It's also no wonder that companies slather apps like Instagram and YouTube with targeted ads aimed at young eyeballs. They know where their customers are. The ad agency Catalyst Group Marketing even posted an article on their website about "Marketing to the Visual Generation," giving tips to marketers on how to best access these young customers.[2]

All this screen time watching entertainment content and scrolling through social media feeds littered with advertisements means that kids today, more than any other generation, must be highly skilled at sorting through the "noise." With the sophistication of today's technology (which will only get more sophisticated over time), and the misleading tactics of advertisers, it can be very hard to tell the "noise" from the real content. When this content is visual, it is also processed and categorized very quickly and subconsciously, as shown by a 2014 Massachusetts Institute of Technology study.

The researchers showed participants images for thirteen milliseconds to see how their brains processed the images. They found that the participants were able to process and categorize these images, despite seeing them so briefly.[3] As the study's author, Mary Potter, explains, "The fact that you can do that at these high speeds indicates to us that what vision does is find concepts. That's what the brain is doing all day long—trying to understand what we're looking at."[4]

Today's young people are mostly looking at social media sites like Instagram or watching videos on YouTube or Netflix. Their brains are often processing multiple kinds of media at the same time, as they may be watching a Netflix show while also scrolling through Instagram. They may see the media they are consuming, and their brain is processing the images, even if they may not be looking at the images for very long. Still, as mentioned in Chapter 1, young people care deeply about what they are posting and interacting with on these sites. They use filters to make their images look better, they hold the camera at certain angles to show their best angle, and they may feel the urge to take a selfie to document their everyday experience. The social media app SnapChat makes this almost like a challenge through its "stories" feature, which can also be found on Instagram. These posts make up users' online personas.

And that is what posts create—a *persona*, a digital fabrication of users' lives. Between the filters and photos taken out of context, it can seem like everyone is doing amazing things and looking amazing 24/7. Young people should understand that images on social media sites depict people's best selves and are often run through multiple filters to the point where the person in the image may not even resemble the real person. Instastyle author Tezza even sells her photo presets that she uses to edit her Instagram photos and the before-and-after images on her site are dramatically different.[5] Or, as in the example of Shudu (@shudu_gram), the person in the images may not be a person at all. This Instagram account, run by the company Diigitals, claims to be the "world's first digital supermodel." The agency has created multiple computer-generated models, and they are stunningly realistic.[6]

These personae also take the form of social media "influencers," people who have gathered a large following and are paid by brands to showcase their products in their social media posts. Because these accounts are often not linked to a celebrity (although "Internet famous" *is* a thing), it can often appear that this person sincerely uses the products in his or her everyday life, which influences others to do the same. The digitally created supermodel Shudu was created to do just that.

According to a recent Stanford University study, kids are not always adept at identifying ads and sponsored content online. In the study, students were given a fake home page to observe and were then asked to categorize content on the page as an article or an advertisement. One of the ads was hidden in plain sight in the form of an article. However, a quick look at the title "Sponsored Content" helped students understand that the article was biased, paid for by the ad company. If it is hard for students to recognized content that is clearly labeled as sponsored, then understanding the sponsored content in the Instagram influencers they follow may be even harder because these are not clearly labeled as ads on the platform.

Advertisers follow a formula: attention, interest, desire, action (AIDA). Created in the early 1900s, this formula has stood the test of time.[7] Social media "influencers" use their accounts, which already have the attention of their followers, to garner interest in a brand and to create desire. In some cases they may offer deals or discounts through their social media account. Once students learn this formula, they will probably recognize it everywhere. For ideas on how to teach this in the classroom, see Textbox 11.1 at the end of this chapter.

The Stanford study also had students analyze an image of mutated daisies posted to the photo sharing site imgur.com (Figure 11.1). The exercise asked, "Does this post provide strong evidence about the conditions near the Fukushima Daiichi Power Plant? Explain your reasoning." Fewer than 20 percent of the 454 high school students in the study questioned the source of the post or the source of the photo. Almost 40 percent believed that the visual evidence in the photo was strong evidence regarding the conditions at the power plant, further showing the power of images to sway and cement our opinions and beliefs.[8]

Those who did not believe that the image provided "strong evidence" often made the claim that the image could be "Photoshopped." Most Internet users have come across an image that has been digitally altered, and this level of healthy skepticism is prevalent, although there is not always a way for the average person to know whether they are looking at the original or an altered version of an image. Some even argue that some image edits don't affect the validity of an image. For example, in November 2018, Instagram user @grantdenham, a resident of Malibu, posted an image to Instagram of a wall of smoke along the bay as he evacuated due to a wildfire.[9] It became an

三悔堂 @san_kaido · 27 May 2015

マーガレットの帯化(那須塩原市5/26)②
右は４つの花茎が帯状に繋がったまま成長し、途中で２つに別れて２つの花がつ
ながって咲いた。左は４つの花茎がそのまま成長して繋がって花が咲き輪の様に
なった。空間線量0.5μSv地点(地上高1m)

🌐 Translate Tweet

   💬 85        🔁 1.9K        ♡ 1.0K        ✉

FIGURE 11.1
Screenshot. Used with permission from author @san_kaido on Twitter. Accessed
November 18, 2018.

iconic image of the Woolsey Fire. However, a second image began circulating,
as pointed out by Twitter user @KdbyProxy.[10] The second image had been
edited, most likely with an Instagram filter, and looked much more dramatic
and was also slightly cropped (Figure 11.2).

The edited image showed up on news sites and was tweeted out by Tech
Crunch journalist Josh Constine, who was covering the story. It was even used
by the LA County Sheriff's department in a tweet about the fire.[11] The edited
image was not originally credited to Denham, although eventually through
the power of social media, he was identified as the original photographer.

**Ira Goldman** 🦫🦫🦫
@KDbyProxy

( Follow )

> On the left: The original, ominous-enough real-life photo by @GrantDenham.
> On the right: A popular tweaked version that's going around, because it seems someone felt the real-life photo wasn't real enough.

#photography #photoshop

9:01 PM - 9 Nov 2018

**592** Retweets **1,070** Likes

💬 76     🔁 592     ♡ 1.1K     ✉

FIGURE 11.2

Screenshot. Twitter. Accessed November 23, 2018. https://twitter.com/KDbyProxy/status/1061076302294216704.

This raises the question of whether an edit like adding a filter to an image to increase its dramatic effect is the same as what we would normally consider a "photoshopped" image. We usually assume that images that are digitally altered are completely different from the original or contain multiple images stitched together, such as putting something in someone's hand or swapping faces. These are obvious changes to the original, but what about when an image's color or saturation is altered? What if the original image is cropped to tell a different story? In the case of the Woolsey Fire image, the edit was not even done by the original photographer. What are the implications of ownership over these images when the content is mostly the same? These questions should always be in the back of our minds when we view images shared through social media sites where these edits can be done in seconds.

## FIRST-HAND EXPERIENCE

While writing this book, I had my own first-hand experience with digging into the source of an image. After communicating with Stanford University regarding their media literacy study, I was left with the task of getting the rights to use the radioactive daisies image in this book. After some research, I discovered that the original image was posted by a Twitter user in Japan. With the aid of the built-in translator in Chrome, I was able to read that, according to the user's biography, the user, @san_kaido, who posted the image, "started Twitter mainly for the purpose of obtaining information on radioactivity and nuclear power plants issues and disseminating opinions." (This is the text translated by Google's Chrome browser.) I reached out to them directly and what ensued was a fascinating Twitter conversation.

@san_kaido, the original photographer, was not aware of why, a few years ago, there was a high level of interest in their daisy photo. While the user was credited with taking the photo, it's not clear that anyone had discussed the image itself with its author. I explained that the image was used in a study at Stanford University to teach students about "fake news," how they shouldn't trust what they see at face value. @san_kaido was, I could tell, a little offended by the idea that this image was "fake news."

@san_kaido, who has asked not to be credited with the image in this book and whose profile picture does not indicate identity, explained that they had been recording radiation levels and documenting the plants in the area near the reactor. Radiation levels in the area were higher than normal, but when they grew a daisy from a seed taken from the daisy pictured, no mutation occurred. @san_kaido believed that to discount the increase in radiation and call it "fake news" was problematic. They added, "However, the number of people who have conditions and means to transmit it is limited, and among them the photograph that I happened to have spread beyond the intention of the person himself."[12] (Again, this is translated by Google's Chrome browser.) The original photographer believes that the image has gone beyond the original purpose of the image and they believe that very little information is being shared by the people directly affected by the disaster.

This image has become iconic in the world of debunking fake news and myths, although it appears that the author's own perspective, which is an important part of the context around the image, has been left out of the discussion. For students, this is an easy step to take. With the quick, easy, direct access that social media provides, it is worth it to reach out, if possible, to the direct source of the image in question.

With a reverse image search (described later in this chapter) it is also possible to track down the original author of an image even if the image itself is being used out of context or by another person or website. @san_kaido continues to document nature in their Japanese prefecture and following those tweets is fascinating. I learned through this experience that, even with our best, most well-intentioned efforts, we can tell the wrong story or at least only part of the story.

The Stanford study and Snopes.com have both "debunked" the image as false, despite its author stating that while the mutation is probably not caused by radiation, that does not mean that radiation did not affect the natural habitats in the prefecture.

## A HEALTHY SKEPTICISM

Because our brains process images so quickly and visual evidence like a photograph seems so reliable, we often trust visual evidence that we shouldn't, even when all the other red flags are there. As recently as 2017, President Donald Trump retweeted posts on Twitter of videos that appeared to show one thing, but really depicted something different. One of the videos depicted a person of color beating up a white Danish boy on crutches and was shared with the caption, "Muslim migrant beats up Dutch boy on crutches." It was shared by Twitter user @JaydaBF, whose real name is Jayda Fransen. She is a leader of the group Britain First, a far-right hate group.

Fransen and her co-leader were arrested in March 2018 for hateful harassment of community members near where a trial involving three Muslim men was being held. The video itself, if taken at face value, does not raise any red flags. However, a quick search of the user posting the video should immediately prompt further investigation. The Danish police responded to the president regarding his tweet, explaining that the man in the video was not a Muslim migrant, but a Danish citizen and had already been detained for the attack.[13]

Although it's easy enough to research the person sharing the video or image to see if it comes from a trustworthy user, it may become harder for us to know whether the image or video being shared is real at all. Technology has brought us to a juncture where images and videos themselves can be doctored so well that detecting fakes is becoming more and more difficult. Take, for example, the 2017 video of former president Barack Obama created by researchers at the University of Washington. Researchers were able to teach a computer how to re-create Obama's mouth shape by feeding it hours of footage and audio of the president. They used this technology to create an entirely fabricated video of Obama delivering a single speech made up of snippets of many different speeches he had given over time.[14] This new technology has come to be known as "deep fakes."

Hany Farid, a computer science professor at Dartmouth College, has been studying deep fakes and working on tools that can detect them. In a 2018 interview with the *Wall Street Journal*, he expressed that he could see these kinds of videos being used to trigger political disputes, even wars. He believes that his work is in itself an "arms race" because every time he and his team come up with a new way to detect fakes, the creators of these videos then learn how to create videos that pass that test.[15]

We are heading into uncharted territory, where telling fact from fiction, even in video, is difficult. In Australia, 24-year-old Noelle Martin has helped pass a law that makes deep fakes created without consent illegal. She is a victim of deep fake videos. Her likeness has appeared in several pornographic videos online. At first, she was ashamed and blamed herself, but eventually she began to speak out about the harassment, even giving a TED talk about her experiences.

By speaking out, unfortunately, she found that the misuse of her images increased, and harassers even released her real name and address alongside of some of the fake videos. Martin's biggest fear was the long-term effect that these images and videos would have on her career. So far, they have not harmed her career, most likely because of her outspokenness about her victimization. Although the law is now on the books, she still has no legal recourse because her perpetrators are anonymous.[16] Similar laws do not yet exist in the United States and in many other countries, and only time will tell how the legal community in the United States will address these kinds of videos.

## PROTECTING OUR OWN ONLINE IDENTITIES

Noelle Martin came upon these images out of curiosity. Like anyone ready to join the job market, she did a simple Internet search of herself. She used a reverse image search using one of her Facebook photos and was shocked by what she found. Reverse image searches are a great way for anyone to see what kind of information about them is online, but it can also be a powerful tool for discovering fake or misused images.

Take, for example, the uphill battle that Canadian educator Alec Couros, author of this book's foreword, has fought for many years against romance scammers using photos of him and his family to swindle women out of thousands of dollars. He has been contacted by some of these women who have fallen victim to the scammers. Many of them were duped on Facebook, where scammers were able to create viable profiles, often with images of his family on them and with carefully crafted "Friends" lists that also include fake profiles of his family members. Alec has been public about this battle and often shares his story and techniques that victims and those suspecting a scammer can use to try to identify whether the person they are talking to is who they say they are.[17] He always recommends doing a reverse image search when talking to a stranger online to see who he or she might really be.

To conduct a reverse image search, you can either drag a photo directly into a web browser's search box or use the Images search tool by clicking the camera icon to upload an image from your computer. This works in most major search engines like Google and Bing. This search will then locate where the image may exist elsewhere on the Internet. In the case of a scammer or any other kind of questionable image, it would be easy to see that the image had appeared elsewhere in a different context. You can also right-click on an image in the Google Images search and choose "Search Google for this image." Doing this with Grant Denham's fire image, for example, shows places where the image (and its altered version) live on the Internet and it even provides a location for the image (Malibu). For more on how to incorporate reverse image search in the classroom, see Textbox 11.1 at the end of this chapter.

## IMAGES AND CONTEXT

Images tell a story, and the context of that story is important. Take the photography of Ansel Adams, possibly one of the world's most famous landscape photographers. His images of farm workers working the fields at the base of a picturesque mountain range seem, at first glance, to be just quaint landscape photos (Figure 11.3). They could even be the kind of image used on the packaging of a farm-produced product. Imagine a slogan like, "From our home to yours," or something similar. However, Adams spent time at the Manzanar

FIGURE 11.3

Adams, Ansel. "Farm, Farm Workers, Mt. Williamson in Background, Manzanar Relocation Center, California." Digital image. Library of Congress. Accessed November 23, 2018. http://hdl.loc.gov/loc.pnp/ppprs.00370.

Relocation Camp, a Japanese internment camp in the early 1940s, documenting the lives of the Japanese families living there.

The farmers in these images are Japanese families forced out of their homes during World War II, not quaint farmers tilling the soil and harvesting their crops. What if the farm workers were cropped out completely and only the mountain range was featured? The significance of the view would be completely erased. For students, discussing the value of the context of an image is an important conversation.

Often, images are taken out of context to elicit an emotional response toward an issue. For instance, a 2016 meme containing an image of violent protesters paired with the words "Claim Trump is going to ruin America as they go out and ruin America" began to circulate on the site Reddit and social media sites like Facebook and Twitter. The meme insinuated that the image was of protesters at recent violent protests against the election of President Donald Trump. However, as Snopes and other sites reported, the image was from a 2012 protest in Greece. Although some of the protests in the United States had been violent, the creator of the meme intentionally chose an image that was extreme enough to cause an emotional reaction to the words and the message.[18]

Even when the image is accurate, the choice of image is often intentionally made to evoke a desired emotional response. An article on a left-leaning website about a Republican politician might choose an unflattering photo of the politician, while a right-leaning site that supports the politician might choose a more flattering image. It is as important to understand the purpose and role of the image in the message being conveyed as it is to understand the source and the placement of the image. Students can easily look for coverage of the same news story on various websites and compare the images chosen by each site that accompany the story.

We live in a visual world, a world of screens, a world where advertisements and news organizations and anyone who wants our attention can grab it within seconds with a carefully chosen (and sometimes manipulated) image placed with the right (although sometimes wrong) context. As the saying goes, "knowing is half the battle," so understanding how images, and even video, can be altered or used out of context can help students question the images and videos they see and hopefully push them to seek out the truth.

There is a darker side to this healthy skepticism, however, if we get to the point where we don't trust anything we see because so much of what we see is carefully manipulated. We are not there yet, but we are close. Whereas some researchers are creating technologies that can make anyone look like they are saying anything, other researchers are building tools to help us spot the fakes. Let's hope that they can stay one step ahead in this "arms race" of image authentication.

TEXTBOX 11.1.

### Elementary Grades

It's easy to plant the seed of skepticism in younger students when they view images and visuals online. Simply projecting an interesting picture or a meme on the board and then asking students to come up with three questions they have about the image can help them begin to think critically about what they are seeing. Students can write their own question on a slip of paper and then pair up or share their question with their table group. Have pairs or tables share their questions with the class and record them on the board. Choose one at random to investigate more deeply to model for students how they can take this a step further to find their answer.

Older elementary students may follow this up with choosing a question to explore. If so, try to choose an image or meme that will lend itself to finding a deeper story. This could also be where you introduce students to a reverse image search.

### Middle Grades

Present students with three images paired with captions explaining what they are or memes that supposedly explain what is in the photo. One of the captions should be false. As in the elementary grades lesson, have students write questions they have about the images and about the paired text. Have them pair up or share their question with their table group. Have students share their questions with the class and ask them how they might find the answer. Accept all answers. Students who may have done this kind of activity before may already know about a reverse image search. If they do, let a student explain how it works. If not, model and explain how to conduct a reverse image search for the class, showing how the one false caption can be found through this method.

Let students conduct their own searches by providing digital versions of the images to them. Then challenge students to find three images and caption them or create memes with them. Instruct students to make one of the captions false and have them challenge their classmates to find the false one. Students should begin to understand how important it is to dig deeper when they see these kinds of images online.

### High School Grades

In high school, include image deconstruction skills in a larger unit or project that requires students to do research. Require them to cite their images and find where they originally came from. This can be done using a reverse image search, or by only choosing images whose veracity can be confirmed through consistent bylines wherever the image appears (e.g., Associated Press or Reuters bylines). Alternately, show students examples of images taken out of context and memes used to sway opinion that pair text and images that are not connected. Also show them the Obama deep-fake video, or a clip of someone saying something taken out of context that could be used to make others think that the person said something very different (think political ads—or make your own).

Have students create their own article, website, flyer, or other material aimed at swaying viewers' opinions about a topic. The material can be highly opinionated or not, but it should misuse an image to sway opinion. Students can also edit clips to make people look like they are saying something they are not. If students have access to video-editing software, they could even attempt to make their own deep fake video. These projects could be shared with middle schoolers, who can be given the task of debunking them.

# 12

# Fake News in the Digital Age

On November 23, 2016, just fifteen days after the presidential election, NPR aired an interview with Jestin Coler, the creator and owner of Disinfomedia.[1] His company is a purveyor of "fake news," and makes tens of thousands of dollars in ad revenue off completely fabricated news stories, including one that claimed that an FBI agent linked to then–presidential candidate Hillary Clinton's email leaks had been found dead in a murder-suicide.[2] The NPR story shone a light on this highly lucrative business of posting and spreading false and exaggerated stories online. A large percentage of the fake stories spread during the election were not written with the intention of swaying the election, but rather were written by individuals who knew how to write catchy headlines and sensational stories that would garner more clicks and therefore more ad revenue. In fact, many of the blatantly false stories being spread around social media sites like Facebook were being written and published by teens in Macedonia trying to make a quick buck off ad revenue.[3]

However, not all false news stories were spread solely for profit. US officials have reported that Russia played a large role in the spread of fake news to sway the election by not only creating false stories, but by spreading and amplifying existing false stories.[4] What's more, according to Chris Jackson of Ipsos Public Affairs, a company that conducted a survey for Buzzfeed, "Public opinion, as reflected in this survey, showed that 'fake news' was remembered by a significant portion of the electorate and those stories were seen as credible."[5] The implications for the influence of fake news on public opinion and individuals are enormous.

A few months later, the Trump administration began its transition into the White House, and the new president had already spent months battling the media over their coverage of him. At his January 11 press conference, President-Elect Trump made multiple references to "fake news," and even refused to take a question from CNN reporter Jim Acosta, calling the news organization "fake news," most likely because he disapproved of CNN's coverage of him during the campaign.[6] Only a few days after that, Trump's campaign adviser, Kellyanne Conway, stated that White House Press Secretary Sean Spicer gave "alternative facts" during his first press briefing while discussing the size of the crowd at President Trump's inauguration.[7] She received quite a bit of backlash for the phrase, which many called a euphemism for "lies."

The term "fake news" started as a way to describe blatantly false stories, stories that were conjured based on little or no actual facts. However, the term has become a synonym for news that does not align with one's worldview or beliefs. It has become a way for people to discredit information that they don't believe is true.

There are deep implications to this use of the term that feed directly into how people consume and seek out information. It should be noted that fake news stories are nothing new. The *Onion* has been printing a satire newspaper since 1988, first as a free newspaper, and now exclusively as a website. The website's Latin tagline, *Tu Stultus Es*, translates to "You are an idiot." The site features articles such as, "GOP Promises Americans Will Be Able to Keep Current Medical Conditions If Obamacare Repealed." Totally and utterly fake, the Onion (http://www.theonion.com) clearly defines itself as satire.

However, more and more sites are peddling headlines and trying to pass off totally, utterly fake stories as real. The most famous case is probably the PizzaGate scandal in which various commenters on the website 4chan posted theories that mentions in John Podesta's emails (leaked by WikiLeaks) of "cheese pizza" were actually references to a child sex trafficking ring that was being run by Hillary Clinton out of a Washington, DC, pizza shop.[8] The site InfoWars picked up the story and ran with it, causing many of its readers to buy into what was debunked as an entirely false story.

InfoWars (http://www.infowars.com), run by controversial radio host Alex Jones, has been under attack for stories it runs that are often loosely based on facts. Jones frequently claims that the information published on the site is protected by free speech. The site itself looks like a viable news site, but contains headlines such as "Tectonic Explosion Soon to Spark Civil Unrest: America Is on the Brink of a Civil War." This extreme headline is paired with a highly opinionated article and video. Unlike the *Onion*, however, InfoWars states that "Alex Jones is a unique voice that sifts through the information and exposes the underlying intentions." Jones wants the information on the site to be treated as a "true" reading of various news stories and events, despite the fact that many of the "facts" on the site have been debunked.

We are living in a complex time for information. The exponential growth of websites and online sources can make seeking out the truth as difficult as finding the proverbial needle in a haystack. The Internet has made the proliferation of misinformation and the viral spread of conspiracy or false stories like those found on InfoWars that much easier. It has also made it easier for people to consume only information that confirms their own beliefs.[9]

If you are looking for a community of people who are hateful toward a specific group of people, a community that shares your religious beliefs, a community that shares your political ideals, or even a community that believes that the September 11th attack on the United States was a government conspiracy, you can find those people and connect with them on the Internet. In their book, *The Knowledge Illusion: Why We Never Think Alone*, authors Steven Sloman and Philip Fernbach describe this phenomenon:

> This is how a community of knowledge can become dangerous: The people we talk to are influenced by us and—truth be told—we are influenced by them. When group members don't know much but share a position, members of the group can reinforce one another's sense of understanding, leading everyone to feel like their position is justified and their mission is clear, even when there is no real expertise to give it solid support.[10]

When we surround ourselves only with people who think like us, it makes it harder for us to unravel these beliefs. The less we know about, say, John Podesta's emails, the more likely we are to believe that there is a secret code hidden in them. Human behavior scientists have been studying the effects of confirmation bias, the idea that people tend to adhere to ideas and statements that confirm their beliefs, despite proof that contradicts their beliefs, for decades. However, the fake news phenomenon that exploded in the 2016 presidential election caused many to revisit how the effects of confirmation bias play out in the proliferation of fake news.

Another factor involved in the proliferation and widespread sharing of falsified or extremely biased articles passed off as "news" is the way that news is written. Factual news should not be funny or witty or include any kind of opinionated or hyperbolic language. With so much competition for readers, news reporting has become more like storytelling. To keep someone reading or to catch readers' attention, journalists have to think differently about how they craft their articles. This often leads to "click bait"—brief articles with catchy titles that lure readers in. Journalists are constantly thinking about how their piece will be read and shared on social media sites.[11]

News, when reported as simple facts, is boring (and some would argue that it should be). Read any article reported by the Associated Press, and it will stand out for its dry, plain regurgitation of facts without using qualifying, biased adjectives, making the news "relatable," or connecting to the reader through the use of a particularly friendly or human voice. Because so much news comes from social media and is read on smartphones, the way journalists write is evolving to meet these new mediums, and as a result, how people define "news" and what they expect from the news they read has evolved.

Many times, articles with catchy headlines, are actually advertisements, not real news at all. Many of these articles contain some facts, but their real intention is to expose you to a product. These kinds of articles are so tricky that when Stanford University completed a study to test the ability of young people to identify bias, false news stories, or even identify ads on a web page, the study found that the test subjects were often unsuccessful.[12] The study, published in November of 2016, right after the election, showed that students at the middle, high school, and college level had huge gaps in their ability to analyze social media posts, websites, and other resources for credibility. The Stanford History Education Group, which conducted the study, released a social studies curriculum for teachers to address some of the study's findings through the lens of historical research.[13]

## FAKE NEWS AND INFORMATION LITERACY IN THE CLASSROOM

This drastic shift in how information is created, shared, and consumed—combined with naturally occurring human behavior around how we process information—means that educators must incorporate more critical thinking skills into their classrooms. Thinking critically about what we read is hardly a new skill, but each day, this task becomes more and more complex. Educators now have the imperative to help their students sift through the overwhelming amount of information at their fingertips to figure out how to tell fact from fiction, and to create their own understanding of the information they find. Table 0.3 in the Introduction lays out a scope and sequence for addressing these critical thinking tasks in the classroom. Textbox 12.1 contains sample lessons related to teaching about fake news in the classroom and Textbox 12.2 contains an example of how one educator keeps fake news in mind when her students are learning how to research.

## WHAT IS A FACT?

One might believe that Kindergarten is too early to start young minds down the path of analyzing and thinking critically about information. However, even a six-year-old can understand the difference between something that is true and something that is false. That said, simply asking, "Is this true?" will not lead to a classroom full of critical thinkers. Educators can help students know how to identify facts as well as understanding how "facts" can differ depending on someone's point of view. This is a concept that must be reinforced continually as students read, write, and watch videos or browse the web. It can help to have a fact-versus-opinion poster in the room to remind students of how to tell the difference, and to have a number of nonfiction books in the class library.

## IS THIS AN AD?

As discovered in the Stanford study mentioned earlier, students in middle, high school, and college had difficulty telling when something on a webpage was an advertisement. However, it is possible for a child as young as kindergarten or first grade to begin to identify ads on webpages. For certain, most of them have seen a commercial on TV or on YouTube and have a basic understanding of the difference between the show they were watching and the commercial that popped up. Many ads on the websites they visit are labeled with the word "Advertisement." If students can identify the letters A and D placed next to each other, they can begin to notice the placement of this word next to flashy content on the sites they visit.

Although they may not be able to understand the sophisticated "Sponsored Content" label, they can understand that if they click on something and it takes them some place completely different that has nothing to do with what they were originally doing, they probably got "tricked" by an ad. By explaining that advertisers try to trick you into clicking on their ads so they can make money, teachers can turn avoiding ads into a game of "don't get tricked by the ad."

## WHAT MAKES SOMEONE AN EXPERT?

If someone has a sudden pain or a rash, most likely the first thing he or she would do is call the doctor. We depend on experts in our society to help us with specific needs and information. If you need help with your math homework, you might ask your uncle who is an engineer. From a young age, people understand that there are particular people in their life who have specific information about specific things. However, it has become harder and harder, as more and more information is brought online, to know where the information we are reading comes from and who wrote it. Many times, students don't even bother to find out, especially if they are in a rush to finish a research paper. Other times, they are reading information on their phone and just the act of navigating to an About page or locating the author can be burdensome or difficult.

A great resource to use with younger learners is *All about Explorers*, a site that intentionally contains false information about famous explorers for use in these kinds of lessons. If students drill down far enough, they can discover the hoax. As an extension, have students compare the information they find on a *Britannica* page with the *All about Explorers* page so they can see how ridiculous some of the facts are, despite the site's design that makes it look legitimate.

Another point to discuss is the implications of the lack of an author on a website. Common sense says not to use the source. However, if students can verify the information in at least three other places, the site may be legitimate, *or* it could be a site created simply for ad revenue (e.g., "I'll teach you about Christopher Columbus as long as you gaze longingly at these ads for a while."). Many students may have been taught not to trust Wikipedia because of its lack of a definitive author. Point out to students that there are warnings that state that an article may be missing references. Scroll down to the bottom of various Wikipedia articles and show them the references that they could navigate to and view on their own. Despite the lack of a definitive author, Wikipedia can be a great starting point for a research project.

## WHY DID THE AUTHOR WRITE THIS?

One of the toughest parts about the "fake news" phenomenon is how hard it can be to tell whether what you are reading is actually "news." Headlines like "WATCH: Fox News Reporter Flees When Interview Goes Hilariously Wrong"[14] from the Huffington Post walk a fine line between news reporting and entertainment. These kind of exaggerated headlines used by the Huffington Post and other sites serve to catch readers' attention, and are often geared toward a specific audience. Journalists are competing with each other in the fast-paced, low-attention span world of social media, so headlines are becoming more and more "catchy." This can blur the line between reporting the news and making something entertaining enough to grab and hold a reader's attention.

## HOW DOES BIAS AFFECT HOW I INTERPRET WHAT I READ?

Reinforcement of healthy skepticism should continue through high school and beyond. However, as students become more sophisticated thinkers and readers, they need to move beyond simple source analysis. In high school, students can begin to explore the psychology behind why people believe false stories or mistake misinformation or entertainment for news. This includes exploring their own biases.

Scientists have studied confirmation bias, or "our tendency to seek out information that confirms what we already know or believe to be true,"[15] for years, but this psychological phenomenon has gained a lot of traction since the 2016 presidential election. Many researchers, psychologists, political scientists, and social media experts wondered why so many people fell prey to completely false stories and even shared them widely during the election. Why was it that, even after these stories had been debunked, people still believed them?

In 1980, researchers at Stanford University conducted a study titled "Perseverance of Social Theories: The Role of Explanation in the Persistence of Discredited Information." They provided participants information about a firefighter. One version of the information described him as a successful firefighter who always chose the safest option. The other version described him as an inferior firefighter who also chose the safest option. Participants were told halfway through that they had been given false information.

Despite this, participants had trouble moving away from their original assessment of the firefighter. As the researchers stated, "[T]hese studies also extend prior research by suggesting that initial beliefs may persevere in the face of a subsequent invalidation of the evidence on which they are based, even when this initial evidence is itself as weak and inconclusive a single pair of dubiously representative cases."[16] In other words, it's pretty hard to change someone's beliefs, even with substantial evidence to prove their beliefs wrong.

Class discussions around beliefs that students hold about a topic or event can help reveal these biases before delving into the content. Students can then become more aware of their own, perhaps skewed, viewpoint, and where their beliefs come from before discussing the facts of the topic or event. The Stanford researchers concluded that this might be a solution to "inoculate" people against this bias. These are uncomfortable and difficult conversations for adults, so it is important, before attempting such a discussion, to set the expectation of respect and tolerance of differing viewpoints. This is not an opportunity for students to prove their point to each other, but rather, to listen, to understand someone's beliefs and how those beliefs could influence how the facts of a topic or event are interpreted. This could also be done individually through a reflective assignment in preparation for such a discussion or just in preparation for analyzing content.

## TEXTBOX 12.1.

### Elementary Grades

Before younger students can analyze or understand sources and assess their validity, they need to understand the difference between fact and opinion and fact and fiction. Discuss the idea of truth with students and what it means. Give them a few statements and ask them which ones they think are true, and how they know that they are true. These should be things that they might know through personal experience (like "ice is cold"), or things that they have learned in class (1 + 2 = 3). Also have students compare statements like "pizza is good" and "pizza is made from bread, cheese, and tomato sauce" to decide which are fact and which are opinions. Also include in these statements items like "dogs say meow" or "the moon is made of cheese" so they can also distinguish fact from fiction. You can them have students sort phrases into "fact," "opinion," "fiction" either by having them glue cut-out phrases into the right column, by having them come up to an interactive white board and dragging the right phrase into place, or by having them cut and paste the phrases into the correct place on a digital document.

## Middle Grades

Provide students with a few questions to explore about famous explorers such as Christopher Columbus, Ferdinand Magellan, or Henry Hudson. These can be simple questions, such as "What did the explorer discover?" or "What country did the explorer sail from?" or even "What year was the explorer born?" You can then provide students with three sites they can use to find their information. One should be *All About Explorers* (http://www.allaboutexplorers.com), a misleading website full of falsified information. The other two could be the *Mariner's Museum* (https://exploration.marinersmuseum.org/type/age-of-discovery) and *Ducksters* (https://www.ducksters.com/biography/explorers). Have students compare their answers and agree.

## High School

In the high school classroom, this fine line can be explored through examining an author's purpose. It is common practice in the classroom to guide students through the exploration of whether something was written to inform, entertain, or persuade. This can be done using local news stories to start the process of breaking apart headlines and categorizing what students are reading online that may or may not be actual news. This lesson should be part of a larger unit that includes multiple opportunities for students to dissect and decipher the author's purpose. In this lesson, students must write their own news story with each purpose (inform, entertain, or persuade) in mind. This can also be paired with having students look for sponsored content at a more sophisticated level by having them figure out whether what they are reading is actually an ad. These discussions and explorations are a blend of understanding what facts are, what makes something an advertisement, how to decipher who is writing what students are reading, and whether this person is an expert, as well as understanding the purpose behind what students are reading.

TEXTBOX 12.2.
CASE STUDY

Educator Lisa Stevens discusses fake news with her students when they are talking about researching online. Figure 12.1 shows an image that she uses for reference. She prints it out and places in her Media Labs so that students can review it when necessary. The infographic can be downloaded at https://groundviews.org /2018/05/11/infographic -how-to-spot-false-news/.

FIGURE 12.1

## CAN NEWS BE FAKE?

Many journalists find issues with calling any news "fake news." In their opinion, if news is "fake," then it isn't actually news at all. They point to the nuances between false stories, falsified stories, and manipulation of facts. These nuances are vital to understanding that even factual information can be skewed. Data visualization is, by far, one of the easiest ways to skew facts to support a particular claim or bias. This matters because so much of the information students consume is visual. These visuals can come in the form of graphs and charts found on infographics as well as in tweets and other social media posts.

The website "Flowing Data," created by author and data visualization expert Nathan Yau, is dedicated to breaking down and analyzing data and data visualization. In one article, Yau demonstrates basic ways that data can be visually manipulated to exaggerate or support a specific claim.

For instance, he shows how simply truncating the axes in a bar graph (having the values start at a number higher than zero) can affect how the data looks and, to the unperceiving eye, tell a different story than the same data shown without truncated axes.[17] The issue here is that the data is real. It is not made-up and it is factual. However, the data has been manipulated to tell a different story than it was meant to tell. Technically, this is not "fake" or "falsified" or "fabricated." It just takes a trained eye to see what's really there.

Using this kind of data manipulation as a background, students can then think about other ways that facts can be skewed to tell a different story. News articles can easily decide to print only part of a quote, which could completely change its meaning. Political ads do this a lot—finding obscure or partial quotes from the opposing candidate and taking them out of context to paint whatever picture they want to paint to make the other candidate look bad. Again, this would not be false or falsified or fabricated information, which makes it that much harder to catch.

If students move away from thinking about "fake news" and rethink the term and its implications, they can move toward a deeper understanding of what news actually is, and the nuances of the truth itself. According to *Merriam-Webster*, news is "a report of recent events, material reported in a newspaper or news periodical or on a newscast, matter that is newsworthy," or a newscast itself.[18] When students use the term "fake news," what are they describing?

If *fake* is defined by *Merriam-Webster* as "counterfeit or sham,"[19] then "fake news" is a counterfeit report of recent events or sham material reported in a newspaper. This definition works when discussing fabricated information, such as PizzaGate, discussed at the beginning of this chapter. However, this definition doesn't hold when the facts are real but the delivery is manipulative.

The misrepresentation of data and factual information is a huge issue and takes many forms. Sometimes, an article may use a real, undoctored photograph and pair it with a completely false story. This happened during the 2016 presidential election with an image from England of a man with a number of black boxes labeled "Ballot Box." The story claimed that the picture was of a man in the United States who had found boxes of "fraudulent ballots" in a warehouse in Ohio. Snopes.com quickly debunked the story.[20] These kinds of hoaxes are easier to debunk than misrepresentation of facts like the ones made on a daily basis by online news outlets, Facebook posts, and TV pundits. Politifact.com has a "Truth-o-Meter" page (https://www.politifact.com/truth-o-meter/statements/) where visitors can see fact-checked ratings of statements on a scale from "True" to "Pants on Fire." Yet misrepresentation of facts can go beyond the political sphere, and there is not as much fact checking involved in smaller, lower-profile statements and memes and information that travels like brushfire through social media outlets.

False news stories are not a new phenomenon, but the way these stories are spread has changed drastically in recent years. Humans are influenced by how others think, no matter whether what they are thinking is completely false or inaccurate, and the way people consume news has changed the way it is written. Journalists now have a lot of competition for eyes. This has led to more figurative and creative language in our news stories rather than dry facts, making it harder to discern which stories are news and which are meant to entertain. By scaffolding critical thinking skills across grade levels, educators can help build more critical media consumers, who, hopefully, will be better able to evaluate what they are reading or watching and minimize the spread of false information.

# 13

# Free Speech in the Digital Age

It may seem out of place to have a chapter focused on the First Amendment wedged into a book about digital and media literacy, but the Internet has opened new doors and new questions about First Amendment rights and protections. It is vital that teachers and students understand how what they say and do with technology is or isn't protected under the Constitution.

The First Amendment states,

> Congress shall make no law respecting an establishment of religion, or prohibiting the free exercise thereof; or abridging the freedom of speech, or of the press; or the right of the people peaceably to assemble, and to petition the Government for a redress of grievances.

The Internet allows for anyone to share pretty much anything they want in a public forum. The ease of posting means that the quantity of posts is exponential. This can make it feel as though anything goes online. It's not uncommon for people to say, "I have free speech," or refer to the First Amendment, especially when posting controversial content.

However, not *all* speech is protected, and it is important to understand the limits of free speech, both as a private citizen, as a student, and as a public employee, as many teachers in public school districts are. The number of cases in which students and teachers are being held accountable for online behaviors or running aground of First Amendment protections gets larger every year. Many, if not all of these online cases have real offline repercussions and many of these online cases use offline precedents as the basis of their decision.

## REGULATING SPEECH ONLINE

The Supreme Court has helped define the First Amendment over hundreds of years, before radio, television, and the Internet. Precedents from these cases are applied to speech as it exists online today. For instance, obscenity is not protected under the First Amendment. The Supreme Court's decision in the 1973 case, *Miller v. California*, set the standard definition of obscenity used by most states today.[1] It is also the standard used in CIPA and COPPA laws that protect children online. (See Chapter 8 for more on these laws.)

In 1997, the Communications Decency Act, part of the Telecommunications Act of 1996, was struck down as unconstitutional. The Supreme Court decided that the law did not clearly define the kind of content that would be regulated because indecent content is protected, while obscene content is not.[2] This left the content on this new, powerful communication technology largely unregulated in the way that the traditional media like TV and radio are.

Regulation of the Internet has been mostly left to the companies themselves. Because speech is only protected from government censorship, private companies are free to censor any speech they want on their platforms. This is usually written into their Terms of Use or, in the case of forums, in their community policies. Outspoken alt-right personality Milo Yiannopoulos found himself on the receiving end of this censorship when Twitter banned his account after he orchestrated a social media "trolling" campaign against African-American actress Leslie Jones. Yiannopoulos had been under scrutiny by Twitter for years, and this last stunt sealed his fate.

Yiannopoulos claimed that Twitter was censoring him, but the platform has every right to ban any user that they believe has broken their policies.[3] Their policy states:

> Twitter's mission is to give everyone the power to create and share ideas and information, and to express their opinions and beliefs without barriers. Free

expression is a human right—we believe that everyone has a voice, and the right to use it. Our role is to serve the public conversation, which requires representation of a diverse range of perspectives. . . . Under this policy, we take action against behavior that targets individuals or an entire protected category with hateful conduct, as described above.[4]

On the other end of the spectrum, a May 2018 Supreme Court decision declared that President Trump's blocking of seven Twitter users amounted to a case of government censorship and that the act of blocking users by the president of the United States violated their First Amendment rights.[5] Even though the account, @realdonaldtrump, is his personal account, it is run by a government entity (the president) and blocking users is no different than the government denying citizens their constitutional right of "redress of grievances."

With billions of users across the globe, Facebook has had its own troubles with content shared on its platform. In April 2017, a fourteen-year-old boy in Chicago was arrested in connection with a rape that was broadcast on Facebook Live. This is just one of many horrific crimes that have been committed using the Facebook Live feature, which allows users to broadcast in real time. According to authorities, forty people watched the crime, but none contacted the police.[6]

Facebook has both human and technological efforts at play at the same time trying to keep on top of the content posted to the site. In 2016, algorithms that are supposed to catch posts containing child pornography took down a post containing the iconic Vietnam War–era image of a little girl running naked toward the camera, her clothes having been burned from her body from a napalm attack. This was an eye-opening look at how algorithms can help but are not a true solution to the problem.[7] Although Silicon Valley often sees tech as the solution to many content-related issues, it is proving quite challenging, and this was an embarrassing mistake for Facebook.

Because of these challenges, Facebook also employs more than seven thousand human content moderators who help police content on the site. One of these moderators filed a lawsuit against the company in June 2018 claiming that the job gave her posttraumatic stress and psychological trauma, and that Facebook did not have policies or supports in place for employees who are subjected to graphic, often horrific, content posted by users.[8]

We are in new territory where it's not clear whose job it is to make sure that the Internet is a safe place to be and that it doesn't become a platform for hate and violence. To reiterate the words of Vint Cerf, often called the "Father of the Internet," the Internet is a mirror that reflects our society, so perhaps fixing the mirror is not the issue. Rather, how do we, as a society, address the underlying causes of these kinds of messages and how do we, as a society, work to make the Internet what we want it to be? Is it appropriate to assign that task to companies like Facebook and Twitter, which are not necessarily interested or invested in online discourse except insofar as it sells ads?

## UNPROTECTED SPEECH

Other kinds of speech are not protected under the First Amendment. Threatening speech, speech that incites violent or illegal acts, and harassment are not protected forms of speech. These restrictions also apply to online speech. It is important for students (and everyone) to understand that if you receive messages that are threatening or incite illegal acts, calling the police is an appropriate response. Online speech is no different than if someone stood on your front lawn and yelled for you to come out so they could fight you, or if someone left a threatening note in your mailbox. Threats are threats. If you feel unsafe, call the police.

Speech that contains false or derogatory statements made with the sole purpose of harming someone's reputation is also not protected. This kind of speech falls under the umbrella of defamation and could be considered libel if it is written and slander if it is spoken (including on radio and other media). These laws are another example of how legal precedents made before the Internet existed are applied to online settings. The Electronic Frontier Foundation even has a dedicated page for bloggers centered on defamation.[9] With the rise of the Internet and Web 2.0 (the interactive web that brought us social media), anyone could start a website or a blog and share their opinion or spread gossip or false rumors.

Surprisingly, one form of speech that *is* protected is hate speech. This is different from a hate crime, which is an act of hate that breaks the law (i.e., a threat based on the race, ethnicity, or other identity of the victim). Unfortunately, this means that saying hateful things is not illegal. This is why the Ku Klux Klan and Black Nationalist groups like the Nation of Islam are allowed to march and spread their message despite their hateful content. (Both groups are designated as hate groups by the Southern Poverty Law Center.[10])

However, it is important to consider that censorship of any speech is censorship of all speech. Once we as a country start telling some people that they are not allowed to say something (no matter how hateful), it opens the door for more censorship. So, by allowing for hate speech, we allow for all speech to be free. It's a risk that we take in the name of protecting what some might argue is the most vital element of our democratic society.

First Amendment protections only apply to protections from government censorship, yet the US government does not regulate Internet speech or censor the Internet (although some would argue that the mandatory content filters required through E-Rate funding for schools and library are a form of censorship.) This is why companies like Twitter and Facebook can suspend users without violating users' First Amendment rights. This is also why First Amendment protections look different in private and public schools and job sectors.

## THE FIRST AMENDMENT IN SCHOOLS

First Amendment rights in public schools are not completely protected because of Supreme Court case decisions regarding student conduct in school. In one of the most famous cases, *Tinker v. Des Moines Community School District*, the Supreme Court defended the right of students to wear black arm bands to school in silent protest of the Vietnam War. In the decision, the court stated that their actions did not "materially and substantially interfere" with the school day. It also stated that students do not "shed their constitutional rights to freedom of speech or expression at the schoolhouse gate."[11] This decision has been a guideline for regulating students' free speech in school, and increasingly, speech outside of school that could potentially affect the school environment.

In May 2013, Wesley Teague, a senior at Heights High School in Wichita, Kansas, was suspended after posting a tweet that poked fun at the high school's football team. The administration claimed that the tweet was sent to incite anger among the student body and that it caused a serious disruption to the school day. Wesley, who was president of the senior class, was suspended for the rest of the school year. Wesley, his family, and many of the students, argued that the tweet was sent in jest and that the punishment was too harsh and infringed on his First Amendment rights.[12]

This is a growing trend as schools and districts desperately try to prevent conflict and disruptions that could potentially start on social media. With the threat of school shootings, this desperation has led to schools and districts investing in social media monitoring tools like Firestorm, which uses algorithms to monitor public social media posts that contain certain keywords and content.[13] This monitoring can also potentially infringe on students' First Amendment rights should they be disciplined for posts that they make outside of the school day on their personal devices. It is at the administration's discretion to decide if a post merits discipline, and, unfortunately, this sometimes means that students are disciplined for sharing unpopular opinions, raunchy jokes, or other content that school finds offensive that isn't necessarily threatening or can't be categorized as bullying or harassment.

In this same thread, classrooms themselves are not considered "public forums," or places where First Amendment rights are fully protected. This designation of various spaces in relation to the First Amendment date back to the 1939 case *Hague v. Committee for Industrial Organization* in which a city ordinance preventing a labor union from meeting in public was struck down because the court defined city streets and sidewalks as open forums where speech is fully protected.[14] Over time, the definitions of spaces has come up in a number of cases. Spaces that are not designated as public, open forums may not have full protection of First Amendment rights. For instance, a government-owned space that is not open to the public is subject to limitations. Classrooms fall into this category.

In 1996, Pennsylvania teacher Diane Murray sued the Pittsburgh Board of Education for not allowing her to use "Learn Ball," a classroom management system with licensed materials. She claimed that her classroom was an open forum and that the district was infringing on her First Amendment rights by not allowing her to use the program and its licensed materials in her classroom. The court disagreed, stating that her classroom qualifies as a "traditional forum" (one that may have limitations), but not as an "open forum."[15]

This case, and others like it, set a strong precedent and should be considered when it comes to what we say and what our students say in our classroom. This includes what is said using online discussion forums in tools like Canvas or Edmodo or Google Classroom. Although teachers and students do not leave their First Amendment rights at the door when they enter the classroom, their full rights are not guaranteed.

This precedent was also set in the 1988 *Hazelwood v. Kuhlmeier* case regarding the censorship of a school newspaper. When the school pulled two articles from the approved proofs for an upcoming issue, the students sued. The court sided with the school, stating that the school had the right to regulate the content of the school publication to maintain a high standard for speech at school.[16] In today's classrooms, this extends to student-run blogs or webpages. As the *Tinker* decision made clear, schools have broad powers to censor student speech if it has potential to incite the student body or disrupt teaching and learning in the school, or if it infringes on the rights of others.

Teachers and students in private or independent schools may have even fewer protected First Amendment rights in their classrooms and school environments. This is because independently run schools are not government entities, and as discussed earlier, the First Amendment only protects citizens from government censorship, not from an employer or private entity.

A teacher in Florida found this out the hard way when she posted pictures of her same-sex wedding to social media. Less than a week later, she was fired from her job at a Catholic school. The school administration claimed that she broke her contract, which contained language about morality.[17] In general, incidents such as this fall under discrimination laws, not First Amendment protections. In this case, the school referred to the teacher's contract language, which left it open for the school to fire her because of her sexual orientation. The school could actually argue that, as a religious institution, it is their First Amendment right to have that language in the contract. However, if an employee is fired in a way that appears to be retaliatory or based solely on race, age, or sexual orientation, a discrimination case could be applicable.

Public school teachers have slightly different First Amendment protections at work. They are technically employed by a district, so are not considered federal employees; however, they are considered public employees. Public school employees do have some protections at work under the First Amendment because they are government employees. This is often limited to "public concern" issues such as "whistleblowing."[18] Being a member of a union also extends protections from being fired without "just cause" or due process. However, as explained previously, a classroom is not considered an open

**Table 13.1. The First Amendment**

| Unprotected Speech | Protected Speech |
|---|---|
| **Defamation** | **Symbolic Speech** |
| Making untrue statements about another person to damage that person's reputation. | Actions that convey a particular message or statement to those viewing it. |
| | **Flag Burning** |
| | In 1984, in front of the Dallas City Hall, Gregory Lee Johnson burned an American flag as a means of protest against Reagan administration policies. The Supreme Court decided that this speech was protected as symbolic speech used to convey a message. |
| **Libel** | **Anonymity** |
| To publish in print (including pictures), writing, or broadcast through radio, television, or film, an untruth about another which will do harm to that person or his or her reputation, by tending to bring the target into ridicule, hatred, scorn or contempt of others. Libel is the written or broadcast form of defamation, distinguished from slander, which is oral defamation. | The freedom to publish any written work anonymously. In 1960, the Supreme Court upheld that anonymous publications were protected speech because they allow for persecuted groups, including the original American revolutionaries, to depend on anonymity to safely criticize oppression in society. |
| **Keira Knightley Libel Suit against British tabloid** | |
| A British tabloid suggested Knightley had an eating disorder and blamed her for the death of an anorexic teen. Knightley won a $6,000 settlement for a libel claim and donated the settlement to charity. | |
| **Slander** | **Freedom of the Press** |
| Oral communication of false and malicious statements that damage the reputation of another. | This part of the first amendment states that the government cannot influence or interfere with the distribution of information or opinions. Recently, this part of the first amendment has come up in discussions around "fake news" and coverage of political events and issues. Although free speech does not include speech that is false (libel or slander), such as articles claiming that a candidate broke the law when she or he did not, simply reporting unflattering stories is |
| Untrue allegations were made against a candidate in a California election through YouTube videos and radio ads. The candidate accused the opponent of slander. | |

not considered libel, slander, or defamation if the allegations in the story are true. This also does not make the news "fake."

## Establishment Clause

The Establishment Clause prohibits the government from making any law "respecting an establishment of religion." This clause not only forbids the government from establishing an official religion, but also prohibits government actions that unduly favor one religion over another. It also prohibits the government from unduly preferring religion over nonreligion, or nonreligion over religion.

Students can pray in school, although they cannot disrupt class time for prayer and public schools cannot require mandatory prayer for students.

## Freedom of Peaceable Assembly

The right to come together for political, social, or entertainment reasons in public or private spaces.

The August 2017 Unite the Right rally in Charlottesville, VA, was defended by the American Civil Liberties Union, a national organization that promotes civil liberties, including freedom of speech. The organization was highly criticized for defending the rights of white supremacists to gather to share hateful and bigoted speech, but it defended itself saying that while detestable, this speech and the right to assembly peacefully are protected under the First Amendment.

## Hate Speech

Although the Supreme Court has decided that specific kinds of threatening or injurious speech is not protected under the First Amendment, there are no prohibitions against hateful speech unless it falls into one of the unprotected categories of speech.

## Fighting Words

Words that one uses to provoke a fight or hostility.

During the 2016 Presidential campaign, Vice President Joe Biden made a comment about "slugging" then candidate Donald Trump. He was accused of uttering "fighting words."

## Nonpeaceable Assembly

The congregating of people for any purpose that leads to violence or lawlessness.

## Obscenity

The character or quality of being obscene; an act, utterance, or item tending to corrupt the public morals by its indecency or lewdness.

continued

**Table 13.1 The First Amendment (continued)**

| Unprotected Speech | Protected Speech |
|---|---|
| Obscenity (cont.) | Hate Speech (cont.) |
| **Roth v. United States** <br> The Court noted that the First Amendment was not intended to protect every utterance or form of expression, such as materials that were "utterly without redeeming social importance." The Court held that the test to determine obscenity was "whether to the average person, applying contemporary community standards, the dominant theme of the material taken as a whole appeals to prurient interest." <br><br> The punk band The Dead Kennedys was part of an obscenity trial centered around their album art. In the end, the courts sided with the band, who pointed out that the art had appeared in galleries and was a social statement, not pornographic or obscene. <br><br> The Bradenburg Test <br><br> This test is applied to speech to determine if it is protected under the First Amendment: The Court used a two-pronged test to evaluate speech acts: (1) speech can be prohibited if it is "directed at inciting or producing imminent lawless action" and (2) it is "likely to incite or produce such action." <br><br> Often, this is connected to the act of yelling "fire" in a crowded movie theater being unprotected speech. This was part of the *Bradenburg v Ohio* Supreme Court decision. <br><br> Free Speech at Work <br><br> Contrary to popular belief, your employer can fire you over what you say and do at work. The First Amendment protects citizens from censorship by the Government, but a private employer can decide what is acceptable and not acceptable at work. A woman who "flipped off" President Trump's motorcade recently learned that lesson. <br><br> This is also why companies like Twitter and Facebook can ban and block users based on what they post. These users have no First Amendment protections when using a private service. <br><br> Most protections at work center around antidiscrimination laws, not First Amendment rights. For instance, firing someone because of his or her religion would be a clear violation of antidiscrimination laws. | In January 2017, the band The Slants won a case in the Supreme Court upholding this protection of hateful speech when they argued that they should not be denied a trademark for their band name just because the name was deemed offensive. As Justice Samuel Alito stated in his opinion on the case, "Speech may not be banned on the ground that it expresses ideas that offend." |

## The First Amendment in Schools

Students who attend public educational institutions (K–12 and colleges and universities) are held to a different standard, although they still maintain their First Amendment rights. The Supreme Court has decided that some speech can be censored by a school if it is deemed disruptive, threatening, or dangerous, or if it will infringe on the rights of others. This was part of the opinion for a case in which a student was reprimanded by the school for delivering a speech that was full of vulgarities to the student body.

The Supreme Court decided in favor of a group of students protesting the Vietnam War by wearing black armbands to school. When the students were disciplined, they sued, and the Supreme Court agreed that their speech was considered protected "symbolic speech" and did not pose a threat or disruption to the school environment.

*To read more about the First Amendment in schools, check out:* http://www.newseuminstitute.org/first-amendment-center/topics/
freedom-of-speech-2/k-12-public-school-student-expression/speaking-out-in-school/.

Sources:

*Texas v. Johnson*, 491 US 397 (1989).
"Libel," Law.com, accessed November 16, 2018, http://dictionary.law.com/default.aspx?selected=1153.
"Knightley Accepts Libel Settlement," *Los Angeles Times*, May 26, 2007, accessed November 18, 2018, http://articles.latimes.com/2007/may/26/entertainment/et-quick26.4.
*Manuel D. Talley v. California*, 362 US 60 (1960).
"Slander," TheFreeDictionary.com, accessed November 28, 2019, http://www.thefreedictionary.com/slander.
Jessica Weston, "Slander; Facebook, Videos, Memes: Local Election Takes an Ugly Turn," *Ridgecrest Daily Independent*, November 4, 2016, accessed November 19, 2018, http://
www.ridgecrestca.com/article/20161104/NEWS/161109757.
"Fighting Words," TheFreeDictionary.com, accessed November 28, 2019, http://www.thefreedictionary.com/fighting+words.
Allie Malloy, "Earnest Defends Biden's Fighting Words against Trump," CNN, October 26, 2016, accessed November 19, 2018, https://www.cnn.com/2016/10/26/politics/
joe-biden-donald-trump-fight/.
"Can Students Pray or Discuss Religion in Public Schools?" Freedom Forum Institute, accessed November 19, 2018, http://www.newseuminstitute.org/about/faq/
can-students-pray-or-discuss-religion-in-public-schools/.
Joan Biskupic, "ACLU Takes Heat for Its Free-speech Defense," CNN, August 17, 2017, accessed November 18, 2018, http://www.cnn.com/2017/08/16/politics/aclu-free-speech-white
-supremacy/index.html.
"Obscenity," TheFreeDictionary.com, accessed November 18, 2018, http://legal-dictionary.thefreedictionary.com/obscenity.
*Roth v. United States*, 354 US 476 (1957).
Michael Silverberg, "The Obscenity Trial That Made H. R. Giger an Icon for Punk Rock and Free Speech," *Quartz*, June 20, 2014, accessed November 19, 2018, http://qz.com/210900/
the-obscenity-trial-that-made-h-r-giger-an-icon-for-punk-rock-and-free-speech/.
David G. Savage, "Supreme Court Rules the Slants May Trademark Their Name, Striking Down Law Banning Offensive Terms," *Los Angeles Times*, June 19, 2017, accessed Novem-
ber 19, 2018, https://www.latimes.com/politics/la-na-pol-court-slants-disparate-trademark-20170619-story.html.
*Brandenburg v. Ohio*, 395 US 444 (1969).
"Government Employees and First Amendment Overview," Freedom Forum Institute, accessed November 19, 2018, http://www.newseuminstitute.org/first-amendment-center/
topics/freedom-of-speech-2/free-speech-and-government-employees-overview/.
Jennifer Bendery, "Woman Fired for Flipping Off Trump's Motorcade," *Huffington Post*, November 7, 2017, accessed November 20, 2018, https://www.huffingtonpost.com/entry/
woman-flips-off-donald-trump-fired_us_59fe0ab4e4b0c9652fffa484.
*Tinker v. Des Moines*—Landmark Supreme Court Ruling on Behalf of Student Expression," American Civil Liberties Union, accessed November 19, 2018, https://www.aclu.org/other/
tinker-v-des-moines-landmark-supreme-court-ruling-behalf-student-expression.</tc>

public forum, and so teachers' speech can be limited in the classroom. This is especially true for political or religious speech in the public sector.

Speaking as a private citizen is also protected. For instance, writing an opinion blog post or a letter about issues in the school or district could be protected if you are speaking as a private citizen. This was part of a 1967 case, *Pickering v. Board of Education.*[19] Marvin Pickering, an educator, wrote a letter to the editor of the local newspaper complaining about a school board proposal. He was fired for voicing his opinion. He sued the board for violating his First Amendment rights and the Supreme Court agreed, stating that Pickering was speaking as a concerned private citizen and that, as far as they could tell, there were no false or reckless claims in the letter. This decision could be applied to Facebook posts, posts to forums, tweets, or other opinions expressed through digital platforms. However, the key here is that educators are speaking as public citizens and *not* as employees of the school or district in which they work.

The First Amendment is broad and complex, and its application in the classroom and in schools is varied and often lacks current precedent. It is vital that educators and their students understand the limitations to their First Amendment rights in school and that they are able to identify when censorship crosses into discrimination. For a "cheat sheet" of basic protected and unprotected forms of speech see Table 13.1.

Teaching students about the First Amendment can seem unwieldy and complex, but the most important part of the process is getting students talking and helping them navigate the complexities of one of our most important democratic rights. Putting this in context around social media and discussing current events can also help them understand their own rights both in how they express themselves but also when speech is directed at them. For ideas on teaching these concepts, see Textbox 13.1.

TEXTBOX 13.1.

## Elementary Grades

Younger students have a sense of what makes a classroom a happy place to be. Depending on their age, ask them to list one to three rights that would be respected in their ideal or perfect classroom. You may need to preface this activity with a discussion of what rights are. Have them share those rights with a partner or with their table group. Have a few students share their answers with the class. List their answers on the board. Ask students what they, their classmates, and the teacher can do to make sure that these rights are respected in the classroom. Explain that our country has a Bill of Rights, a document that states what rights our citizens have. Show them the First Amendment and break it down however is best for their age group. Have them make connections between the rights in the First Amendment and the rights that they created for their classroom.

## Middle Grades

Have students reflect on what they know about democracy and the most important things that make our democracy work. Have them write down three things that make democracy work. Then either pair students or have them share their ideas with their table group. If students are paired, have them pair up with another group and create a new list based on their answers. Table groups can compare answers and come up with their own list. Have groups share out and record their answers on the board. Save these for a later time.

During the next class period, review the First Amendment with students so they understand each aspect of the amendment. Then compare these with their list from the previous class and see which of their "important things" also fall under the First Amendment. Students should understand that these protections are only from government censorship, and that these protections sometimes don't apply in the same way at school or at work. They should also understand why hateful speech is protected and why protecting all speech matters.

Provide students with a few examples to explore. These can be examples such as articles online critical of the president, hateful tweets, comments that threaten violence, or other examples. Make sure to have a few that are protected speech examples and a few that aren't. Also provide students with a "cheat" sheet of the First Amendment text and any court cases or other information that you reviewed in class (alternatively, students can use their notes from class if you required notes to be taken). Have students work with a partner to examine each example and decide if it is an example of protected or unprotected speech and provide their reasoning.

### High School Grades

Spend some time in the classroom reviewing court cases mentioned in the chapter or general information about the protections students have and don't have when it comes to the First Amendment in school. Start by reading over the First Amendment itself, breaking down each part so students understand the various protections under the Constitution. Share the story of Wesley Teague with students. Either hold a general class discussion, or something more structured such as giving the class a statement such as "The school was right to suspend Wesley," and having the students stand in areas of the room based on whether they agree or disagree with the statement. Require students to back up their statements with what they have learned. Another way to discuss the topic would be to have some students be the school administrator and some represent the student. Hold a trial where both sides must defend their position with legal precedent and specific applications of the First Amendment.

# Conclusion

Writing this book was like trying to hit a moving target, and likewise, teaching digital and media literacy can often feel like an exhausting task. Technology is constantly evolving, and it seems like every day there are new developments in how these technologies affect both our physical and mental health. Data breaches and privacy concerns make headlines on a weekly basis, and social media plays a larger and larger role in politics and society at large. When today's students enter the adult world, it's not clear what technologies will be available or in what new ways technology will be integrated into their every day lives. A few things are sure: privacy concerns will persist and technology will still battle for our attention spans. We are already seeing the effects of pervasive technology, constant connectedness, and social media on our youngest adults as they enter adulthood.

In January 2019, right before Alexandria Ocasio-Cortez became the youngest Congressperson ever elected at twenty-nine years old, a video posted to YouTube emerged of Ocasio-Cortez dancing to a pop song. The video was made while she was a student at Boston University, and edited clips were shared by conservative news outlets and social media accounts to discredit her as a "nitwit."[1] Today's students have been using social media and posting to YouTube and other sites at younger and younger ages, and even parents are posting videos and images of their children as babies, toddlers, and young children, sometimes in embarrassing situations. A quick search of "David after the Dentist" on YouTube will show a potentially embarrassing video of a seven-year-old boy still groggy from a trip to the dentist that his dad posted, most likely without David's consent.[2] It's hard to know what kind of effect this video could have on David as he enters adulthood, although he will soon find out. David is now seventeen according to the date that the video was uploaded to YouTube.

In 2011, the author Nicholas Carr sparked a dialogue around the long-term effects that the pervasiveness of the Internet could have on our attention spans in his book *The Shallows: What the Internet is Doing to Our Brains*. Carr explained, "Whether I'm online or not, my mind now expects to take in information the way the Net distributes it; in a swiftly moving stream of particles."[3] Educators often complain that their students' attention spans are getting shorter, and that they feel pressured to make their instruction more and more like the fast-paced world of video games and to cater to smaller and smaller attention spans created by the constant distraction of technology that students carry around in their pockets.

This is more than a kid or student problem, as former Google engineer Tristan Harris explains in his TED talks centered around the ethics related to technology design. He explains that smartphones and apps are intentionally designed to garner our attention because more attention leads to more ad revenue. He compares these tiny, handheld devices to carrying around a slot machine in our pockets. We swipe and scroll mindlessly, hoping that we will come across a post or receive a notification the same way that we pull the slot machine lever hoping to see three of a kind. These devices and apps take advantage of the dopamine released in our brains when we do get that gratification.[4] As these efforts are brought into the light, it's not clear if companies will be forced to rethink their designs because of public push back or whether we will shrug and accept this as a trade-off for the utility of these devices and the ways that they make our lives easier.

We are at an important time in the use of technology in classrooms. Technology integration in the classroom has gone beyond simply teaching students how to use technology tools and has entered the age of leveraging technology to do things that were previously impossible. The next decade will take educators to new applications and integrations of technology that we have never seen or experienced. It will also pose challenges as educators, schools, and districts continue to grapple with the ethics and responsibilities involved in bringing new technology to their students.

This book does not address all technologies available in the classroom, and one that has gained a lot of traction and has made leaps in ease of use and availability is virtual reality (VR). Facebook acquired Oculus, a VR headset company, in 2014 for $2 billion.[5] In August 2018, the company announced that it was providing schools in Japan, Taiwan, and Seattle with free headsets to pilot how their headsets could provide immersive three-dimensional experiences in the classroom.[6] There are privacy concerns around the Oculus headsets both because Facebook, the company's owner, has been embroiled in privacy controversies, and because the technology is so new that there is little information about how and what kind of data VR companies collect about their users. Still, there will be schools that want to get ahead on a new technology and will bring these into their classrooms with the potential for VR to become commonplace.

In Europe, the passage of the EU General Data Protection Regulations legislation has had a ripple effect on how companies handle and think about user data across the globe. Most likely, the United States and other non-EU countries will see more privacy regulations placed on tech companies. However, it's not clear how far these regulations will go. It is also clear that there is a heightened awareness of the effects that technology has on our brains and attention spans. It's not clear whether there are lasting effects that will permanently change our brains and how they function. Studies have also made connections between our "always on" society and social media and mental health, specifically anxiety and depression. One study linked specific social media apps to mental health and discovered that Instagram contributed more to anxiety and depression than any other app they studied.[7] It is also unclear if these kinds of apps and potentially even more connectedness will have long-term effects on young people as they enter adulthood.

As more and more information moves online and user-generated content balloons, it is also unclear how the prevalence of misinformation and disinformation will affect society as a whole. Some historians worry that the current state of media in the United States and elsewhere may have a damaging effect on democratic systems and how they function. These concerns stem from both disinformation campaigns aimed at swaying elections, like Russia's attempts to influence the 2016 US presidential election, as well as ways that governments can leverage technology to gather private data about their citizens and digitally track them. China is already doing this through its new facial recognition technology, which it has deployed in public spaces to track its citizens.[8] There is no way to know the lasting effects of misinformation and disinformation campaigns and privacy violations, but there is no doubt that this is just the beginning of the fight against these complex technological challenges.

All these unknowns mean that there is a huge potential for young people today to decide the future of how digital technologies will play a part in everyday life. This places a large responsibility in the lap of today's educators to understand and teach students about how the technologies they use and the media they consume work, and the direct effects they have on how students live their lives and perceive the world around them. In his dystopian novel *Feed*, author M. T. Anderson explores this potential future with a world where people have implants in their brains called "feeds" that interoperate with their brains and are run by large corporations. The feed bombards them twenty-four hours a day with advertisements and creates consumer profiles based on their activity to sell them products. Even more, the "feed" influences what the teens in the novel like, their fashion trends (which change a few times a day), and it attempts to reduce their lives to mere consumerism so they ignore the larger issues in the world like a threat of world war and a dying planet. This is one vision of the future, but it is not the only one. In the near future, we could also see digital technologies bring us together like never before and allow us to explore worlds that we only dreamed existed. It could help cure illnesses on a global scale and help societies spread freedom and fight oppression. The Internet is young and ever evolving. Educators play an important role in modeling and guiding young people toward responsible and thoughtful use and consumption of digital technologies so that they can be leaders in creating the best version of the future we can imagine.

# Appendix

This appendix contains sample lessons for elementary, middle, and high school students. They are meant to be a guide and can, obviously, be adjusted as needed. They are intentionally accessible for classrooms with limited access to technology and they are technology agnostic in that they do not suggest any one technology tool or device over another, but provide a number of options to try. Some lessons require an Internet connection, but all can be done with students sharing a computer if necessary.

Each lesson is paired with an International Society for Technology in Education (ISTE) Standard for Students as well as a goal. Some lessons have prerequisite understandings and some are meant to be part of a larger unit or series of lessons, although all can be taught individually.

*Elementary grades* refer to grades K–4. *Middle grades* refer to grades 5–8. *High school grades* refer to grades 9–12. Some lessons will work well across multiple grade levels and some are more limited to their specific grade level.

## CHAPTER 2 SAMPLE LESSONS: LIVING IN THE DIGITAL WORLD
### ISTE Standard for Students: Digital Citizen
2a—Students cultivate and manage their digital identity and reputation and are aware of the permanence of their actions in the digital world.
2b—Students engage in positive, safe, legal, and ethical behavior when using technology, including social interactions online or when using networked devices.

**Grade Level:** Elementary Grades

**Lesson Goal:** To know how and why people use digital devices and what kinds of responsibilities come with the use of digital devices.

**Materials:** Chart paper, interactive white board, or traditional classroom board for recording ideas. Markers or other writing utensils for the chart paper.

**Process:**

1. Explain that the class will be discussing digital devices and how people use them.
2. Ask students to raise their hand if they have ever used a smartphone, a tablet, a computer, a game console, or any other electronic device. (This can easily be turned into a visual graph of some kind to tie into math instruction.) This is to gauge the familiarity that students have with digital devices and how many students interact with these devices outside of school.
3. As a class, brainstorm a list of things that people can do on these devices.
4. Give each small group of students a piece of chart paper. Have them write or draw pictures of what they do on a device. If they do not have access to a device at home, they can share their experiences using digital devices at school.
5. Have each table or group share some ideas from their table or have each group hold up their paper so the rest of class can see it and point out a few things on the paper.
6. Explain that these are powerful tools that can do a lot of different tasks. Make sure to point out ways that they are used for learning and entertainment.
7. Ask students to share out rules that they have at home and school when it comes to digital devices. Make sure to discuss whether they have screen time rules or times when they are not allowed to use their devices.
8. Explain the importance of limiting screen time before bed.

For older elementary students who may be thinking about or have social media accounts, discuss how they use these sites and why they use them. Help them understand that, by law, they are not supposed to have an account without their parents' permission if they are younger than thirteen. Discuss the implications of lying about your age. If you are lying, who else is also lying? Why might putting a fake age online be problematic if you are a minor? Make sure to highlight the positive uses of social media as well.

For a wrap-up or exit ticket, have students write, draw, or explain three ways that people use digital technologies, including one positive use and one negative use.

**Grade Level:** Middle Grades
**Lesson Goal:** To know and understand best practices when using social media to build good digital habits.
**Materials**: Chart paper and markers for student groups.
**Process:**

1.  Explain that students will be discussing "digital habits."
2.  Ask students to define *social media*. Help them if they need clarification.
3.  Ask them how many of them use social media (they don't have to have an account, usually, to use it as an onlooker).
4.  Explain that they will be thinking about their use of social media today.
5.  Break students up into groups of no more than four.
6.  Distribute chart paper and markers.
7.  Model for students how to break their chart paper into four boxes.
8.  Have them write "Why" in the top left-hand box.
9.  Have them write "Who" in the top right-hand box.
10. Have them write "When" in the bottom left-hand box.
11. Have them write "What" in the bottom right-hand box.
12. Explain that each group will brainstorm:
    -   "Why I use social media."
    -   "Who do I connect with on social media?"
    -   "When do I use social media?"
    -   "What do I share on social media?"

They will write their answers in the corresponding boxes. Give them fifteen to twenty minutes to complete the task. Either have groups present, or do a gallery walk (walk around and read each other's charts). Come back together and discuss similarities, differences, things that surprised them, and questions they have.

Make sure to highlight the timing of when they are using social media (e.g., while doing homework, while in bed at night) and discuss the pros and cons of their timing choices. Also discuss their "friends" and whether they actually know all of the people they follow and who follow them, and what the implications of that might be, both good and bad. Discuss any other items of interest from their lists. Wrap up by having them either write or state verbally one takeaway from the activity and the conversation.

**Grade Level:** High School
**Goal:** To understand the potential long-term effects of our online choices.
**Materials:** Link to article about Harvard rescinding admission to incoming freshmen over social media posts (https://www.thecrimson.com/article/2017/6/5/2021-offers-rescinded-memes/). Links to articles about Justine Sacco, Alexandra Wallace, Tyler Clementi, or Megan Meier. Internet-enabled devices for each student or student pairs.
**Process:**

1. Ask students if they have ever shared anything on social media that they have regretted or seen someone post something questionable.
2. Allow a few students to share their stories if they are willing.
3. Have students read the *Crimson* article about Harvard rescinding admission to incoming students.
4. Ask students to decide if they agree with the decision. They can either write their response or just prepare their response in their head.
5. Have them either turn to a partner to share their thoughts or share their thoughts with their table group.
6. Have a few students share their thoughts with the class. Make sure to touch on:
   - What are the privacy concerns with a private Facebook group? (How do you think Harvard found out?)
   - What are students' thoughts on being, essentially, punished for something that they did using their own personal account on their own personal time?
   - Why do they think that Harvard made this decision? (They are an elite, Ivy League school. Why might that matter?)

- But if these memes were just jokes, why does it matter? (Some posts were anti-Semitic, racist, or promoted violence toward certain groups of people—how does Harvard know what kind of person someone is if they see these kinds of "jokes?")

7. Explain that students in this Facebook group gave a bad first impression. Ask students what kind of first impression they think people would have when looking them up online. Have them describe their online persona in three words. Have a few students share their three words with the class.

8. Have students put their own name into a search box to see what they find. Make sure that they use their whole name and the town or city they live in, and have them try adding the name of the school or any other organization they are a part of. See if they can find themselves.

9. Regroup. Who found themselves? Who found someone with their same name who was not them? Why might this matter? Who found nothing? Why might this matter?

10. Ask students: Who decides who you are online? (Guide them toward understanding that it is both up to them and up to the perception of others that they have no control over.)

## CHAPTER 3 SAMPLE LESSONS: HOW DOES THE INTERNET WORK?
**ISTE Standard for Students: Empowered Learner**
**1d**—Students understand the fundamental concepts of technology operations; demonstrate the ability to choose, use, and troubleshoot current technologies; and are able to transfer their knowledge to explore emerging technologies.

**Grade Level:** Elementary Grades
**Goal:** Be able to explain what the Internet is and how people use it.
**Materials:** Chart paper, interactive white board, or traditional classroom board for recording ideas.
**Process:**

1. Ask students to raise their hand if they have ever used the Internet.
2. Ask students to share things they have used the Internet to do. Make a list on the board.

3.  Have students try to categorize the list by placing similar actions together. For example, watching videos and playing games might fall under "entertainment" or "having fun," while research and school work might fall under "learning."
4.  Ask students where they think the information they find comes from. Make sure that they understand that this information comes from other people who put that information up online.
5.  Conclude the discussion by summarizing that the Internet is a place where people can learn, have fun (using whatever categories the class came up with), and share ideas and information with others.
6.  Explain that the Internet is like a worldwide community.
7.  Have students draw their own visual depiction of the Internet.

**Grade Level:** Middle Grades
**Goal:** Be able to explain in basic terms how the Internet works.
**Materials:** Two pieces of paper for each student or two pieces of chart paper for a group of students to share, writing utensil for each student or a marker for a group of students to share, Code.org Packets, Routing and Reliability video (https://youtu.be/AYdF7b3nMto). Optional: A slip of paper for each student for an exit ticket.
**Process:**

1.  Ask students to raise their hand if they have ever used the Internet.
2.  Ask students to keep their hand up if they can explain how the Internet works.
3.  Have a few students share out their thoughts.
4.  Explain that, today, students will explore how the Internet works, but first, they are going to create a diagram explaining what they think happens when they access a website. Make sure that students understand what you mean by "diagram." Their diagrams can include both pictures and words.
5.  Tell students to draw a diagram on their paper that shows their understanding of how information travels over the Internet. Give them about five to ten minutes (closer to ten for groups, smaller amount of time if students are working individually). Explain that there is no wrong

answer because you want to know what they know before exploring further.

6. Have a few students share and explain their diagrams with the class. Write down any pertinent vocabulary used (ISP, cable, modem, router, etc.) on the board.

7. Show students the Packets, Routing and Reliability video, asking them to write down any questions they have after watching it. You may need to show it twice for better comprehension.

8. Address and clarify any questions that students may have.

9. Ask for one or more students or student groups to explain their new understanding of how the Internet works. Clarify any misconceptions.

10. Have students draw a new diagram to explain how the Internet works.

11. Have one or more students or student groups share their new diagrams. Clarify any misrepresentations or mistakes in their drawings and explanations.

12. An accurate student diagram should include two internet-connected devices, multiple cables or "pathways," and a router. Explanations should include terms like *router*, *packets*, and *IP address*.

13. For a snapshot of what the students understand, ask for an exit ticket on which each student writes, in sentence form, his or her understanding of how the Internet works. This can be done on paper or through a digital LMS system used by the school.

Follow-up lessons can include subsequent videos from the Code.org playlist (https://www.youtube.com/playlist?list=PLzdnOPI1iJNfMRZm5DDxco3Ud sFegvuB7) and a conversation around ISPs and the companies that students' families pay to access the Internet.

**Grade Level:** High School
**Goal:** Understand what an IP address is and how it can be used to locate a user on the Internet.
**Prerequisite:** A basic understanding of how the Internet works.
**Materials:** An Internet-connected device for each student or one per three to four students. A slip of paper for each student and a writing utensil for an exit ticket. The websites http://who.is and http://www.infosniper.net/.

**Process:**

1.  Ask students to recap how the Internet works. Have one or two students explain to the class.
2.  Ask students how computers know where to send packets of data.
3.  Explain that, today, students will see how those computer addresses (IP addresses) can be traced to a physical location.
4.  Navigate to the site http://who.is and explain that this site will show you who owns any website in the world.
5.  Have students share some of their favorite websites (e.g., Twitter, Instagram, ESPN).
6.  Choose one website and type its URL into the search box.
7.  Show students the information listed such as registration date (when the domain was first purchased), expiration date (when the domain registration expires), as well as the address and phone number of the company.
8.  At the top of the page are similar domains. Ask students why they think some are listed as "Taken," and, if any are for sale, why they are priced the way they are. (HINT: Ask students if they have ever mistyped a URL and gotten to a page of ads—companies make money from the "wrong" URL.)
9.  Have students explore websites on their own using http://who.is to see what they find. Give them about ten to fifteen minutes.
10. Come back together and ask students to share what they found. Ask them if anything surprised them, if they learned anything new, or simply what they are thinking now that they have seen this tool.
11. Bring students' attention back to the board and show them the homepage of http://who.is. Point out that, under the search bar, it tells the user his or her IP address.
12. Have students navigate to the homepage and click on their IP address. This should show them the name of the ISP that provides the Internet service to the school. If they do this at home, it will show their home Internet provider.
13. Direct students to the site http://www.infosniper.net/ and have them input the IP address of their machine as listed on http://who.is.
14. Ask them what they found. (HINT: It should be a map showing their location.)

15. Ask a few students to share out what they are thinking now that they have seen this information.

16. Have students write down one thing they learned about IP addresses today on their exit ticket slip.

## CHAPTER 4 SAMPLE LESSONS: SEARCH ENGINES
### ISTE Standard for Students: Knowledge Constructor
3a—Students plan and employ effective research strategies to locate information and other resources for their intellectual or creative pursuits.

**Grade Level:** Elementary Grades

**Prerequisite:** Adequate comfort with typing and preparation around the content area, including specific questions or basic background knowledge.

**Goal:** To successfully locate accurate information based around a topic or question.

**Materials:** Kid-friendly search engine such as SweetSearch (http://sweetsearch.com) or Kiddle (http://www.kiddle.co), a projector and board, computer for each student or each student group or pair.

Prior to this lesson, have students brainstorm questions that they have about whatever they will be researching. Or, give them a scavenger hunt–style template with prepopulated questions based on content they are learning. They should have the questions in front of them along with some way of recording what they find. They should also have space to add questions that arise during their research.

It is also helpful to have the search engines bookmarked or easily available with one click so students don't have to type in the URL each time.

Prepare a checklist of criteria that students can check off to make sure that a site or resource is a good match for their topic and their reading level. One strategy is to have them hold up a finger each time they don't know a word. If all five fingers go up quickly, then it's probably not at their reading level.

**Process:**

1. Explain that students will be exploring questions and seeking answers using a search engine. Ask students for examples of search engines. Guide them to names like Bing, Google, and Yahoo.

2. Ask students if they have ever tried to find an answer to a question online. How did they do it?
3. Ask them what was easy and what was hard about the experience. (Some possible answers: hard to read, too many results, not sure which result to click.)
4. Explain that students will be using a "kid-friendly" search engine that will help them find information.
5. Pull the search engine up on the board and ask students what they should look for.
6. Model out loud how to turn their question into a search term (e.g., "How fast can a cheetah run?" becomes "cheetah speed.")
7. Model how to read the search results by talking through your thought processes ("I see that the first website is. . . . I wonder. . . . I see. . . .")
8. Model how to use the features of the particular search engine to narrow down or better understand their results.
9. Point out sponsored results or ads at the top of the results page. Even kindergarteners and first graders can recognize "AD" as an ad.
10. Give students ten to fifteen minutes to start their search. Walk around and assist students, observing their behaviors.
11. Come back together and ask them to share what they found and how they found it. You can do this by pairing students up before having them share aloud.
12. Allow students more time to explore and record what they find. Make sure that they record the website where they found the information. If they are writing by hand, the name of the site can suffice.
13. Circulate to support students.

**Grade Level:** Middle Grades
**Goal:** Use keywords and search terms effectively in Internet searches.
**Prerequisites:** Research questions developed by students.
Prepare a checklist of criteria that students can check off to make sure that a site or resource is a good match for their topic and their reading level. One strategy is to have them hold up a finger each time they don't know a word. If all five fingers go up quickly, then it's probably not at their reading level. This checklist should also ask if the site is relevant to their topic.

**Materials:** One internet-enabled device per student or student group, written questions (either digitally or on paper), highlighter (if questions are on paper).

**Process:**

1.  Explain that students will be seeking answers to their research questions using a search engine.
2.  Ask students to define *search engine* and give examples.
3.  Explain that students first need to turn their questions into search terms—terms that search engines better understand.
4.  Model for them how search engines "read" by typing in a question and showing them the bolded words. These are the search terms that the search engine uses to find the answer to what someone is searching for.
5.  Have student use the highlighter or the highlighter tool in their digital document to highlight the search terms—the most important terms in their question—and have them do a search.
6.  Similar to the elementary grades lesson, you can also model aloud your process for analyzing the results page.
7.  Have students experiment with different combinations of words to see how their choice of search terms affects their results.
8.  Give students fifteen minutes to find a site that they think will be helpful.
9.  Have students write down or record the site name and URL and explain why they think it will be helpful and what they found there.
10. Time permitting, have students experiment with a new question or search term.

**Grade Level:** High School

**Goal:** Be able to conduct complex searches, including those using databases or repositories of scholarly works.

**Process:**

1.  Ask students the difference between *fact* and *opinion*.
2.  Ask them how they know if something they are reading is fact or opinion. What are the clues?
3.  Model for students how to use search terms to find different kinds of file types and different kinds of resources (e.g., typing *filetype:pdf* in front of

a search, using the word *blog* in a search, searching http://scholar.google
.com). Also point out sponsored results on the search results page of the
search engine they are using.

4.  Have students find three kinds of online resources based around the con-
    tent they are studying. One should be an opinion resource; one should
    be a nonfiction, mostly unbiased source; and one should be an advertise-
    ment or other kind of click bait resource.

5.  To add a little fun, don't have students label which is which and have
    them provide the direct URLs and try to stump each other to see if they
    can figure out which is which by looking at each other's resources.

## CHAPTER 5 SAMPLE LESSONS: SOCIAL MEDIA
### ISTE Standard for Students

**2d**—Students engage in positive, safe, legal, and ethical behavior when using
technology, including social interactions online or when using networked
devices.

**Grade Level:** Elementary Grades
**Goal:** To be able to share work to an online platform for a global audience.
**Materials:** Class blog at a site like https://edublogs.org or http://kidblog.org,
writing sample from each student or student group, computing device for
each student or student group, projector and screen or whiteboard. Educator
Linda Yollis' great resource for leaving quality comments: http://yollisclass
blog.blogspot.com/2016/10/quality-commenting-five-tips.html.

This "lesson" spans a number of months. Before starting, it is helpful to
have a blog set up with posts on it and have students interact with your content first to see how the blog is set up and how to access posts. It is also helpful for students to have a piece of writing that they have already completed
before starting their first blog post so they can just transfer their writing into
their post.
**Process:**

1.  Ask students if they know what a blog is and why people have blogs.
    Discuss their responses.

2.  Show them the class blog and explain that you will be sharing their work and things that are happening in class on this special website just for their class—their class blog.

3.  Use the blog to share news with family (NOTE: Permission should be gotten from parents if student photos are to uploaded to the site).

4.  Post a few simple assignments to the blog for kids to see and complete (e.g., directions and resources).

5.  Introduce them to commenting, sharing with them the video at Linda Yollis' class blog (linked in Materials).

6.  Allow students to leave comments on your posts as part of their homework or class assignments.

7.  Gather required permission slips from families and from administrators. Explore privacy settings for the platform you have chosen. Create student accounts on the site. After a few months, explain that students will be getting to write their own posts.

8.  Teach students how to log in and create a new post.

9.  Have them give their post a title (based on the writing sample that they have from class).

10. Have them type their writing into the blog post. If they are already working in a digital tool like Google Docs, they can copy and paste. *Make sure that you have the posts set up to require teacher review before going live. This way you can catch any errors or concerns and address them with the student.*

11. Students should learn how to save their posts, how to come back to them to add to them, and how to find them once they are published.

12. Depending on your privacy settings, you can send the link to the blog to families to share the exciting work.

13. Once kids get the hang of posting, turn on commenting for their posts and have them leave each other posts.

14. For an added fun factor, depending on your privacy settings, share the blog widely and have your colleagues or friends or family leave them comments. Students will be excited to see that people they don't know are reading their work and loving it.

**Grade Level:** Middle Grades

**Goal:** To learn about other cultures and communities through a video chat game.

**Materials:** A computer with Internet connection, camera, and microphone. Projector and screen or whiteboard. A Skype or Google account. Mystery Skype resources from Microsoft: https://education.microsoft.com/skype-in -the-classroom/mystery-skype. Parental and administrative permission for students to participate.

**Process:**

1. Go to https://education.microsoft.com/skype-in-the-classroom/mystery -skype and sign up for Mystery Skype. *You will need a Microsoft account to do this.* Or scan the #mysteryskype hashtag on Twitter to find others to connect with. This can also be done with a Google Hangout if Skype is not available or one or both partners don't have a Microsoft account. If you decide to find your own connections outside of the Microsoft network, *choose a partner that can easily connect with what you are learning in the classroom.*

2. Reach out to potential partners.

3. Once you are connected, do a test call with the teacher from your classroom to make sure that the technology aspect will work on your network and devices. This can be done without your students.

4. Use the resources at the Microsoft Mystery Skype page listed previously to prepare for the conversation. *Your class will ask questions of the other class or expert to try to find out where they are and who they are.*

5. Introduce your students to how the game works and help them prepare by giving them jobs, discussing communication skills, or even practicing with a game of Twenty Questions.

6. Decide how the class will sit during the game. Will they sit on the floor? At their desks?

7. On the big day, do a test of the equipment.

8. Play the game by asking questions of each other. The first class or person who figures out where the other is wins the game.

9. Debrief with the class by discussing what they learned, what went well, what they could improve on for next time. This could also be done on paper.

**Grade Level:** High School

**Goal:** To connect with peers around academic content and build a library of shared resources.

**Prerequisite:** A social bookmarking account (if student is thirteen or older) for each student. If using Diigo Educator account (https://www.diigo.com/education), student accounts can be created with no email required. Scrible integrates with Google Classroom, so classes can be imported from there.

**Materials:** A social bookmarking tool like Diigo (http://diigo.com) or Scrible (http://www.scrible.com). Administrative permission to have students use social bookmarking and information for parents about the site you will be using.

**Process:**

1. Choose a topic or unit of study that you will be teaching that will require students to do research.

2. Sign up for a free Diigo or Scrible account and explore the tools and features.

3. Introduce the tool as part of the unit, explaining that students will be able to collaboratively share resources. Talk about why that might be helpful and ask students how this might make doing research different. Talk about ways that students can use social bookmarking in the classroom.

4. Have students sign up for an account using their school email address, or if using Diigo, you have the option to create their accounts for them.

5. Have students install the browser extension that will allow them to use the tool on any webpage.

6. Give students a small task to do in the tool (e.g., bookmark a site, annotate it, add a comment, etc.) so you can make sure that they know how to use the features that you want them to use. *Emphasize the importance of tagging and organizing their resources. Model proper tagging practices, explaining that consistent tagging and organizing makes for more productivity.*

7. Guide students through the process of making a shared library or sharing resources. Have them share one resource to a shared space.

8. Once students are comfortable with using the tool collectively sharing resources, annotating, and so on, then give them a more complex task or

assignment. This can be a research project, a presentation, or anything else that requires them to do research.

9.  Alternatively, have students use the tool for the rest of the year as they are learning together as a place to put resources for homework, classwork, projects, and so on.

10. Have students reflect from time to time on how they are using the resource and how it could be used better.

## CHAPTER 6 SAMPLE LESSONS: TARGETED ONLINE ADVERTISING
### ISTE Standard for Students

**2d**—Students manage their personal data to maintain digital privacy and security and are aware of data-collection technology used to track their navigation online.

**Grade Level:** Elementary Grades
**Goal:** Be able to identify ads on various websites.
**Materials:** Age-appropriate websites that have ads and websites that don't have ads. Sample sites: http://www.starfall.com, http://www.abcya.com (free version only), http://coolmath.com.
**Process:**

1.  Ask students if they ever see commercials on TV. Ask them what they see in commercials (students should talk about toys or other kinds of products). Ask if they have ever asked their parent to buy them something that they saw in a commercial. Explain that commercials try to get people excited to buy things. Explain that commercials, also called *advertisements*, exist on websites, too.

2.  Tell students that they will now use their eyes to try to spot the commercial or ad.

3.  Pull sites up one by one on large screen for the whole class. Each time, give students ten seconds to look at the site before you ask them to raise their hand if they see an ad.

4.  If you have an interactive whiteboard, students can circle the ads digitally. If not, you can circle them with a dry erase marker or just point them out. Have students explain why they think it's an ad.

5. You can point to the word that says "Advertisement"; you can also click on the ad to see where it takes you (to a different site that has nothing to do with what you were doing).

6. Tell students that advertisers try to "trick" you into clicking on their ads so that they can make money—don't let them trick you!

Continue to reinforce this as students navigate websites online throughout the year. If they get to a strange site, ask them if maybe they got tricked? Explain that students can close the window or click the "back" button to get back to where they were.

**Tips:** Starfall does *not* have ads. If your school blocks ads through filtering software, access the sites at home and take screenshots to show to your students in school.

**Grade Level:** Middle Grades

**Goal:** To recognize "baked-in" ads and sponsored content on various websites and to understand how these ads can be tailored to students individually.

**Materials:** An Internet-enabled device for each student or pair of students. Stanford University's *Evaluating Information Online* resource (https:// purl.stanford.edu/fv751yt5934), marketing websites that show examples (e.g., https://www.wordstream.com/blog/ws/2014/07/07/native-advertising -examples). Local news sites, Instagram (if not blocked at school), http:// gizmodo.com.

**Process:**

1. Ask students to explain what an advertisement is.

2. Ask students where they usually see advertisements. How do they know that they are advertisements?

3. Show students the advertising example from the Stanford resources. See if they can properly identify all of the ads.

4. Ask students why companies might want to make it hard to tell when something is an ad.

5. If Instagram is blocked, asked students about the ads they see there. If it is not blocked, or if students have access to their phones, have them find an ad on their feed. Discuss how they are integrated into the "stream" as if they are someone the students follow. Why might that be?

6. Explain how advertisers make their revenue.
7. Show students other examples from the article. Have students navigate to their local news site or Gizmodo.com and have them find sponsored content that is somewhat hidden or "sneaky." Have them screenshot this to turn it in if you need evidence of what they found.
8. Discuss the ads you found. Ask students if they ever feel "creeped out" by the ads that they see online. Do they feel like someone is "watching them?"
9. Explain how targeted online ads work and how they track students. Ask students how that makes them feel. Explain the pros and cons of tracking (you see more stuff that interests you versus companies have a lot of data about you). Are they okay with the trade off, yes or no?
10. As an exit ticket, have students explain what they now know about online advertising.

As a follow up, share ways that students can manage their privacy online.

**Grade Level:** High School
**Goal:** To know how to take active measures to protect your online privacy from advertisers.
**Prerequisite:** Students should know how to spot online ads of all kinds and understand how they are used to track them and how advertisers use their data to personalize their "ad experience."
**Materials:** Internet-enabled device for each student (this can also be a phone). Ghostery extension (https://www.ghostery.com/products/), AdBlock extension (https://adblockplus.org/), Duck Duck Go Search Engine (https://duckduckgo.com/), Opt-out site (http://optout.networkadvertising.org). *Be sure to check with your school or district IT department about installing browser extensions in case that feature is restricted for your students.*
**Process:**

1. Ask students what they know about online advertising and how it works.
2. Ask students what they know about how companies track them online. Have they ever seen an ad pop up on a different site that contains something that was in their cart on another site?
3. Explain how targeted ads work and fill in any gaps or misunderstandings about how cookies and other tracking methods work.

4.  Explain that students will be learning ways to protect their information from advertisers.

5.  If students have smart phones, have them navigate to their iPhone settings, or on an Android, to their Chrome settings (if they have the app) and turn on the "Do Not Track" feature. Explain that this will help on websites that comply with the request, but it is not foolproof because websites are not required to comply.

6.  Have students install the Ghostery extension. This will show them how many advertisers are tracking them on each site they visit.

7.  Have students install the AdBlock extension. This will show them how many ads are loading on each page they visit. Remind them that some sites will not load properly with an ad blocker running. Ask them why they think that is.

8.  Have students navigate to the Opt-out link and have them run the tool to see how many advertisers have cookies installed on their machine. Students can manually opt out of these if they wish.

9.  Show students the Duck Duck Go search engine, explaining that this search engine does not send identifying information about you to the sites you visit and does not track your search history to sell it to third parties. Have students do a few searches to see how it works.

10. Ask students how they feel about companies tracking them. Ask them three things that they will do based on what they have learned. This can be an exit ticket.

Revisit these conversations throughout the school year.

### CHAPTER 7 SAMPLE LESSONS: PRIVACY IN THE DIGITAL AGE
### ISTE Standard for Students

2d—Students manage their personal data to maintain digital privacy and security and are aware of data-collection technology used to track their navigation online.

**Grade Level:** Elementary Grades
**Goal:** To understand the difference between private and personal information.

**Materials:** Chart paper and markers or projector and screen or board. (Optional) T-chart template for each student with *personal* and *private* on each side.

This lesson should be part of a larger set of lessons around best practices when using the Internet.

**Process:**

1. Ask students what it means when someone is a *stranger*.
2. Ask students if they have ever met or talked to a stranger before.
3. Ask students what kinds of things they might tell a stranger. Record these either on T-Chart on chart paper or on the board.
4. Ask students what kinds of things they would never tell a stranger. Record these items on the T-Chart as well.
5. Explain that *private* information is information that you would never tell a stranger. Review their list and go over each item, making sure that it belongs in that column. (Examples: your full name, your address, birthday, phone number.)
6. Explain that *personal* information is information that is safe to tell a stranger. Review their list and make sure that each item is in the right column. (Examples: your favorite color, what kind of pet you have, your favorite season.)
7. Ask students if they ever play games online or visit websites.
8. Ask students if they have ever been asked by a website to give private information in order to use the site. Did they give the information? Why or why not?
9. Discuss why students shouldn't be giving private information to websites.
10. Follow up by having students complete their own T-Chart as an exit ticket (for older elementary only). *Be sure to check with your school or district IT department about installing browser extensions in case that feature is restricted for your students.*

**Grade Level:** Middle Grades

**Goal:** To understand that when we post online, it is like saying something out loud in public. We never know who is listening.

**Materials:** T-Chart with *coffee shop* and *my bedroom* on each side for each student or pair of students.

**Process:**

1. Ask students if they have ever been surprised by something that somebody has shared publicly about themselves, for instance, something that they themselves wouldn't share. If applicable, ask for examples or provide your own if students don't have their own.

2. Ask students if they have ever gone to a restaurant. What kinds of things do they talk about there? What about in their room at home?

3. Give students the T-chart template and have them work independently or with a partner to list things they would talk about in a coffee shop and things they would only talk about in the privacy of their own room. If needed, provide students with examples to get them started (Examples: your report card grades, your favorite color).

4. Have students share answers with the class. If they worked with a partner, ask if they ever disagreed on where to put a topic of conversation. If they worked individually, point out or ask if anyone put a topic of conversation in a different column than a peer.

5. Make sure that students can differentiate between private information like phone numbers, addresses, credit card numbers, and personal information like favorite food or movie.

6. Ask students if they have ever seen people share things in the "coffee shop" column online. Ask for examples if applicable. Discuss the differences in people's comfort level sharing things online.

7. Explain that people sometimes call it "oversharing" when someone shares a lot of personal information online. Explain that there can be more to be concerned about than simply sharing too much about yourself.

8. Explain that the Internet is like a coffee shop. It's a public place. Ask students why they should keep this in mind when sharing online. Make sure they understand that they may not know who is "listening." It could be a future employer, a parent, law enforcement, or a stranger who may use that information to steal their identity or locate them in "real life."

9. Discuss ways that students can maintain privacy on the Internet. Ask students to share how they protect their privacy before giving them ideas.

**Grade Level:** High School

**Goal:** To know how to adjust technology settings to protect your privacy from advertisers and companies who collect data from their users.

**Materials:** Internet-enabled device for each student, access to the settings of a browser, account access to change settings. (Optional: paper and writing utensil for each student.) For some accounts, students may want to use their phones because some sites may be blocked by a school network filter.

This lesson is only appropriate for students thirteen and older who are legally allowed to have accounts on most websites. All informational links are subject to change but were current at the time of publication.

**Process:**

1.  Ask students what they know about how their information is being shared by the websites that they use. If they don't know, ask them where they can find that information.
2.  Discuss and define *Privacy Policies* with students. Make sure they understand what "third party" means.
3.  Have students explore the Privacy Policies of sites that they use regularly. Students can record something surprising or something they don't understand in what they find on each site.
4.  Ask students about what they found and how it made them feel.
5.  Explain that, for sites that give your information to a third party or where advertisers track you, there may be some things that you can do. Examples are:
    a.  Turning on "Do Not Track" for their browser and their phone. Make sure to explain that this is *voluntary* for sites and most ignore it and track you anyway, but it's worth trying. (iOS directions: https://support.apple.com/guide/safari/prevent-websites-from-tracking-you-sfri40732/mac; Android directions: https://support.google.com/chrome/answer/2790761?co=GENIE.Platform%3DAndroid&hl=en)
    b.  Updating their privacy settings on social media sites they use. This may need to be done on a phone.
    c.  Learning how to download their data from Google (https://support.google.com/accounts/answer/3024190?hl=en) and Facebook (https://www.facebook.com/help/1701730696756992?helpref=hc_global_nav).

d. Checking whether location services are turned on for apps and services they use. (In other words, which apps and services are tracking their location?)

e. Checking to see what permissions they are giving apps and services they use, and which apps and services are linked to their Google Account. (https://support.google.com/accounts/answer/3466521?hl=en)

f. Guide students through these steps at their own pace based around which accounts and services apply to them.

g. Have students share their thoughts on the experience and any changes they may plan on making moving forward. What is one thing they changed about their privacy settings during class? Are there any apps or services that they may stop using now that they know what information they have about them?

## CHAPTER 8 SAMPLE LESSONS: LAWS IN THE DIGITAL CLASSROOM

**ISTE Standard for Students**

**2c**—Students demonstrate an understanding of and respect for the rights and obligations of using and sharing intellectual property.

**Grade Level:** Elementary Grades

**Goal:** To understand that creative works are owned by the person who created the work and why that person might want to let others use their work or why they might not.

**Materials:** Examples of creative works. These could be student created or recognizable famous works.

**Process:**

1. Ask students if they have ever made something. Ask them to share examples.
2. Ask students how they felt about the work and why they created it.
3. Ask students if anyone has ever copied something they created. Discuss how that did or would make them feel and why.
4. Share a work that a classmate or a famous artist, musician, or writer created that they might recognize (e.g., a song that they might know or a children's book they've read).

5. Ask students who made the work and why.

6. Ask them how they think the creator would feel if someone copied their work and why.

7. Explain that there are laws called *copyright laws* that protect the right of the creator of a work to protect their work from other people copying it.

8. Ask students why someone might want to copy someone else's work.

9. Ask students how they think that the famous artist, musician, or writer makes a living. (Students will probably say through their art or works.) Why might they not want someone to copy their work?

10. Explain that it is important to think about the creator of a work before we use it for ourselves. We can always ask permission from the original creator to use their work, and some creators actually tell people how they can use their work so they don't have to ask permission.

11. Ask students to share with a partner or at their table what kinds of ways they'd be okay with others using their work.

12. Ask for students to share their ideas with the class.

Over the school year, the class can create a library of works by students that other students can use in their projects, but they must ask permission from the author first. This could be a bin of drawings, three-dimensional projects, songs, song lyrics, poems, or stories, clearly labeled with the author's name. These would clearly not be able to be submitted as assignments for classwork, but could be added onto an existing project the same way an image from an Internet search might be used.

**Grade Level:** Middle Grades

**Goal:** To know how to find copyright-free images on the Internet and use them, with citation, in a project.

**Materials:** An Internet-enabled device for each student or student pair, access to sites like http://pexels.com, http://pixabay.com, http://commons .wikimedia.org, or http://search.creativecommons.org. Publishing software like Microsoft PowerPoint, Google Slides, or Google Draw (Google Suite for Education is required to use Google products with students younger than thirteen). Students can also use the site Poster My Wall (http://postermywall .com), even if they are younger than thirteen.

This lesson should be a precursor to the project and just a simple way for students to find copyright-free images. A suggested project is a simple, five-slide research presentation related to the unit they are studying that requires at least one copyright-free image *or* a copyright-free image on every slide.

**Process:**

1. When introducing students to their project, explain that they will need to use copyright-free images.
2. Ask students what they know about copyright laws. Clarify any misunderstandings and discuss why copyright law exists and why it matters.
3. Ask students if they have ever used a copyright-free image in a project. If they did, where did they get it from and how did they know that they had permission to use the image?
4. Share the sites in "Materials" with students. This can be done through a shared document, a class webpage, or an online course so they can easily click on the links.
5. Have students search Google images for an image related to the project. Then have them search the other sites and compare what they find.
6. Ask students if they noticed any differences and why they think those differences exist.
7. Explain that students will be using the provided sites to find images for their presentation instead of using a general web search.
8. Model for students how to download the image and how to get the image on their slide as well as how to put a caption indicating where the image came from. This can be very small at the bottom of the slide. For instance, if the image came from Pixabay, they would type, "Image courtesy of (insert user) on Pixabay.")
9. Have students search for images and put one on one of their slides with the correct citation.

**Grade Level:** High School

**Goal:** To properly cite the source of a direct quote, paraphrase, or idea in a paper or project.

**Prerequisite:** Lessons around where to place citations (this will depend on the project type). Also, lessons around what needs to be cited and why. Which form is desired for citation? The most common citation style in high school is MLA citation.

**Materials:** A site like http://citationmachine.net or http://scrible.com or the "Explore" feature in Google Docs. An essay, presentation, or other project that requires citation.

**Process:**

1. Ask students to name a few facts that they know. Ask them where they got those facts and who said them. Tell students that this, essentially, is citation. It is the proof for where information comes from *and* it also gives credit where credit is due when the idea or information we are sharing is not our own.

2. Explain that students will need to use proper academic citations for their projects, which is the way that they will be expected to cite sources in college and academia, and even the workplace. Explain that citations tell the reader about the author, the date of publication, and the title of the piece being referenced.

3. Give students time to do some research to find applicable sources that they can use. If they are using a social bookmarking tool like Scrible, have them bookmark the relevant sites so they don't lose them.

4. If students are using Google Docs to write an essay, show them how they can use the "Explore" feature to search the web for resources and then add the citation directly into their doc.

5. Students can use the citation tool in Scrible to create citations for their sources.

6. If they do not have access to these tools, then Citation Machine is a great resource. They can paste a URL and Citation Machine will populate the citation, which can then be copied and pasted.

7. Remind students that they will need to cite everything that is not their idea, even if they put it in their own words.

8. Have students work on a short paragraph that includes a proper citation and submit it to make sure that they are citing properly. You will want to clarify whether you want endnotes or footnotes as well as the citation format (e.g., MLA, APA).

**CHAPTER 10 SAMPLE LESSONS: ANALYZING SOURCES**
**ISTE Standard for Students**
**3b**—Students evaluate the accuracy, perspective, credibility, and relevance of information, media, data, or other resources.

**Grade Level:** Elementary Grades
**Goal:** To have a basic understanding of how to read webpages.
**Materials:** Internet-enabled device for each student or pairs of students. Projector and board or screen to project onto. A kid-friendly website like National Geographic Kids (http://kids.nationalgeographic.com), FunBrain (http://funbrain.com), Fact Monster (http://factmonster.com), or Scholastic News (https://scholasticnews.scholastic.com/). A checklist of items to find (see Process for ideas).
**Process:**

1. Explain that students will be learning how to read a website.
2. Ask students how reading a website is different than reading a book or magazine.
3. Ask students what kinds of things they read on websites.
4. Explain that students will be going on a reading scavenger hunt on a website to test their website reading skills. Students can work in pairs or individually, depending on your preference. Having them work together could allow stronger readers to be paired with struggling readers.
5. Provide students with links to the sites in "Materials" so they can easily click on them. This can be done through a doc, a class website, or your school's learning management system (e.g., Google Classroom, Edmodo).
6. Students can complete a different checklist for each website, depending on their grade level and time constraints. Or spread out the scavenger hunts over a couple of lessons. Each site has different qualities to explore.
7. Provide students with the scavenger hunt checklist. You can also provide blanks for students to fill in. Sample items include:
   a. Find three advertisements.
   b. What is the name of the website?
   c. Are there places to play games on the website?
   d. Does the website have a store? If yes, what can you buy there?
   e. Do you have to log into the website to use it?

    f.  Find an article or story.
       i.  Who wrote the article or story?
      ii.  When was it written?
    g.  Is there an area of the website specifically for your age or grade level?

8. Have students share their answers with each other or with another partner pair.

9. Review students' answers by having them come up to the front to show where they found items on the list on at least one of the websites. Make sure that students have found all items, guiding them to any they missed. Explain that students now know how to "read" a website.

**Grade Level:** Middle Grades

**Goal:** To be able to analyze a site and decide whether it is accurate or helpful based on evidence.

**Materials:** Internet-enabled device for each student or pairs of students. Projector and board or screen to project onto. Sites related to a topic students are researching, or have students compare the Sierra Club (https://www .sierraclub.org/) with DHMO (http://dhmo.org). A paper or digital template for students to fill out what they find for each letter of the acronym. A paper or digital "cheat sheet" explaining what each letter of the acronym stands for.

    This lesson should be done in conjunction with a research project or unit as a way to prepare students for the project or unit.

**Process:**

1. Ask students if they have ever used a website to find information.

2. Ask them to name websites they have used. Why did they use them? How did they find them?

3. Ask students if they have ever discovered that information that they have found on a website wasn't accurate or true.

4. Explain that students will be completing a research project and that it is important that they know how to find accurate information that they can trust.

5. Explain that they will be using a special method for analyzing websites call *CRAAP* detection (or *PARCA*, if *CRAAP* is not appropriate for your classroom).

6. Distribute the "cheat sheet" (it could be a double-sided paper with "cheat sheet" on one side and the template on the other)

7.  Review each letter of the acronym, explaining what it means, or have students read each one aloud, clarifying the meaning.

8.  Make sure that students have a copy of the template they will be using. Explain how to use the template, even modeling using it with one of the sites if necessary.

9.  Show students the two sites they will be looking at. Make sure to treat both sites equally because students do not, at this point, know whether either site is trustworthy or not.

10. If necessary, do the first letter together with one of the sites (have the class choose which site they want to start with).

11. Have students work independently or in pairs (pairs will allow you to put stronger readers with struggling readers) to complete the template as you walk around and check in on their progress and understanding.

12. Once students have analyzed both sites, have them decide which of the sites they would use (or if they would use both sites) for research around environmental and health concerns.

13. Discuss each site with students, making sure that they understand how to find the information for each of the letters in the acronym and what it means.

14. As a class, decide if you would use these sites for research.

15. Have each student explain why they would or wouldn't use each site and why as an exit ticket to check for student understanding.

**Grade Level:** High School

**Goal:** To be able to independently analyze sites for accuracy.

**Materials:** Internet-enabled device for each student or pairs of students. Projector and board or screen to project onto. Fake News "game" (https://www .channelone.com/feature/quiz-can-you-spot-the-fake-news-story/). Sites related to a topic that students are researching, or have students compare articles on the same topic on different sites. Examples are an AP News article on immigration (https://apnews.com/0a7e7ec16cd743e4840c321a99e005ef) and an immigration article on Breitbart.com (https://www.breitbart.com/ border/2018/12/28/california-police-officer-killed-by-alleged-illegal-alien- was-a-legal-immigrant/). A paper or digital template for students to fill out what they find for each letter of the acronym. A paper or digital "cheat sheet" explaining what each letter of the acronym stands for.

This lesson should be done in conjunction with a research project or unit as a way to prepare students for the project or unit.

**Process:**

1. Ask students what they know about "Fake News," a term that they probably hear a lot these days. Be sure to explain that news is only fake if the story is completely made up or the facts are not true. Sometimes stories can be misleading or spread misinformation and still be about real events.
2. Explain that students will be learning how to analyze sites so that they can decide if what they are reading is trustworthy or not.
3. Explain that first, students will take a short "quiz" to test their ability to judge if something they are reading is fake news.
4. Have students go through the quiz here: https://www.channelone.com/feature/quiz-can-you-spot-the-fake-news-story/.
5. Review the answers, pointing out the clues provided that help distinguish a story as real or fake.
6. Explain that students will now have to analyze sites to see if they are trustworthy or not.
7. Show students the *CRAAP* acronym and ask if any students have ever seen it or used it. If they have, ask them to help explain what each letter means, clarifying as necessary.
8. Provide students with the paper or digital "cheat sheet" and template and have them work individually or in pairs to analyze the two sites.
9. Walk around and check in with students to make sure that they are on track and ask them questions about what they are finding and whether they think the site they are looking at is a quality source and why.
10. Once students have evaluated both sites, pull them up one at a time and ask students if they would use the site and why. Review each aspect of the acronym.
11. Make sure that students have noticed the biased language of Breitbart and the store on the site. Make sure that students have looked up the authors of both articles and noticed that the AP author has a verified Twitter account. Be sure that students have researched the publisher (website) of each story as well.
12. As a follow up, provide this cheat sheet as students build their own list of sites to use for their research.

## CHAPTER 11 SAMPLE LESSONS: DECONSTRUCTING IMAGES
### ISTE Standard for Students

**3b**—Students evaluate the accuracy, perspective, credibility, and relevance of information, media, data, or other resources.

**Grade Level:** Elementary Grades
**Goal:** To analyze images by asking questions.
**Materials:** One to two engaging images. Samples: http://hdl.loc.gov/loc.pnp/fsa.8a37082 (Greene County Fair Whites Only day), https://flic.kr/p/dKR2nr (Children in the snow). These images can be projected on a board or printed for students to view at their seats or provided digitally for students to access on a device. For older elementary students, provide paper and a writing utensil or another way to record their thoughts about the image.

This lesson should be part of a larger unit around research or inquiry or even visual storytelling.
**Process:**

1. Ask students to name their favorite picture book. If needed, give them examples from class to help them understand what you mean by "picture book."

2. Have students share why this is their favorite book. Have them talk about the pictures in the book. Do they think that the pictures could tell the story of the book even if there were no words?

3. Explain that pictures do tell stories, and we can even find our own stories in pictures.

4. Explain that today, students will be telling their own stories about a picture kind of like their favorite picture books. However, they will only be using one picture to tell their story.

5. Tell students that when you show them the image, you want them to look at it for ten seconds without saying anything and think about what is going on in the picture.

6. Show students an image and count down from ten, reminding them to look carefully at the image and think about the story behind the image. Older elementary students can write down the story. You may want to give them more time.

7.  When time is up, ask students who they think is in the picture. Make sure to have them justify their answers. What clues do they see in the picture? For example, in the case of the children at the gate, why do they think the children in the foreground are watching the other children?

8.  Have students explain what they think is going on in the picture. Where is this happening? How do they know? For example, in the case of the children in the snow, they should consider what parts of the world have snow.

9.  Continue to pose questions. What kind of clothing are they wearing? When do they think the picture was taken? Who took the picture? Make sure to let students ask their questions first, only prompting if they need it.

10. Ask students how they could find out if they are right about the image. After soliciting ideas, make sure that they understand that someone took the photograph, so that person should know the whole story.

11. Show students the origin of the image and tell the true story of the image.

12. Have students compare the true story with their imagined story. What did they get right? What did they get wrong? What clues did they get and which did they miss?

13. Explain that while images can tell stories, it's not always clear what the real story is unless we can talk directly to the person who took the picture. In this case, the photographer left some information about the image to help us out.

14. Explain the importance of understanding the difference between the story we see in an image and the real story. Asking questions helps us better understand what may be going on in an image and finding the person who took the image is our best bet.

Continue to prompt students to ask questions when they come across images in their research, their textbooks, and other books that they read.

**Grade Level:** Middle Grades

**Goal:** To understand that sometimes captions on images can be misleading and how to find out if the image they are looking at matches the meme text or caption it is paired with.

**Materials:** Three images paired with text either as a caption or in "meme" style. At least one of these should be incorrectly described by the text. Example links and captions:

- NYC Subway flooded after Hurricane Sandy (https://gizmodoemergency .files.wordpress.com/2012/10/48.jpg).
- John McCain started a fire on a navy ship (https://www.factcheck .org/2018/08/after-mccains-death-a-false-claim-resurfaces/).
- Donald Trump *People Magazine* meme (https://www.snopes.com/fact -check/1998-trump-people-quote/).
- Photo of a fire on the Cuyahoga River in Ohio (http://time.com/3921976/ cuyahoga-fire/).

These images and their captions should be provided digitally for students so they can access them on their own devices. You can also make your own using a meme generator like https://imgflip.com/memegenerator.
**Process:**

1. Ask students to describe their favorite meme. Make sure they describe the image. Ask them where the image came from. If they provide an answer, ask them to explain how they know the origin.
2. Explain that we often see images paired with text online and it's not always clear where the images come from, but we often trust the caption or text more than we should.
3. Show students the image of a flooded subway tunnel. Ask them what they know about the image and what is in the image. Ask them what they know about the text paired with the image. Is the fact correct?
4. Ask students how the image made them feel. Did they feel sad? Did they feel scared? Were they indifferent? Why might that matter?
5. Confirm or debunk the image as a class by modeling how to do a reverse image search of the image. A reverse image search of the flooded subway should show multiple articles related to the disaster. Click on a few and review them as a class. Alternately, have students do their own reverse image search once they are shown how to do it.
6. Discuss what students find and decide if the image and caption match.

7. Give students the McCain image along with a misleading caption, the Trump meme, and the Cuyahoga River fire image with an accurate caption. Have them work individually or in pairs to try to discover whether the text and the images match. Give students fifteen to twenty minutes.
8. Come back together and discuss what students found.
9. Ask students what they learned about images that they see online. Explain that they should always do their own research when they see images online.

**Grade Level:** High School
**Goal:** To understand how images can be misused to sway opinions and influence people.
**Materials:** Story about fake ballot boxes in Ohio during 2016 presidential campaign (https://www.snopes.com/fact-check/clinton-votes-found-in-warehouse/). Fake tweet generator (http://www.prankmenot.com/?twitter_tweet) or fake news headline (https://breakyourownnews.com/).
**Process:**

1. Ask students if they have ever seen someone share a meme or image that later was exposed as fake. Why do they think someone would share something that is not true?
2. Show students one of the real examples from the middle school lesson as well as an image from the Snopes article listed in the materials. Ask students which one they think is real and why. If possible, provide them with digital versions of the images so they can do a reverse image search.
3. Ask students why someone would go through the trouble of digitally altering an image and pairing it with that article. How did they feel when they saw the headline and the image? Why does that matter?
4. Explain that images can easily be taken out of context to prove a point or tell a false story and often people will believe them blindly because the altered image reinforces their own beliefs.
5. Show students the *prankmenot.com* and the *breakyourownnews.com* sites. Challenge them to create a fake post that misuses a real image to tell a different story and sway others' opinions.
6. Time permitting, hold a "fake news awards" competition and have them vote for the most convincing fake story.

7. Wrap up by reinforcing that students should always do their research before trusting something just because it has an image to back it up.

## CHAPTER 12 SAMPLE LESSONS: FAKE NEWS IN THE DIGITAL AGE
**ISTE Standard for Students: Knowledge Constructor**
**3b**—Students evaluate the accuracy, perspective, credibility, and relevance of information, media, data, or other resources.

**Grade Level:** Elementary Grades
**Goal:** To understand the difference between fact, fiction, and opinion.
**Materials:** Sample phrases that are fact, fiction, and opinion. A projector and screen or board (interactive white board optional). Paper, scissors, glue, or digital document containing phrases.

This lesson should be part of a larger series of activities and lessons around fact and opinion in order for it to be reinforced.
**Process:**

1. Ask students how they know if someone is telling the truth. (Answers might range from their body language and eye contact to the fact that they already know what is true.)
2. After students share, give them two statements such as "ice is cold," and "seven plus three is four." Ask them if either one is true, and how they know that it is true. Explain that when something is true, it can be proven 100 percent of the time.
3. Explain that we can often tell what is true based on our own personal experiences and observations or we can prove whether something is true through our own research. Everyone has held an ice cube or put one in their mouth at some point and knows that they are cold. Students can use mathematical reasoning to figure out the seven plus three is *not* four. Explain that when things are not true, we call them *fiction* or *false*.
4. Now give students the phrases "pizza is good" and "pizza is made of bread, cheese, and tomato sauce." Ask them which one is true. They may argue that the first one is true, but ask them if it is possible that someone does not like pizza. If this is possible, then is that phrase true? If people do like pizza, then is it false? Guide students through the idea that this is

an *opinion* and that opinions are not facts. They cannot be proven 100 percent of the time.

5.  Next, either give students a worksheet with various phrases on it that they can cut out (or have them precut) and a chart with three sections labeled *fact*, *fiction*, and *opinion*. Have students glue the phrases in the correct area of the chart.

6.  Alternatively, do this as a whole class using an interactive white board to drag phrases to the correct areas of the chart, or provide them with a digital document where they can cut and paste the phrases into the correct areas of a digital chart.

**Grade Level:** Middle Grades

**Goal:** Understand what an *expert* is and how to find the author of articles we read online.

**Materials:** All About Explorers (https://allaboutexplorers.com), Mariner's Museum (https://exploration.marinersmuseum.org/type/age-of-discovery), Duckster Explorers Information (https://www.ducksters.com/biography/explorers), ESPN.com (http://www.espn.com).

**Process:**

1.  Ask students to name someone they trust when it comes to getting help with their math homework. This can include the teacher, but should include at least two other people. Write some examples somewhere for easy viewing and referencing by the class, and have the students explain why they would ask these people. Make these notes next to the people named.

2.  Review the responses as a class and ask if they would ask these same people for help with their Spanish homework. Make sure to ask students why they would or wouldn't ask these same people. Answers should include that the people they would ask for help with their math homework have experience or knowledge of math; although there is a possibility that the math experts might have experience with Spanish, they would probably find someone with expertise in the subject area.

3.  Explain that, as the students have explained, some people we know have more information about a topic than others, and we tend to rely on these

people when we need information about a topic. We call these people *experts*.

4. Ask if students know where to find the author of a website or online article. If they do, let them come up to the class and point one out on an ESPN.com article. If not, have them scan the article and look for an author's name.

5. Ask students how you can find out more about the author. Explain that, most of the time, by clicking on an author's name, you can find out more about who wrote the story. On ESPN.com, hovering your mouse over the author's name gives you more information.

6. As a class, decide if the author of the article would qualify as an expert for the article or not.

7. Explain that students will be trying to find information about an explorer (e.g., Christopher Columbus, Ferdinand Magellan, Henry Hudson). Provide them with a few simple questions such as "What did the explorer discover?" or "When did the explorer do most of the exploring?"

8. If students have access to their own device or can share one, have them navigate to each of the sites (All About Explorers, Mariner's Museum, Ducksters) and look for answers to their questions. They should locate the authors of each site or article to decide whether they think the author is an expert. Tell them to be ready to defend their answer.

9. Have students write down what they find and on which site and then have them compare their answers with a peer or peer group.

10. Ask students as a whole group if they found any information that didn't match the others (this should be information from the All About Explorer's site). Ask students about the authors on the site that had the different information. Do they believe that the author is an expert or not?

11. Ask students what might have happened if they were asked to do a research assignment about Christopher Columbus and they used the All About Explorers site without looking to see if the author was an expert. (Answers should be along the lines of failing the assignment, getting the wrong information, etc.)

12. Ask students, "What if you can't find an author? Would you still use the source?" The main idea here is that, ideally, no. If you can verify the information in at least three other places, you may be okay, but don't make that site one that you use a lot.

13. Wrap up by reminding students to think about whether the information they are reading comes from an expert or not before using it or believing it.

Continue to reinforce this as students navigate websites online throughout the year for research and other purposes. Have them continue to practice trying to find the author on various sites and checking the "About" page because it looks different and can be found in different places on different sites.

**Grade Level:** High School
**Goal:** Understand how the author's purpose affects the reporting of the news.
**Materials:** A local news website, paper for each student, or a template with three columns with headings. *If your community does not have a local news website, try to find one that is closest to your community.*
**Process:**

1. Ask students where they would go to find out what is going on in their neighborhood, town, or city.
2. Discuss various sites and then show students the local news website and look through some of the headlines. Jot a few down on the board.
3. Ask students, just based on the headlines, what they think the articles are about and why.
4. Explain that articles usually have one of three goals: to inform, to entertain, or to persuade. This is called the *author's purpose.* Headlines often help an author get his or her purpose across.
5. Discuss which headlines seem like they are meant to inform, which are meant to entertain, and which are meant to persuade.
6. Explain that students will be writing their own news story with a purpose.
7. Brainstorm some topics for the news stories. They could be based on school events, community events, or even classroom news.
8. Have students create three columns on a piece of paper or have pre-made templates. Students should put "Inform" at the top of one column, "Entertain" at the top of another, and "Persuade" at the top of another.
9. Students then need to choose a news event and write a sample headline that matches each purpose on their template. This may require more detailed instruction and modeling, so you may want to have a sample ready.

10. Students then work on their news article. They can choose one of their headlines and write a very brief article that matches the purpose of the headline (inform, entertain, or persuade).

11. When they are done, have them read their articlees to each other. To make it a game, have them read the story out loud to a neighbor to see if their classmate can determine the author's purpose.

12. Explain that it is important to understand the purpose behind what we are reading because sometimes entertainment and persuasion (bias) are made to look like informational news stories. Remind them to look at the headlines, too.

Continue to reinforce this as students work through nonfiction texts and news stories throughout the year. Continue to ask them why they think the author wrote the article, and whether what they are reading is actually news. This should cross over into anything and everything they read.

**TIPS:** Preview the website ahead of time to choose a page or places where students can find headlines that meet all three criteria (inform, entertain, persuade). If students have their own machines, you can give them the links and have them collaborate to try to figure out what a story is about just through the headline.

## CHAPTER 13 SAMPLE LESSONS: FREE SPEECH AND THE INTERNET
### ISTE Standard for Students

**2b**—Students engage in positive, safe, legal, and ethical behavior when using technology, including social interactions online or when using networked devices.

**Grade Level:** Elementary Grades

**Goal:** To understand the rights laid out in the First Amendment and why they matter.

**Materials:** Writing utensils and paper for each student, the text of the First Amendment (also prepare a version that is suitable for students' grade level/). This lesson can be done as a classroom culture building activity or as part of a unit around freedom of speech. Before the lesson, make sure that students understand what "rights" are.

**Process:**

1.  Ask students to list on a piece of paper two rights that they think are most important for students to have in order for the classroom to be a safe and happy place.
2.  Have students share their rights with two other students, or with their table group. Have the partners or table group combine their lists, eliminating duplicate answers.
3.  Walk around and listen to students share and discuss, helping them build their new lists.
4.  Have each new group share their lists with the class.
5.  Ask students to name which rights they heard repeated the most.
6.  Write these on the board or on chart paper or record them digitally.
7.  Explain that students just went through the same process that the founders of our country went through when the United States was first formed. The founders created a "Bill of Rights" to protect the rights of citizens and help make the country safe and happy.
8.  Ask students if they have ever heard people mention "Freedom of Speech."
9.  Explain that this freedom is in the Bill of Rights.
10. Read the First Amendment to students and, depending on their age, help them break it apart so that they can understand what it means.
11. Ask students to make connections to the First Amendment and their list of classroom rights.
12. Explain that students should keep these rights in mind as they interact in the classroom.

Continue the discussion by making similar connections to other areas of the Bill of Rights in classes that follow.

**Grade Level:** Middle Grades
**Goal:** To understand what kinds of speech are protected and which kinds aren't.
**Materials:** A copy of the First Amendment, sample forms of speech (some legal, some illegal), important court cases, a "cheat sheet" of protected and unprotected speech (see Chapter 13 for a table explaining the most common kinds of protected and unprotected speech).

**Process:**

1. Ask students to name what they think are the most important aspects of our democracy. What makes us a "free country?" Record their ideas on the board.
2. Ask students if they are familiar with the Bill of Rights. What is it?
3. Show students the First Amendment and read it over as a class. Have students explain each aspect of the amendment according to their best knowledge and clear up any misconceptions or misunderstandings. Be sure that students understand that the First Amendment is the first part of the Bill of Rights.
4. Ask students if they think that all speech is protected. If they answer "no," ask them what they think is not protected. If they say "yes," ask them for some examples.
5. Explain that there are some kinds of speech that are not protected. Give an example of speech that threatens someone's safety.
6. Distribute the "cheat sheet." This can be done digitally or on paper. This sheet should be as complex or simple as needed for your grade level.
7. Briefly review the cheat sheet with students.
8. Give students a sample scenario (see Textbox 13.1 in Chapter 13 for examples) and ask them if they think the speech is protected. They must back up their answer with evidence from the cheat sheet.
9. Give students three to five scenarios and have them work with partners to try to figure out if the speech is protected or not.
10. Have students compare their answers with another partner group.
11. Go over the answers together as a class to clear up any misunderstandings.
12. Have students complete an exit ticket explaining two things they learned about the First Amendment.

**Grade Level:** High School
**Goal:** To understand how the First Amendment plays out in schools and social media.
**Prerequisite:** The Middle Grades lesson or a similar lesson that provides students a basic understanding the First Amendment.
**Materials:** Examples of First Amendment cases involving students and social media (see Chapter 13 for examples).

This lesson assumes that students have already spent time discussing and understanding the First Amendment.

**Process:**

1. Ask students what they know about First Amendment rights and how they extend (or don't extend) into schools.
2. Provide students with an example of a school disciplining a student over a social media post. This could be a real or imagined example.
3. After reviewing the story, either project or write a statement such as "The school was right to suspend the student" on the board.
4. Direct students to stand on one side of the room if they agree with the statement, and on the other if they disagree. If they are not sure or are undecided, they can stand in the middle. If, at any point, students change their stance, they can move to a different part of the room.
5. Once students are situated, have them take turns sharing why they are standing where they are. It may be helpful to have something for them to hold or toss as they take turns. Make sure that they back up their statements with references to the First Amendment and even specific examples that can be compared with the example given.
6. Once all students have had a chance to share their thoughts, either give a quick recap of what you heard by simply restating the major points that were made or ask a student to do a recap.
7. You can have students complete an exit ticket explaining either their takeaway from the discussion or explaining a new perspective that they heard in the discussion.

As a follow up lesson, give students a real or imagined scenario and have them choose a stance and argue that stance in an essay that is well-researched and contains legal precedents and specific applications of the First Amendment. Or have students participate in a debate around a similar First Amendment topic. Be sure that they are required to provide legal precedences and research.

# Notes

## CHAPTER 1

1. "Digital Literacy," ALA's Literacy Clearinghouse, July 17, 2017, accessed October 5, 2018, https://literacy.ala.org/digital-literacy/.

2. Jazzy Wright, "ALA Task Force Releases Digital Literacy Recommendations," United for Libraries, June 18, 2013, accessed October 5, 2018, http://www.ala.org/news/press-releases/2013/06/ala-task-force-releases-digital-literacy-recommendations.

3. "About Us," DigitalLiteracy.gov, accessed October 5, 2018, https://digitalliteracy.gov/about.

4. "ISTE Standards for Students," International Society for Technology in Education, accessed October 8, 2018, https://www.iste.org/standards/for-students.

5. *Advancing Educational Technology in Teacher Preparation*, US Department of Education, Office of Educational Technology, Education Technology and Teacher Preparation Brief, Washington, DC, 2016.

6. "ISTE Standards for Educators," International Society for Technology in Education, accessed November 9, 2018, https://www.iste.org/standards/for-educators.

**CHAPTER 2**

1. "Kids and Tech: The Evolution of Today's Digital Natives," *Influence Central*, accessed July 27, 2018, http://influence-central.com/kids-tech-the-evolution-of -todays-digital-natives/.

2. V. Rideout, *The Common Sense Census: Media Use by Kids Age Zero to Eight* (San Francisco, CA: Common Sense Media, 2017).

3. Rideout, *The Common Sense Census.*

4. Rideout, *The Common Sense Census.*

5. V. Rideout and M. B. Robb, *Social Media, Social Life: Teens Reveal Their Experiences* (San Francisco, CA: Common Sense Media, 2018).

6. "Multitasking: Switching Costs," American Psychological Association, accessed November 1, 2018, https://www.apa.org/research/action/multitask.aspx.

7. danah boyd, *It's Complicated: The Social Lives of Networked Teens* (New Haven, CT: Yale University Press, 2015).

8. boyd, *It's Complicated.*

9. D. G. Krutka and J. P. Carpenter, "Participatory Learning through Social Media: How and Why Social Studies Educators Use Twitter," *Contemporary Issues in Technology and Teacher Education* 16, no. 1 (2016): 38–59.

10. Taylor Lorenz, "'Flop Accounts' Are the New Teen Thing on Instagram." *Atlantic*, July 30, 2018, accessed August 15, 2018, https://www.theatlantic.com/ technology/archive/2018/07/the-instagram-forums-where-teens-go-to-debate-big -issues/566153/.

11. Amanda Lenhart, "Meeting, Hanging Out and Staying in Touch: The Role of Digital Technology in Teen Friendships," Pew Research Center: Internet, Science and Tech, August 6, 2015, accessed August 15, 2018, http://www.pewinternet .org/2015/08/06/chapter-1-meeting-hanging-out-and-staying-in-touch-the-role-of -digital-technology-in-teen-friendships/.

12. Matt Ivester, *lol . . . OMG! What Every Student Needs to Know about Online Reputation Management, Digital* (Createspace, 2011).

13. Jon Ronson, "How One Stupid Tweet Blew Up Justine Sacco's Life." *New York Times*, February 12, 2015, accessed August 18, 2018, https://www.nytimes .com/2015/02/15/magazine/how-one-stupid-tweet-ruined-justine-saccos-life.html.

14.   "UCLA Student Leaves School over Anti-Asian Rant," *New York Times*, March 19, 2011, accessed August 18, 2018, https://www.nytimes.com/2011/03/20/us/20rant .html.

15.   "Fire Lindsey Stone and Jamie Schuh," Change.org, accessed August 20, 2018, https://www.change.org/p/life-living-independently-forever-fire-lindsey-stone-and -jamie-schuh.

16.   Ed Pilkington, "Tyler Clementi, Student Outed as Gay on Internet, Jumps to His Death," *Guardian*, September 30, 2010, accessed September 28, 2018, https:// www.theguardian.com/world/2010/sep/30/tyler-clementi-gay-student-suicide.

17.   "Authorities Subpoena Rutgers for E-mails Regarding Tyler Clementi Complaint of Roommate's Webcam," NJ.com, October 7, 2010, accessed September 28, 2018, https://www.nj.com/news/index.ssf/2010/10/middlesex_prosecutor_ subpoenas.html.

18.   Mark Ward, "What the Net Did Next," *BBC News*, January 1, 2004, accessed September 28, 2018, http://news.bbc.co.uk/2/hi/technology/3292043.stm.

19.   Tristan Harris, "How a Handful of Tech Companies Control Billions of Minds Every Day," *TED: Ideas Worth Spreading*, 2017, accessed October 07, 2018, https:// www.ted.com/talks/tristan_harris_the_manipulative_tricks_tech_companies_use_ to_capture_your_attention.

20.   American Academy of Child and Adolescent Psychiatry, "Teen Brain: Behavior, Problem Solving, and Decision Making," accessed September 06, 2018, https://www.aacap.org/aacap/Families_and_Youth/Facts_for_Families/FFF-Guide/ The-Teen-Brain-Behavior-Problem-Solving-and-Decision-Making-095.aspx.

21.   "Corrigendum: The Pen Is Mightier Than the Keyboard: Advantages of Longhand Over Laptop Note Taking." *Psychological Science* 29, no. 9 (2018): 1565– 568, doi:10.1177/0956797618781773.

22.   Nellie Bowles, "A Dark Consensus about Screens and Kids Begins to Emerge in Silicon Valley," *New York Times*, October 26, 2018, accessed November 04, 2018, https://www.nytimes.com/2018/10/26/style/phones-children-silicon-valley.html.

## CHAPTER 3

1.   Barry Leiner, Vinton Cerf, David Clark, Robert Kahn, Leonard Kleinrock, Daniel Lynch, Jon Postel, Larry Roberts, and Stephen Wolff, "Brief History of the

Internet," Internet Society, accessed July 10, 2017, http://www.internetsociety.org/internet/what-internet/history-internet/brief-history-internet.

2.    Defense Advanced Research Projects Agency (DARPA), "Where the Future Becomes Now," accessed July 31, 2017, https://www.darpa.mil/about-us/darpa-history-and-timeline.

3.    "Lawrence Roberts," Internet Hall of Fame, accessed July 11, 2017, http://internethalloffame.org/inductees/lawrence-roberts.

4.    DARPA, "ARPANET," accessed July 09, 2017, http://www.darpa.mil/about-us/timeline/arpanet.

5.    "The Invention of the Internet," History.com, accessed July 10, 2017, http://www.history.com/topics/inventions/invention-of-the-internet.

6.    Jonathan Strickland, "How ARPANET Works," HowStuffWorks.com, accessed July 11, 2017, http://computer.howstuffworks.com/arpanet1.htm.

7.    Vangie Beal, "Packet Switching," Webopedia.com, accessed July 09, 2017, http://www.webopedia.com/TERM/P/packet_switching.html.

8.    Leonard Kleinrock, "The Day the Infant Internet Uttered Its First Words," accessed July 8, 2017, https://www.lk.cs.ucla.edu/internet_first_words.html.

9.    "TCP/IP," History-Computer.com, accessed July 12, 2017, http://history-computer.com/Internet/Maturing/TCPIP.html; "RFC 793—Transmission Control Protocol," faqs.org, accessed July 12, 2017, http://www.faqs.org/rfcs/rfc793.html.

10.    Vangie Beal, "TCP—Transmission Control Protocol," Webopedia.com, accessed July 11, 2017, http://www.webopedia.com/TERM/T/TCP.html.

11.    Leiner, Cerf, Clark, et al., "Brief History of the Internet."

12.    "Paul Mockapetris," Internet Hall of Fame, accessed July 10, 2017, http://internethalloffame.org/inductees/paul-mockapetris.

13.    "Raymond Tomlinson." Internet Hall of Fame, accessed July 12, 2017, http://internethalloffame.org/official-biography-raymond-tomlinson.

14.    "The Inventor of Email Is VA Shiva Ayyadurai," accessed July 13, 2017, http://www.inventorofemail.com/.

15.    "RFC 561—Standardizing Network Mail Headers," faqs.org, accessed July 12, 2017, http://www.faqs.org/rfcs/rfc561.html.

16. National Science Foundation, "A Brief History of NSF and the Internet," accessed July 13, 2017, https://www.nsf.gov/news/news_summ.jsp?cntn_id=103050.

17. "History of the Web: Sir Tim Berners Lee," World Wide Web Foundation, accessed July 13, 2017, http://webfoundation.org/about/vision/history-of-the-web/.

18. National Science Foundation, "A Brief History."

19. "Netscape IPO 20th Anniversary: Read Fortune's 2005 Oral History of the Birth of the Web," Fortune.com, accessed July 13, 2017, http://fortune.com/2015/08/09/remembering-netscape/.

20. "What You Need to Know about the FCC's 2015 Net Neutrality Regulation," Cnet.com, accessed July 13, 2017, https://www.cnet.com/news/13-things-you-need-to-know-about-the-fccs-net-neutrality-regulation/.

21. "Meet the Man John Oliver Just Called 'Doofy,'" Cnet.com, accessed July 13, 2017, https://www.cnet.com/news/fcc-chair-dishes-on-plan-to-rewrite-net-neutrality-rules/; Federal Communication Commission, "FCC Acts to Restore Internet Freedom," FCC News, December 14, 2017, accessed September 10, 2018, https://docs.fcc.gov/public/attachments/DOC-348261A1.pdf.

22. Tim Berners-Lee, "Frequently Asked Questions," accessed July 13, 2017, https://www.w3.org/People/Berners-Lee/FAQ.html.

23. "Ethernet," TechTerms.com, accessed July 13, 2017, https://techterms.com/definition/ethernet.

24. Curt Franklin, "How Routers Work," HowStuffWorks.com, accessed July 13, 2017, http://computer.howstuffworks.com/router2.htm.

25. "Transatlantic Cable," Enyclopedia.com, accessed July 24, 2017, https://www.encyclopedia.com/science-and-technology/technology/technology-terms-and-concepts/transatlantic-cable#3406400955.

26. "Aboard the Ship Laying the Groundwork for Global Communications," accessed July 14, 2017, http://www.cbsnews.com/news/transatlantic-cable-150-years-new-installment-undersea-te-connectivity-subcom-global-communications/.

27. "This Is How a Router Really Works," Mashable.com, accessed July 14, 2017, http://mashable.com/2013/02/04/router-faq/.

28. Vangie Beal, "Intranet," Webopedia.com, accessed July 13, 2017, http://www.webopedia.com/TERM/I/Intranet.html.

29.   Megan Ellis, "How Does a Router Work? A Simple Explanation," MakeUseOf .com, accessed July 13, 2017, http://www.makeuseof.com/tag/technology-explained -how-does-a-router-work/.

30.   Andrew Meola, "How the Internet of Things Will Affect Security and Privacy," *Business Insider*, accessed July 13, 2017, http://www.businessinsider.com/internet-of -things-security-privacy-2016-8.

31.   "Security Tip (ST04-015): Understanding Denial-of-Service Attacks," US Department of Homeland Security CISA, accessed July 14, 2017, https://www.us -cert.gov/ncas/tips/ST04-015.

32.   "Dyn Analysis Summary of Friday October 21 Attack," Oracle Dyn, accessed July 14, 2017, https://dyn.com/blog/dyn-analysis-summary-of-friday-october-21- attack/; "DDoS Attack That Disrupted Internet Was Largest of Its Kind in History, Experts Say," *Guardian*, accessed July 14, 2017, https://www.theguardian.com/ technology/2016/oct/26/ddos-attack-dyn-mirai-botnet.

33.   "Ransomware," Department of Homeland Security CISA, accessed July 31, 2017, https://www.us-cert.gov/security-publications/Ransomware.

34.   Department of Homeland Security, "Recognizing and Avoiding Email Scams," accessed July 15, 2017, https://www.us-cert.gov/sites/default/files/publications/ emailscams_0905.pdf.

35.   "Google Docs Phishing Campaign," Department of Homeland Security CISA, accessed July 15, 2017, https://www.us-cert.gov/ncas/current-activity/2017/05/04/ Google-Docs-Phishing-Campaign.

36.   "Protect against Wifi Hacking—What You Need at the Coffee Shop," Truthfinder.com, accessed July 14, 2017, https://www.truthfinder.com/infomania/ safety/protect-against-wifi-hacking/.

37.   "Seymour Papert's Legacy: Thinking about Learning, and Learning. . . ," accessed July 15, 2017, https://tltl.stanford.edu/content/seymour-papert-s-legacy -thinking-about-learning-and-learning-about-thinking.

38.   "Internet Access in US Public Schools and Classrooms: 1994–2005," US Department of Education, accessed July 15, 2017, https://nces.ed.gov/ pubs2007/2007020.pdf.

39.   Natasha Lomas, "Google's Right to Be Forgotten Appeal Heading to Europe's Top Court," TechCrunch.com, accessed July 15, 2017, https://techcrunch

.com/2017/07/19/googles-right-to-be-forgotten-appeal-heading-to-europes-top
-court/.

## CHAPTER 4

1. "Archie," Techopedia.com, accessed July 23, 2018, https://www.techopedia.com/definition/5338/archie.

2. "What Was the First Search Engine?" wiseGEEK.com, accessed August 1, 2017, http://www.wisegeek.com/what-was-the-first-search-engine.htm.

3. "How Search Algorithms Work, accessed August 1, 2017, https://www.google.com/insidesearch/howsearchworks/algorithms.html.

4. "Bing," Britannica.com, accessed August 12, 2017, https://www.britannica.com/topic/Bing-search-engine.

5. "Baidu," Wikipedia.com, accessed August 12, 2017, https://en.wikipedia.org/wiki/Baidu.

6. "Mission and History," JSTOR, accessed December 18, 2018, https://about.jstor.org/mission-history/.

## CHAPTER 5

1. Mizuko Ito, Heather Horst, Matteo Bittanti, danah boyd, Becky Herr
-Stephenson, Patricia G. Lange, C. J. Pascoe, and Laura Robinson, "Living and
Learning with New Media: Summary of Findings from the Digital Youth Project,"
*The John D. and Catherine T. MacArthur Foundation Reports on Digital Media and
Learning,* November 2008, http://digitalyouth.ischool.berkeley.edu/files/report/
digitalyouth-WhitePaper.pdf.

2. "About LiveJournal," LiveJournal.com, accessed October 5, 2018, https://www.livejournal.com/about/.

3. danah m. boyd, Nicole B. Ellison, "Social Network Sites: Definition, History,
and Scholarship," Journal of Computer-Mediated Communication 13, no. 1
(October 1, 2007): 210–30, https://doi.org/10.1111/j.1083-6101.2007.00393.x.

4. Ito et al., "Living and Learning."

5. "Social Media," *Merriam-Webster.com*, accessed November 5, 2018, https://www.merriam-webster.com/dictionary/social media.

6.   Amanda Lenhart, "Teens, Technology and Friendships," Pew Research Center, August, 2015, http://www.pewinternet.org/2015/08/06/teens-technology-and -friendships/.

7.   "Instagram Ranked Worst for Young People's Mental Health," Royal Society for Public Health, May 19, 2017, accessed October 4, 2018, https://www.rsph.org.uk/ about-us/news/instagram-ranked-worst-for-young-people-s-mental-health.html.

8.   Bo Burnam, dir. "Eighth Grade," 2018, New York, NY: A24. For more information, visit IMDb, August 3, 2018, accessed November 26, 2018, https://www .imdb.com/title/tt7014006/.

9.   Jean M. Twenge, Thomas E. Joiner, Megan L. Rogers, and Gabrielle N. Martin, "Increases in Depressive Symptoms, Suicide-Related Outcomes, and Suicide Rates among US Adolescents after 2010 and Links to Increased New Media Screen Time," *Clinical Psychological Science* 6, no. 1 (January 2018): 3–17. doi:10.1177/2167702617723376.

10.   Tristan Harris, "How Better Tech Could Protect Us from Distraction," TED, December 2014, accessed November 6, 2018, https://www.ted.com/talks/tristan_ harris_how_better_tech_could_protect_us_from_distraction/.

11.   "Instagram Ranked Worst."

12.   G. S. Okeeffe and K. Clarke-Pearson, "The Impact of Social Media on Children, Adolescents, and Families," *Pediatrics* 127, no. 4 (April 2011): 800–804. doi:10.1542/peds.2011-0054.

13.   "Instagram Ranked Worst."

14.   Jonah Engel Bromwich, "How the Parkland Students Got So Good at Social Media," *New York Times*, March 7, 2018, accessed December 12, 2018, https://www .nytimes.com/2018/03/07/us/parkland-students-social-media.html.

15.   Jared Keller, "Evaluating Iran's Twitter Revolution," *Atlantic*, June 18, 2010, accessed November 16, 2018, https://www.theatlantic.com/technology/ archive/2010/06/evaluating-irans-twitter-revolution/58337/.

16.   S. Tuzel, and R. Hobbs, "The Use of Social Media and Popular Culture to Advance Cross-Cultural Understanding," *Comunicar* 25, no. 51 (2017). doi:10.3916/ c51-2017-06.

## CHAPTER 6

1. Neil Morse, "PPC.," Search Engine Watch, September 14, 2018, accessed September 19, 2018, https://searchenginewatch.com/category/ppc/.

2. "Using Google Ads for Online Marketing," Google, accessed August 18, 2018, https://support.google.com/google-ads/answer/6227565.

3. "How to Make Money from Your Website with Google AdSense," Google AdSense, accessed August 19, 2018, https://www.google.com/adsense/start/how-it -works/#/.

4. "2019 Media Kit," *Ad Age*, https://adage.com/images/bin/pdf/Ad_Age_Media_ Kit.pdf; "CPM," MarketingTerms.com, accessed August 17, 2018, https://www .marketingterms.com/dictionary/cpm/.

5. Vangie Beal, "Cookie—Web Cookie," Webopedia, accessed August 05, 2018, https://www.webopedia.com/TERM/C/cookie.html; "How Advertisers Use Internet Cookies to Track You," *Wall Street Journal*, July 30, 2010, accessed September 5, 2018, https://www.wsj.com/video/how-advertisers-use-internet-cookies-to-track -you/92E525EB-9E4A-4399-817D-8C4E6EF68F93.html.

6. "Magic Cookie," Wikipedia.com, January 29, 2019, en.wikipedia.org/wiki/ Magic_cookie.

7. Simon Hill, "Are Cookies Crumbling Our Privacy? We Asked an Expert to Find Out," *Digital Trends*, March 27, 2015, accessed August 15, 2018, https://www .digitaltrends.com/computing/history-of-cookies-and-effect-on-privacy/.

8. "The Facebook Pixel," Facebook Business, accessed October 5, 2018, https:// www.facebook.com/business/learn/facebook-ads-pixel.

9. Scott Shane, "These Are the Ads Russia Bought on Facebook in 2016," *New York Times*, November 1, 2017, accessed September 5, 2018, https://www.nytimes .com/2017/11/01/us/politics/russia-2016-election-facebook.html.

10. Honest Ads Act, S. 1989, 115th Congress (2017–2018), accessed August 5, 2018, https://www.congress.gov/bill/115th-congress/senate-bill/1989/text.

11. "Welcome to Medium, Where Words Matter," Medium, accessed August 5, 2018, https://medium.com/about.

12.    "How Can I Adjust How Ads Are Targeted to Me Based on My Activity On or Off of Facebook?" Facebook Help Center, accessed October 5, 2018, https://www .facebook.com/help/568137493302217.

13.    Yuxi Wu, Panya Gupta, and Miranda Wei, "Your Secrets Are Safe: How Browsers' Explanations Impact Misconceptions about Private Browsing Mode," in *Proceedings of the 2018 World Wide Web Conference*, 217–26. Lyon, France: 2018, accessed August 15, 2018, https://doi.org/10.1145/3178876.3186088.

14.    "What Happened to Tracking Protection?" Mozilla Support, accessed August 17, 2018, https://support.mozilla.org/en-US/kb/tracking-protection; "Prevent Cross-Site Tracking in Safari on Mac," Safari User Guide, accessed August 17, 2018, https://support.apple.com/guide/safari/prevent-websites-from-tracking-you -sfri40732/mac.

15.    "Instructions for Disabling AdBlock Extensions on Forbes," *Forbes*, accessed September 6, 2018, https://www.forbes.com/adblock/instructions/#25ef14922739.

16.    "Improving Advertising on the Web," *Chromium Blog*, June 1, 2017, accessed August 23, 2018, https://blog.chromium.org/2017/06/improving-advertising-on-web .html.

17.    Justin Pot, "Google, the World's Biggest Advertising Company, Will Block Ads Soon. Is That Good?" How-To Geek, December 27, 2017, accessed August 16, 2018, https://www.howtogeek.com/336952/google-the-worlds-biggest-advertising -company-will-block-ads-soon.-is-that-good/; Coalition for Better Ads, accessed August 17, 2018, https://www.betterads.org/.

18.    Benjamin Herold, "Google Under Fire for Data-Mining Student Email Messages," *Education Week*, June 20, 2018, accessed August 13, 2018, https://www .edweek.org/ew/articles/2014/03/13/26google.h33.html.

19.    "Smart Compose in Gmail Now Available for G Suite," *G Suite Updates* Blog, September 26, 2018, accessed October 6, 2018, https://gsuiteupdates.googleblog .com/2018/09/gmail-smart-compose-gsuite.html.

## CHAPTER 7

1.    "Big Data," Merriam-Webster.com, accessed October 23, 2017, https://www .merriam-webster.com/dictionary/big%20data.

2.    "How Target Figured Out a Teen Girl Was Pregnant before Her Father Did," *Forbes*, February 16, 2012, accessed November 8, 2017, https://www.forbes.com/

sites/kashmirhill/2012/02/16/how-target-figured-out-a-teen-girl-was-pregnant
-before-her-father-did/.

3.  "Alexa, Can You Help with This Murder Case?" CNN.com, accessed August
2, 2018, https://www.cnn.com/2016/12/28/tech/amazon-echo-alexa-bentonville
-arkansas-murder-case-trnd/index.html.

4.  "Guidance on the Protection of Personal Identifiable Information," US
Department of Labor, accessed October 4, 2018, https://www.dol.gov/general/ppii.

5.  "True Story: The Case of a Hacked Baby Monitor (Gwelltimes P2P Cloud),"
SEC Consult, accessed August 2, 2018, https://www.sec-consult.com/en/
blog/2018/06/true-story-the-case-of-a-hacked-baby-monitor-gwelltimes-p2p-cloud/.

6.  "Hacking the Doors Off: I Took Control of a Security Alarm System from
5,000 Miles Away," *Forbes*, accessed August 2, 2018, https://www.forbes.com/sites/
thomasbrewster/2016/02/17/hacking-smart-security-alarms/.

7.  "Amazon Key Home Kit," Amazon.com, accessed August 2, 2018, https://www
.amazon.com/b?ie=UTF8&node=17861200011.

8.  "Pretty Sure Google's New Talking AI Just Beat the Turing Test," Engadget
.com, accessed August 2, 2018, https://www.engadget.com/2018/05/08/pretty-sure
-googles-new-talking-ai-just-beat-the-turing-test/.

9.  Sam McNeill, "Artificial Intelligence in the Classroom," *Microsoft Education*,
March 1, 2018, accessed October 4, 2018, https://educationblog.microsoft
.com/2018/03/artificial-intelligence-in-the-classroom/.

10.  "Can AI Fix Education? We Asked Bill Gates," *The Verge*, accessed August 3,
2018, https://www.theverge.com/2016/4/25/11492102/bill-gates-interview-education
-software-artificial-intelligence.

11.  "Predicting Student Dropout Risks, Increasing Graduation Rates with
. . . ," accessed August 2, 2018, https://customers.microsoft.com/story/
tacomapublicschoolsstory.

12.  Kurt Wagner, "Here's How Facebook Allowed Cambridge Analytica to Get
Data for 50 Million Users," March 17, 2018, accessed August 3, 2018, https://www
.recode.net/2018/3/17/17134072/facebook-cambridge-analytica-trump-explained
-user-data.

13.   Radhika Sanghani, "'I Downloaded All My Facebook Data and It Was a Nightmare,'" *BBC Three*, June 21, 2018, accessed August 3, 2018, https://www.bbc.co.uk/bbcthree/article/93d1393a-1c12-485f-b7fe-5146cd48c12c.

14.   "Privacy and Data Security Update (2016)," *Federal Trade Commission*, January 2017, accessed August 3, 2018, https://www.ftc.gov/reports/privacy-data-security-update-2016.

15.   Ashraf Khalil, "DreamHost Ordered to Release Some Trump Protest Website Data to US Justice Department," August 25, 2017, accessed August 6, 2018, https://www.nytimes.com/2017/08/25/business/dreamhost-trump-doj-privacy-ddos-dailystormer.html.

16.   "What Is Search Retargeting?" *ExactDrive*, accessed August 7, 2018, http://www.exactdrive.com/search-retargeting.

17.   A Joint Resolution Providing for Congressional Disapproval under Chapter 8 of Title 5, United States Code, of the Rule submitted by the Federal Communications Commission Relating to "Protecting the Privacy of Customers of Broadband and Other Telecommunications Services," S.J.Res.34, 115th Cong. (2017–2018), accessed August 7, 2018, https://www.congress.gov/bill/115th-congress/senate-joint-resolution/34.

18.   Heather Kelly and Scott McLean, "Your Browser History Is for Sale, Here's What You Need to Know," *CNN Money*, April 6, 2017, accessed August 7, 2018, https://money.cnn.com/2017/04/05/technology/online-privacy-faq/.

19.   Benjamin Herold, "Google Under Fire for Data-Mining Student Email Messages," March 13, 2014, accessed August 7, 2018, https://www.edweek.org/ew/articles/2014/03/13/26google.h33.html.

20.   "Privacy Pledge: K–12 School Service Provider Pledge to Safeguard Student Privacy," Student Privacy Pledge, accessed August 7, 2018, https://studentprivacypledge.org/privacy-pledge/.

21.   "G Suite for Education FAQ," Google Support, accessed August 7, 2018, https://support.google.com/a/answer/139019?hl=en.

22.   Natasha Singer, "Privacy Concerns for ClassDojo and Other Tracking Apps for Schoolchildren," November 16, 2017, accessed August 7, 2018, https://www.nytimes.com/2014/11/17/technology/privacy-concerns-for-classdojo-and-other-tracking-apps-for-schoolchildren.html.

23.  "Privacy Policy," ClassDojo, accessed August 7, 2018, https://www.classdojo
.com/privacy_10_24_14.

24.  Sydney Johnson, "This Company Wants to Gather Student Brainwave Data
to Measure 'Engagement,'" October 26, 2017, accessed August 8, 2018, https://www
.edsurge.com/news/2017-10-26-this-company-wants-to-gather-student-brainwave
-data-to-measure-engagement.

25.  "Terms of Service," BrainCo, accessed August 8, 2018, https://www.brainco
.tech/privacy.

26.  "Privacy Policy," BusinessDictionary.com, accessed August 24, 2018, http://
www.businessdictionary.com/definition/privacy-policy.html.

27.  "Privacy and Security," Federal Trade Commission, accessed August 24, 2018,
https://www.ftc.gov/tips-advice/business-center/privacy-and-security.

28.  "VPN Beginner's Guide," TheBestVPN.com, accessed August 8, 2018, https://
thebestvpn.com/what-is-vpn-beginners-guide/.

29.  "How Do I Turn on the Do Not Track Feature?" Mozilla Support, accessed
August 8, 2018, https://support.mozilla.org/en-US/kb/how-do-i-turn-do-not-track
-feature.

30.  "Onion Routing," accessed August 8, 2018, https://www.onion-router.net/.

31.  "Libraries Are Banding Together in Support of Tor," *The Verge*, September
16, 2015, accessed August 8, 2018, https://www.theverge.com/2015/9/16/9341409/
library-tor-encryption-privacy.

32.  Amanda Lenhart, "Teens, Technology and Friendships," Pew Research Center,
August 6, 2015, http://www.pewinternet.org/2015/08/06/teens-technology-and
-friendships/

33.  Benjamin Herold, "Teens Worry about Online Privacy: Q&A with Researcher
Claire Fontaine," *Education Week*, accessed August 15, 2018, https://blogs.edweek
.org/edweek/DigitalEducation/2018/04/teens_worry_social_media.html.

34.  "Making It Easier to Share with Who You Want," Facebook Newsroom, May
22, 2014, accessed August 15, 2018, https://newsroom.fb.com/news/2014/05/making
-it-easier-to-share-with-who-you-want/.

35. "Facebook Alerts 14M to Privacy Bug That Changed Status Composer to Public," TechCrunch.com, accessed August 15, 2018, https://techcrunch .com/2018/06/07/facebook-status-privacy-bug/.

36. Hang Do Thi Duc, "Public by Default," *22.8miles*, accessed August 15, 2018, https://22-8miles.com/public-by-default/.

37. danah boyd, *Its Complicated: The Social Lives of Networked Teens* (New Haven, CT: Yale University Press, 2015).

38. Herold, "Teens Worry about Online Privacy."

39. "GDPR FAQs," EU GDPR.org, accessed September 20, 2018, https://eugdpr .org/the-regulation/gdpr-faqs/.

## CHAPTER 8

1. "Legislative History of Major FERPA Provisions," US Department of Education, December 19, 2005, accessed August 9, 2018, https://www2.ed.gov/ policy/gen/guid/fpco/ferpa/leg-history.html.

2. Sarah Schwartz, "Beyond FERPA: Five Tips for Protecting Student Data," *Education Week*, June 25, 2018, accessed August 9, 2018, https://blogs.edweek.org/ edweek/DigitalEducation/2018/06/beyond_ferpa_five_tips_for_protecting_student_ data.html.

3. Federal Trade Commission. "Children's Online Privacy Protection Rule: 16 CFR Part 312." Washington, DC: Office of the Federal Register, 2013.

4. "Universal Service Fund," Federal Communications Commission, August 30, 2013, accessed August 10, 2018, https://www.fcc.gov/general/universal-service-fund.

5. "Advocates Say Google/YouTube Violates Federal Law and Children's Privacy Law," April 9, 2018, accessed August 8, 2018, https://www.studentprivacymatters .org/advocates-say-googleyoutube-violates-federal-law-and-childrens-privacy-law/.

6. "Data, Analytics, and Adaptive Learning," Pearson, accessed August 10, 2018, https://www.pearson.com/us/higher-education/why-choose-pearson/thought -leadership/data-analytics-adaptive-learning.html.

7. "PSD Digital Vendor Security Requirements, 2022F2," Puyallup, WA: Puyallup School District, March 7, 2017.

8.   Joseph Cox, "Hacker Steals Millions of User Account Details from Education Platform Edmodo," *Vice*, May 11, 2017, accessed August 12, 2018, https://mother board.vice.com/en_us/article/ezjbwe/hacker-steals-millions-of-user-account-details -from-education-platform-edmodo.

9.   Jenny Abamu, "Massive Data Breaches, Billions in Wasted Funds: Who Is Holding Edtech Vendors Accountable?" *EdSurge*, May 24, 2017, accessed August 12, 2018, https://www.edsurge.com/news/2017-05-24-massive-data-breaches-billions-in -wasted-funds-who-is-holding-edtech-vendors-accountable.

10.   Rainey Reitman, "Roseville City School District Embraces Chromebooks, but at What Cost?" Electronic Frontier Foundation, December 1, 2015, accessed September 10, 2018, https://www.eff.org/studentprivacy-casestudy.

11.   Faith Boninger, Alex Molnar, and Kevin Murray, "Asleep at the Switch: Schoolhouse Commercialism, Student Privacy, and the Failure of Policymaking," National Education Policy Center, August 15, 2017, accessed November 29, 2018, https://nepc.colorado.edu/publication/schoolhouse-commercialism-2017.

12.   *Reproduction of Copyrighted Works by Educators and Librarians* (Washington, DC: US Copyright Office, August 2014).

13.   *Harper and Row, Publishers, Inc. v. Nation Enterprises*, Oyez, accessed November 10, 2018, https://www.oyez.org/cases/1984/83-1632.

14.   *Leibovitz v. Paramount Pictures Corporation* (2nd Circuit 1998).

15.   Randy Kennedy, "Shepard Fairey Is Fined and Sentenced to Probation in 'Hope' Poster Case," *New York Times*, September 7, 2012, accessed September 12, 2018, https://artsbeat.blogs.nytimes.com/2012/09/07/shephard-fairey-is-fined-and -sentenced-to-probation-in-hope-poster-case/.

16.   Tim Walker, "Legal Controversy over Lesson Plans," National Education Association, accessed October 21, 2018, http://www.nea.org/home/37583.htm.

17.   "Open Educational Resources," William and Flora Hewlett Foundation, August 3, 2016, accessed September 12, 2018, https://hewlett.org/strategy/open -educational-resources/.

18.   Kristina Ishmael et al., "Creating Systems of Sustainability: Four Focus Areas for the Future of PK-12 Open Educational Resources." New America, October 9, 2018, https://www.newamerica.org/education-policy/policy-papers/creating-systems -sustainability-four-focus-areas-future-pk-12-open-educational-resources/

19.  Alex Caton and Grace Watkins, "Trump Pick Monica Crowley Plagiarized Parts of Her Ph.D. Dissertation," *Politico*, January 9, 2017, accessed October 18, 2018, https://www.politico.com/magazine/story/2017/01/monica-crowley-plagiarism -phd-dissertation-columbia-214612.

### CHAPTER 9

1.  "Media," Dictionary.com, accessed November 2, 2018, https://www.dictionary .com/browse/media?s=ts.

2.  "Media Literacy: A Definition and More," Center for Media Literacy, accessed July 17, 2018, http://www.medialit.org/media-literacy-definition-and-more; "Media Literacy Defined," National Association for Media Literacy Education, March 10, 2017, accessed July 17, 2018, https://namle.net/publications/media-literacy -definitions/; "Topic Backgrounder: News and Media Literacy," Common Sense Education, https://d1e2bohyu2u2w9.cloudfront.net/education/sites/default/files/tlr -asset/topicbackgrounder-newsmedialit_2017_final.pdf.

3.  E. Thoman and T. Jolls. "Media Literacy—A National Priority for a Changing World," *American Behavioral Scientist* 48, no. 1 (2004): 18–29. doi:10.1177/0002764204267246

4.  E. Thoman and T. Jolls, *Literacy for the 21st Century: An Overview and Orientation Guide to Media Literacy Education* (Malibu, CA: Center for Media Literacy, 2008).

### CHAPTER 10

1.  "Internet Live Stats," accessed January 13, 2019, http://www.internetlivestats .com/.

2.  Paul G. Zurkowski, *The Information Service Environment Relationships and Priorities. Related Paper No. 5* (Washington, DC: National Commission on Libraries and Information Science, 1974).

3.  "Presidential Committee on Information Literacy: Final Report," Association of College and Research Libraries, November 21, 2012, accessed October 13, 2018, http://www.ala.org/acrl/publications/whitepapers/presidential.

4.  "National Vaccine Information Center," Wikipedia, January 9, 2019, accessed January 13, 2019, https://en.wikipedia.org/wiki/National_Vaccine_Information_ Center.

5.   Carl Sagan, *Science as a Candle in the Dark* (New York: Ballantine Books, 2000).

6.   Brian Stelter, "Three Journalists Leaving CNN after Retracted Article," *CNN Business*, June 27, 2017, accessed December 13, 2018, https://money.cnn.com/2017/06/26/media/cnn-announcement-retracted-article/index.html.

7.   Philip Gourevitch, *The Paris Review: Interviews, I* (New York: Picador, 2006).

8.   Alex Hider, "Lance Armstrong Takes to Instagram to Prove He Isn't Dead," KNXV, May 12, 2017, http://www.abc15.com/news/national/lance-armstrong-takes-to-instagram-to-prove-he-isnt-dead.

9.   Jim Wasserman and David W. Loveland, *Middle Schoolers, Meet Media Literacy: How Teachers Can Bring Economics, Media, and Marketing to Life* (Lanham, MD: Rowman & Littlefield, 2019).

10.   Sarah Blakeslee, "The CRAAP Test," LOEX Quarterly 31, no. 3, https://commons.emich.edu/loexquarterly/vol31/iss3/4

11.   Howard Rheingold, "Crap Detection 101," *SFGate*, June 30, 2009, http://blog.sfgate.com/rheingold/2009/06/30/crap-detection-101/.

12.   "Part 2 of 4: Why Measuring Political Bias Is So Hard, and How We Can Do It Anyway: The Media Bias Chart Horizontal Axis," Ad Fontes Media, August 28, 2018, accessed November 16, 2018, https://www.adfontesmedia.com/part-2-of-4-why-measuring-political-bias-is-so-hard-and-how-we-can-do-it-anyway-the-media-bias-chart-horizontal-axis/.

13.   "Presidential Committee on Information Literacy."

## CHAPTER 11

1.   V. Rideout, *The Common Sense Census: Media Use by Teens and Tweens* (San Francisco, CA: Common Sense Media, 2015).

2.   Chris Hartley, "Marketing to the Visual Generation," Catalyst Group Marketing, June 6, 2018, accessed October 19, 2018, https://thinkcatalyst.co/marketing-visual-generation/.

3.   Mary C. Potter, Brad Wyble, Carl Erick Hagmann, and Emily S. McCourt, "Detecting Meaning in RSVP at 13 Ms Per Picture," *Attention, Perception, and Psychophysics* 76, no. 2 (December 28, 2013): 270–279.

4.   Anne Trafton, "In the Blink of an Eye," *MIT News,* January 16, 2014, accessed October 19, 2018, http://news.mit.edu/2014/in-the-blink-of-an-eye-0116.

5.   By Tezza, accessed October 12, 2018. https://www.bytezza.com/.

6.   "Models," TheDiigitals.com, accessed October 19, 2018, https://www
.thediigitals.com/models.

7.   "AIDA (marketing)," Wikipedia, November 8, 2018, accessed November 1, 2018, https://en.wikipedia.org/wiki/AIDA_(marketing).

8.   Sarah McGrew, Joel Breakstone, Teresa Ortega, Mark Smith, and Sam Wineburg, "Can Students Evaluate Online Sources? Learning from Assessments of Civic Online Reasoning," *Theory and Research in Social Education* 46, no. 2 (2018): 163–93.

9.   Grant Denham, Instagram post, November 9, 2018, https://www.instagram
.com/p/Bp-qm09nvT5kXl9BuouSABW_x4aeoD_3zUznnU0/.

10.   Ira Goldman, Twitter post, November 9, 2018, 9:01PM, https://twitter.com/
KDbyProxy/status/1061076302294216704

11.   LA County Sheriff's Department, Twitter post, November 9, 2018, 8:51 pm.

12.   @san_kaido, Twitter direct message, August 3, 2018.

13.   Megan Specia, "The Stories Behind Three Anti-Muslim Videos Shared by Trump," *New York Times*, November 29, 2017, accessed October 23, 2018, https://
www.nytimes.com/2017/11/29/world/middleeast/anti-muslim-videos-trump-twitter
.html; Lizzie Dearden, "Britain First Leaders Jailed: Police Release Mugshots of Jayda Fransen and Paul Golding because of Impact on Community," *Independent*, March 9, 2018, accessed October 23, 2018, https://www.independent.co.uk/news/uk/crime/
britain-first-leaders-jayda-fransen-paul-golding-jailed-mugshots-police-muslim
-hate-crime-kent-a8246571.html.

14.   Jennifer Langston, "Lip-syncing Obama: New Tools Turn Audio Clips into Realistic Video," *UW News*, University of Washington July 11, 2017, accessed October 23, 2018, https://www.washington.edu/news/2017/07/11/lip-syncing-obama
-new-tools-turn-audio-clips-into-realistic-video/.

15.   Hilke Schellmann, "Deepfake Videos Are Getting Real and That's a Problem," *Wall Street Journal*, October 15, 2018, accessed November 3, 2018, https://www.wsj
.com/articles/deepfake-videos-are-ruining-lives-is-democracy-next-1539595787.

16.    Ally Foster, "Teen's Google Search Reveals Sickening Online Secret about Herself," News.Com.Au, June 29, 2018, accessed November 3, 2018, https://www .news.com.au/technology/online/security/teens-google-search-reveals-sickening -online-secret-about-herself/news-story/ee9d26010989c4b9a5c6333013ebbef2.

17.    Alec Couros, "Info for Romance Scam Victims," *Open Thinking*, accessed November 13, 2018, http://educationaltechnology.ca/information-for-romance -scam-victims.

18.    Dan Evon, "FALSE: Anti-Trump Protesters Destroy America," Snopes.com, November 11, 2016, accessed November 4, 2018, https://www.snopes.com/fact -check/anti-trump-protesters-destroy-america/.

## CHAPTER 12

1.    Laura Sydell, "We Tracked Down a Fake-News Creator in the Suburbs. Here's What We Learned," NPR, November 23, 2016, http://www.npr.org/sections/ alltechconsidered/2016/11/23/503146770/npr-finds-the-head-of-a-covert-fake-news -operation-in-the-suburbs.

2.    "FBI Agent Suspected in Hillary Email Leaks Found Dead in Apparent Murder-Suicide," *Denver Guardian*, November 10, 2016, http://web.archive.org/ web/20161115023815/http://denverguardian.com/2016/11/05/fbi-agent-suspected -hillary-email-leaks-found-dead-apparent-murder-suicide/.

3.    Emma Jane Kirby, "The City Getting Rich from Fake News," BBC News, December 5, 2016, http://www.bbc.com/news/magazine-38168281.

4.    Ned Parker, Jonathan Landay, and John Walcott, "Putin-linked Think Tank Drew Up Plan to Sway 2016 US Election—Documents," *Reuters*, April 21, 2017, http://www.reuters.com/article/us-usa-russia-election-exclusive-idUSKBN17L2N3.

5.    Craig Silverman, and Jeremy Singer-Vine, "Most Americans Who See Fake News Believe It, New Survey Says," BuzzFeed, December 6, 2016, https://www .buzzfeed.com/craigsilverman/fake-news-survey?utm_term=.obE79V3RgM# .sqy9kPDemb.

6.    "Donald Trump's News Conference: Full Transcript and Video," *New York Times*, January 11, 2017, https://www.nytimes.com/2017/01/11/us/politics/trump -press-conference-transcript.html.

7.  "Conway: Press Secretary Gave 'Alternative Facts.'" NBCNews.com, January 22, 2017, http://www.nbcnews.com/meet-the-press/video/conway-press-secretary -gave-alternative-facts-860142147643.

8.  Kim LaCapria, "FALSE: Comet Ping Pong Pizzeria Home to Child Abuse Ring Led by Hillary Clinton," Snopes.com, December 4, 2016, http://www.snopes.com/ pizzagate-conspiracy/.

9.  Farhad Manjoo, "How the Internet Is Loosening Our Grip on the Truth," *New York Times*, November 2, 2016, https://www.nytimes.com/2016/11/03/technology/ how-the-internet-is-loosening-our-grip-on-the-truth.html?_r=0.

10.  Steven A. Sloman and Philip Fernbach, *The Knowledge Illusion: Why We Never Think Alone* (New York: Riverhead Books, 2017).

11.  "Storytelling in the Age of Social News Consumption," Edelman, March 6, 2017, http://www.edelman.com/post/storytelling-age-social-news-consumption/.

12.  Brooke Donald, "Stanford Researchers Find Students Have Trouble Judging the Credibility of Information Online," Stanford Graduate School of Education, November 22, 2016, https://ed.stanford.edu/news/stanford-researchers-find -students-have-trouble-judging-credibility-information-online.

13.  "Reading Like a Historian," Stanford History Education Group, accessed April 17, 2017, https://sheg.stanford.edu/rlh.

14.  Ed Mazza, "WATCH: Fox News Reporter Flees When Interview Goes Hilariously Wrong," *Huffington Post*, May 11, 2017, http://www.huffingtonpost .com/entry/fox-news-run-away-diner_us_59150a7ae4b0031e737c8aa7.

15.  "Fake News: Why We Fall For It," *Psychology Today*, December 28, 2016, https://www.psychologytoday.com/blog/contemporary-psychoanalysis-in -action/201612/fake-news-why-we-fall-it.

16.  Craig Anderson, Mark Lepper, and Lee Ross, "Perseverance of Social Theories: The Role of Explanation in the Persistence of Discredited Information," *Journal of Personality and Social Psychology* 39 (1980): 1037–49.

17.  Nathan Yau, "How to Spot Visualization Lies," FlowingData, April 11, 2017, https://flowingdata.com/2017/02/09/how-to-spot-visualization-lies/.

18.  "News," Merriam-Webster.com, accessed May 3, 2017, https://www.merriam -webster.com/dictionary/news.

19. "Fake," Merriam-Webster.com, May 3, 2017, https://www.merriam-webster .com/dictionary/fake.

20. Dan Evon, "FALSE: Tens of Thousands of Fraudulent Clinton Votes Found in Ohio Warehouse," Snopes.com, October 6, 2016, http://www.snopes.com/clinton -votes-found-in-warehouse/.

## CHAPTER 13

1. *Miller v. California*, 413 US 15 (1973).

2. *Reno v. ACLU*, 521 US 844 (1997).

3. Mike Isaac, "Twitter Bars Milo Yiannopoulos in Wake of Leslie Jones's Reports of Abuse," *New York Times*, July 20, 2016, accessed November 27, 2018, https:// www.nytimes.com/2016/07/20/technology/twitter-bars-milo-yiannopoulos-in -crackdown-on-abusive-comments.html.

4. "Hateful Conduct Policy," Twitter Help Center, accessed January 28, 2019, https://help.twitter.com/en/rules-and-policies/hateful-conduct-policy.

5. Bill Hutchinson, "Here Are the 7 Tweets That Led to Landmark Court Decision against Trump," ABC News, May 24, 2018, accessed November 27, 2018, https://abcnews.go.com/beta-story-container/US/tweets-led-landmark-court -decision-trump/story?id=55407710.

6. Tim Stelloh, "Second Teen Arrested in Live-streamed Sexual Assault in Chicago," NBCNews.com, April 3, 2017, accessed December 28, 2018, https://www .nbcnews.com/news/us-news/second-boy-arrested-gang-rape-chicago-teen-streamed -facebook-live-n742341.

7. Sam Levin, Julia Carrie Wong, and Luke Harding, "Facebook Backs Down from 'Napalm Girl' Censorship and Reinstates Photo," *Guardian*, September 9, 2016, accessed December 28, 2018, https://www.theguardian.com/technology/2016/ sep/09/facebook-reinstates-napalm-girl-photo.

8. Christine Lagorio-Chafkin, "Facebook's 7,500 Moderators Protect You From the Internet's Most Horrifying Content. But Who's Protecting Them?" *Inc.com*, September 26, 2018, accessed December 28, 2018, https://www.inc.com/christine -lagorio/facebook-content-moderator-lawsuit.html.

9.   "Online Defamation Law," Electronic Frontier Foundation, December 22, 2014, accessed November 29, 2018, https://www.eff.org/issues/bloggers/legal/liability/defamation.

10.   "Black Nationalist," Southern Poverty Law Center, accessed December 27, 2018, https://www.splcenter.org/fighting-hate/extremist-files/ideology/black-nationalist.

11.   *Tinker v. Des Moines Independent Community School District*, 393 US 503 (1969).

12.   Suzanne Perez Tobias, "Heights High Suspends Senior Class President over Twitter Post," *Wichita Eagle*, accessed November 27, 2018, https://www.kansas.com/news/article1114918.html.

13.   Tom Simonite, "Schools Are Mining Students' Social Media Posts for Signs of Trouble." *Wired*, August 20, 2018, accessed November 27, 2018, https://www.wired.com/story/algorithms-monitor-student-social-media-posts/.

14.   *Hague v. Committee for Industrial Organization*, 307 US 496 (1939).

15.   *Murray v. Pittsburgh Board of Public Education*, 919 F. Supp. 838 (W.D. Pa. 1996).

16.   *Hazelwood School District v. Kuhlmeier*, 484 US 260 (1988).

17.   Rachel Gribble, "Openly Gay Teacher Fired after Posting Wedding Pictures on Social Media," WCMH, February 10, 2018, accessed November 30, 2018, https://www.nbc4i.com/news/u-s-world/openly-gay-teacher-fired-after-posting-wedding-pictures-on-social-media/1096379143.

18.   "Retaliation—Public Employees and First Amendment Rights," Workplace Fairness, accessed November 30, 2018, https://www.workplacefairness.org/retaliation-public-employees.

19.   *Pickering v. Board of Education*, 391 US 563 (1968).

## CONCLUSION

1.   Faith Karimi, "Alexandria Ocasio-Cortez Responds to Dance Video Critics with More Dancing," CNN, January 5, 2019, accessed January 09, 2019, https://www.cnn.com/2019/01/04/politics/ocasio-cortez-dancing-video-trnd/index.html.

2.   Booba1234, "David after Dentist," YouTube, January 30, 2009, accessed December 9, 2018, https://www.youtube.com/watch?v=txqiwrbYGrs.

3.   Nicholas G. Carr, *The Shallows: What the Internet Is Doing to Our Brains* (New York: W. W. Norton, 2011).

4.   Chris Weller, "A Former Google Executive Reveals the Tricks Tech Companies Use to Grab Your Attention," *Business Insider*, August 28, 2017, accessed October 10, 2018, https://www.businessinsider.com/why-phones-are-addicting-according-to-former-google-exec-2017-8.

5.   Josh Constine, "Facebook's $2 Billion Acquisition of Oculus Closes, Now Official," TechCrunch, July 21, 2014, accessed October 10, 2018, https://techcrunch.com/2014/07/21/facebooks-acquisition-of-oculus-closes-now-official/.

6.   Steven Musil, "Oculus to Study Possible Role of VR in the Classroom," CNET, August 28, 2018, accessed October 10, 2018, https://www.cnet.com/news/oculus-pilot-to-study-the-role-of-vr-in-the-classroom/.

7.   "Instagram Ranked Worst for Young People's Mental Health," Royal Society for Public Health, May 19, 2017, accessed October 10, 2018, https://www.rsph.org.uk/about-us/news/instagram-ranked-worst-for-young-people-s-mental-health.html.

8.   Paul Mozur, "Inside China's Dystopian Dreams: AI, Shame and Lots of Cameras," *New York Times*, July 8, 2018, accessed November 9, 2018, https://www.nytimes.com/2018/07/08/business/china-surveillance-technology.html.

# Index

# About the Author

**Mary Beth Hertz** has been teaching in Philadelphia since 2003. She holds a master's degree in instructional technology from St. Joseph's University, and a bachelor of arts in French from Oberlin College. She is certified in K–6 elementary education, K–12 business/technology education, and K–12 art education, and has an Instructional Technology Specialist certificate. She currently teaches her students technology and art at Science Leadership Academy at Beeber in Philadelphia, Pennsylvania, and is the technology coordinator for the school as well.

Mary Beth was named an International Society for Technology in Education Emerging Leader in 2009, Pennsylvania Association for Educational Communications and Technology's 2013 Outstanding Teacher of the Year, and is a member the 2013 class of ASCD's Emerging Leaders. Outside of teaching, Mary Beth has been a co-organizer of the Philly EdTech Meetup, sat on the board of the Edcamp Foundation for two years, and is a founding organizer of Edcamp Philly. In May 2013, she organized WebSLAM, Philadelphia's first hackathon for high school students.

She has presented at ISTE conferences and the #140 Character Conference, as well as a number of edcamps and Educon, an innovative local conference in Philadelphia. Mary Beth has a website at http://marybethhertz.me, maintains a blog on Edutopia.org, and can be found on Twitter as @mbteach. When she is not tweeting, writing, or teaching, she likes to read science fiction, make things, watch movies, and explore her South Philadelphia neighborhood with her husband and two young children.